Socrates

Classic Thinkers

Richard T. W. Arthur, *Leibniz*
Terrell Carver, *Marx*
Daniel E. Flage, *Berkeley*
J. M. Fritzman, *Hegel*
Bernard Gert, *Hobbes*
Thomas Kemple, *Simmel*
Ralph McInerny, *Aquinas*
Dale E. Miller, *J. S. Mill*
Joanne Paul, *Thomas More*
A. J. Pyle, *Locke*
James T. Schleifer, *Tocqueville*
Céline Spector, *Rousseau*
Andrew Ward, *Kant*

Socrates

William J. Prior

polity

First published in 2019 by Polity Press

Polity Press
65 Bridge Street
Cambridge CB2 1UR, UK

Polity Press
101 Station Landing
Suite 300
Medford, MA 02155, USA

ISBN-13: 978-1-5095-2973-5
ISBN-13: 978-1-5095-2974-2(pb)

A catalogue record for this book is available from the British Library.

Library of Congress Cataloging-in-Publication Data

Names: Prior, William J., author.
Title: Socrates / William J. Prior.
Description: Cambridge, UK ; Medford, MA : Polity Press, 2019. | Series: Classical thinkers | Includes bibliographical references and index.
Identifiers: LCCN 2019009943 (print) | LCCN 2019015932 (ebook) | ISBN 9781509529766 (Epub) | ISBN 9781509529735 (hardback) | ISBN 9781509529742 (pbk.)
Subjects: LCSH: Socrates. | Philosophy, Ancient.
Classification: LCC B317 (ebook) | LCC B317 .P75 2019 (print) | DDC 183/.2–dc23
LC record available at https://lccn.loc.gov/2019009943

Typeset in 10.5 on 12 pt Palatino
by Toppan Best-set Premedia Limited
Printed and bound in Great Britain by CPI Group (UK) Ltd, Croydon

For further information on Polity, visit our website: politybooks.com

For my grandchildren

Contents

Preface

A story is told about an institutional review at Oxford in the 1990s. "When … the visiting team of assessors met the philosophers, they asked them what innovations in teaching methods had been developed over the last two or three years. It is reported that the stunned silence that followed was broken by Christopher Peacocke, then Waynflete Professor of Metaphysics, who observed that Socrates had discovered the right way to teach philosophy 2,500 years ago, and nobody had ever been able to make any significant improvements to it since."[1]

This is a book intended for beginners in the study of Socrates. It is not a book for scholars. It contains views, some of them controversial, on some issues of concern to scholars, but it generally avoids debate on those views. Nothing in this book presupposes familiarity with the scholarly literature on Socrates. The book does presuppose some familiarity with Plato's works, including the *Apology*, *Crito*, *Republic*, and some other dialogues. It should be read in conjunction with those. The first chapter should be read in connection with Plato's *Apology*, the fourth in connection with the *Euthyphro*, the seventh in connection with the *Crito*, and so on with the other chapters. There are many good translations of Plato's works available today. The book draws quotations from the Hackett edition of Plato's complete works, because it is the version most familiar to today's readers, but it refers to the passages in the way that is standard among scholars, using the Stephanus pagination in the margins of the pages of most translations. The reader can check the Hackett translations against any others that are available.

Most of this book concerns the character Socrates, as he is depicted in a certain set of Platonic works, which I refer to as the elenctic dialogues. The first chapter is concerned with the life of the person who stands behind that character, and attempts to place that life in the context of the major events of its time. Because Socrates left no written record of his philosophical views it is impossible to state definitively what the relation is between the historical Socrates and the character in Plato's works. This is the "Socratic problem" and it has no solution. Even when we read about the trial of Socrates, a public event witnessed by approximately five hundred jurors as well as by other Athenians, we rely on accounts of Plato and another associate of Socrates, Xenophon, for our understanding of that event.

Beginning with the second chapter, the book offers an account of the nature of the philosophy presented as Socratic in a set of dialogues in which Socrates practices a distinctive method of inquiry, the elenchus. The elenchus is a negative method, aimed at the refutation of the people Socrates has conversations with, his interlocutors, most of whom claim to have expert knowledge on a moral subject, usually the definition of a moral term. In certain dialogues, such as the *Crito*, this method is put to a positive use; in the *Meno* this positive use is justified by the introduction of a theory concerning the acquisition of knowledge, the doctrine of recollection. The doctrine of recollection changes our understanding of the elenchus.

Socrates typically professed ignorance concerning the answers to the questions he raised for others. He presented himself, not as a moral expert, but as an inquirer. In the *Theaetetus* he describes himself as "barren." He says that he does not express his view concerning the issues he raises because he is aware that he lacks wisdom. At the same time, however, he suggests possible answers to those questions. He is, in terms of the contrast drawn in the *Theaetetus*, fertile. Yet he cannot be both. One way of reconciling these two portraits is through the claim that Socrates' profession of ignorance is ironic, a claim made by Thrasymachus in the *Republic* and Alcibiades in the *Symposium*. Most interpreters do not accept this ironical interpretation; it is not clear, however, that the tension between the two portraits can be resolved in any other way.

Beginning with the fourth chapter of the book, we consider how these two portraits of Socrates characterize several of Plato's elenctic dialogues, beginning with the *Euthyphro*, a dialogue on the nature of piety. In Chapter 5 the book discusses a well-known view of the fertile Socrates, known as intellectualism. According to this view, virtue is a matter of knowledge, produced by an art of measurement. Socrates describes vice as ignorance and denies the possibility of moral weakness. This is the moral theory most often associated with the Socrates of the elenctic dialogues. This theory has a problem, however, with stating the end that virtue seeks. This end is happiness. In one dialogue, the *Protagoras*, it is suggested that happiness is pleasure, but this suggestion is rejected in another dialogue, the *Gorgias*. In the *Gorgias* and *Crito* a different conception of happiness is defended, based on psychological health. In the *Gorgias* this conception is associated with the idea of proper order among parts of the soul, including reason and appetite. Socrates defends this conception of happiness against the views of two of his interlocutors, Polus and Callicles. The happy life, according to this view, is the just life, which is identified as the life devoted to philosophy. This conception of happiness is discussed in Chapter 6.

Chapter 7 is devoted to a question generated by Socrates' conception of the just life, namely the relation between Socrates and the state. This was a question that arose after Socrates' trial: it has been claimed that Socrates was tried as an enemy of the democratic government of Athens. This chapter considers an argument put forward in the *Crito* by the laws of Athens in favor of civic obedience. Plato presents Socrates as a loyal citizen of Athens; he was also, however, a critic of democracy. Socrates wanted the Athenians to care about virtue rather than wealth or power. He thought that it was moral knowledge that qualified one to rule in the state, and he retains this view in the *Republic*. The eighth chapter discusses the relation between the Socrates of the elenctic dialogues and the Socrates of the "middle" dialogues, who is generally thought to be a spokesman for Plato's own views. The chapter compares the two sets of dialogues with respect to several issues: method, metaphysics (including the theory of Forms and the conception of the good), epistemology, psychology, moral theory, and political theory. I argue that the views of the "middle" dialogues in general grow out of the views expressed in the elenctic dialogues in a gradual manner.

The final chapter discusses the philosophical legacy of Socrates from his time to the twentieth century. It pays special attention to his influence in ancient philosophy and in the nineteenth century. Socrates, the virtuous man, the barren inquirer, the fertile theoretician, and the martyr, has been one of the most influential philosophers in the Western intellectual tradition. Not everything he said was true, but nearly everything he said was worth, and has received, philosophical discussion. This book attempts to portray Socrates' views on a variety of topics, so that readers may judge them for themselves. It also tries to show why Socrates has been regarded throughout the history of Western philosophy as a model of the philosophical life.

Acknowledgments

I am grateful to Nick Smith, who suggested that I put my thoughts on Socrates in a book. I am also grateful to three anonymous referees for this press, who offered many valuable suggestions. I also want to thank my colleague Philip Kain, who helped me with the interpretation of Hegel in Chapter Nine, and my former colleague Justin Remhof, who helped me with the interpretation of Nietzsche. I am especially grateful to the editor of this book, Pascal Porcheron, who guided the project from start to finish. Of course, none of these people are responsible for whatever errors the book may contain.

1

Socrates' Times and Trial

The Athenian philosopher Socrates is a cultural hero in Western civilization. Tried in 399[1] on charges of impiety and corrupting the youth, convicted and put to death, he is seen by his admirers, and even by his critics, not as a criminal but as a martyr on behalf of free speech and the unfettered pursuit of truth. If philosophy made saints, he would be considered a saint. The ancient Roman orator and philosophical writer Cicero credited him with changing the course of Western philosophy. Before Socrates, philosophy was primarily concerned with the explanation of nature. Socrates, said Cicero, "was the first to call philosophy down from the heavens and to place it in cities, and even to introduce it into homes and compel it to inquire about life and standards and goods and evils" (*Tusculan Disputations* V.10). Socrates made philosophy, we would say today, relevant to human life. These claims alone make Socrates worthy of study.

Socrates the Man: His Life and Times

Socrates was both a creature of his times and a shaper of those times. In order to understand his philosophy we must understand the events that shaped his life. Socrates was born in about 469, and he was an Athenian citizen. His father Sophroniscus was a stone-cutter, who would surely have passed on his trade to his son. We do not see Socrates practicing this trade in Plato's dialogues, though he does refer to the legendary sculptor, Daedalus, as his ancestor at

Euthyphro 11b–c. His mother Phainarete, whose name means something like "brings virtue to light," was a midwife. It is his mother's trade to which he refers as being similar to his own at *Theaetetus* 149a–151b. Socrates grew up in a period of Athens' greatest power and glory, and experienced her downfall in his adulthood. The rise to power of Athens is described by the Greek historian Herodotus. In 490 the Athenians at the battle of Marathon defeated an invading force sent by the Persian king Darius. In 480, under the leadership of the Athenian statesman Themistocles, a Greek fleet, made up primarily of Athenian ships, defeated another, much larger, Persian fleet under the command of Darius' son Xerxes at the battle of Salamis. In the following year, the Persians were defeated again in battle and expelled from Greece. The leading Greek military power at the time was Sparta, with whom the Athenians fought in coalition against the invading Persians. Following the defeat of the Persians the Athenians organized an alliance of Greek city-states in the area around the Aegean Sea to prevent another Persian invasion. This alliance became an Athenian empire, and Athens became the leading naval power in the eastern Mediterranean. The rise of Athenian power threatened the Spartans, and tensions grew between Athens and Sparta throughout the fifth century, culminating in the Peloponnesian War (431–404), the story of which is told by Thucydides (down to 411) and Xenophon (after that date). This war led to the complete defeat of Athens and the loss of her empire.

Socrates was born following the great victories of the Persian Wars, and lived as an adult during the Peloponnesian War. Plato tells us that he served in the Athenian army in three campaigns; two characters in Plato's dialogues, the general Laches and Alcibiades, praise him for his courage. Following the Athenian defeat in 404 the Spartans imposed on Athens, which had been the leading democracy in Greece, an oligarchic government known as "the Thirty." This government was so hated and feared by most of the citizens of Athens that it acquired the name, "the Thirty Tyrants." The Thirty ruled in Athens only briefly, from 404 to 403, but their rule was a reign of terror, in which many innocent Athenians were put to death and their fortunes confiscated. Many partisans of democracy went into exile. In 403 the democratic exiles defeated the forces of the Thirty in battle and restored the democracy. Socrates remained in Athens throughout this time, which may have caused some resentment among the exiles. The restored democracy passed an amnesty for all who might have participated in the crimes committed prior to or during the rule of the Thirty, except for the Thirty themselves and their associates.

The Intellectual Revolution of the Fifth Century

The latter half of the fifth century was a period of intellectual ferment in Greece, and especially in Athens. Numerous Greek city-states, following the lead of Athens, established democratic governments, supplanting older monarchies and oligarchies. Ancient Greek democratic government was direct, not representative. That is, the citizens of a democracy did not elect representatives to vote on laws for the state; rather, they met in assemblies themselves to vote. These public meetings could be tumultuous. A great premium was placed in a democratic government on the ability of a speaker to express his views clearly and persuasively. This gave rise to a group of teachers who traveled among the city-states, especially the democratic ones, offering courses on rhetoric, the art of public speaking. Some of these teachers also taught other subjects as well, including in some cases mathematics, natural science, and political theory. These itinerant teachers were known collectively as "Sophists," a term that literally means "wise men." In Plato's dialogues we meet several of these Sophists. Plato contrasted Socrates strongly with the Sophists, and he had a rather low opinion of them as a group. As a result the term "sophist" has acquired a negative connotation. To some extent this negative view of the Sophists could be found among the ordinary citizens of Athens. The Sophists taught people how to argue persuasively; some people charged that they made the worse or weaker argument appear the better or stronger. That is, they thought the Sophists were guilty of some form of intellectual chicanery. In the minds of many Athenians Socrates was indistinguishable from the Sophists. Plato, of course, thought this confusion completely unjustified, but not many Athenians knew Socrates as well as he did.

Though some Athenians distrusted the Sophists, what they promised – the ability to speak persuasively in public – was highly prized, and the Sophists commanded large fees for their teaching. Socrates was an exception to this practice; he did not charge his associates[2] for conversing with him, and he denied being a teacher. The Sophists brought new ideas, and not just ideas concerning rhetoric, wherever they went. The most famous member of the group, Protagoras, professed agnosticism about the traditional gods, and famously declared that "man is the measure of all things." These new ideas prompted much discussion, both in public and in private, as new ideas continue to do today. In the latter half of the fifth century the Sophists and Socrates, with the help of a few philosophers of nature, such as Anaxagoras, brought an intellectual revolution to Athens.

The best "snapshot" of this intellectual revolution may well be found in the opening pages of Plato's dialogue, the *Protagoras*. The dramatic date of this dialogue is usually thought to be just before the start of the Peloponnesian War. In this dialogue Socrates narrates a conversation he has just had with Protagoras, "the wisest man alive" (309d).[3] His narration begins with an account of a visit to Socrates' home from a young man named Hippocrates, who desires an introduction to Protagoras. Hippocrates wants to study with Protagoras, to acquire his wisdom, and he is willing to pay dearly for it, though it turns out that he has no idea what Protagoras teaches. After a warning from Socrates about receiving into his soul the teachings of the Sophists without having them tested by an expert, Socrates and Hippocrates go to the house of Callias, one of the richest Athenians and a man noted for spending money on the Sophists. After eventually gaining entrance, they are greeted with a sight that Socrates describes, complete with echoes of Homeric poetry. First there is Protagoras, walking back and forth followed by a group that parts ways when he changes direction; then Hippias of Elis, answering questions on physics and astronomy; and Prodicus, in a former storeroom and still in bed, speaking to others with a deep, reverberating voice that obscures what he says. Other intellectuals, some familiar from other Platonic dialogues, are present in attendance on these teachers. No doubt Socrates' description, with its Homeric overtones, is somewhat ironic, but the impression it gives is that of an assemblage of intellectuals, conversing freely on matters that might engage a university audience today. For a lover of such conversation, it must have seemed like heaven; and Socrates, however much Plato wants to distinguish him from the Sophists, is right at home in it. This account is a Platonic description of an assemblage that may never in fact have occurred, but the atmosphere of free discussion and inquiry is one that, he wants to tell us, characterized this period of Athenian life.

The loss of the Peloponnesian War produced a backlash against this intellectual revolution. Part of the evidence for this backlash is the trial of Socrates. The kind of free thought that the Sophists and other intellectuals, such as Anaxagoras, displayed toward traditional religion came to be seen by some as undermining Athenian values. The ability of the Sophists to teach people to argue both or all sides of important questions was also thought to undermine traditional values. By the end of the war in 404 most of the first generation of Sophists were dead and the tradition of free public and private debate seems largely to have died with them. The atmosphere of intellectual inquiry that characterized Athens in the period before the war was now a thing of the past. Athenians were searching for reasons for the loss of the war, and some fastened on the influence of intellectuals on traditional beliefs. Socrates, unlike most of the Sophists a native Athenian, was unusual in that he was still carrying on the tradition of inquiry that characterized the earlier age. Socrates was hardly unaware of the war; as noted above, he had served in the army. He had been through the Athenian defeat and the rule of the Thirty that followed it, but he seemed unaffected by these events. As both Plato and Xenophon portray him, he continued to philosophize as if the war and its catastrophic conclusion had not occurred. The Athenians were noted for their love of free speech, but the circumstances that brought on their defeat, including a blockade of Athens and the resulting starvation of numerous Athenians, no doubt led many Athenians to question whether there were not limits to such speech. The circumstances in which the Athenians found themselves at the end of the fifth century no doubt contributed to the trial of Socrates.

Socrates' Trial

Four years after the restoration of democracy in Athens, Socrates was brought to trial. The bare facts of the trial as we know them today are these: Socrates was charged with impiety – literally, not believing in[4] the gods the city believed in, but in other new (strange) spiritual things – and corrupting the youth. His chief accuser was an otherwise unknown man named Meletus; his other accusers were Lycon, also obscure, and Anytus, a well-known Athenian politician. Athenian juries were quite large, to protect against corruption and to reflect the diversity of the Athenian population. Socrates was tried by a jury of approximately five hundred members. He was convicted by a majority of jurors and sentenced to death. Beyond these facts we have to deal in speculation. Athenian trials consisted of speeches by and for the prosecution followed by speeches by and for the defense. We do not possess the speeches of the prosecutors. We do not know what they said, and we do not know their motives in prosecuting Socrates. We do have two accounts of Socrates' defense speech, both entitled *Apology of Socrates*, one written by Plato and another by Xenophon. Plato and Xenophon were both associates of Socrates during the last decade of his life. Plato was present at the trial, but Xenophon was not. We also have a discussion of the trial in Xenophon's memoirs of Socrates, his *Memorabilia*. Neither Plato nor Xenophon was a neutral, objective reporter of the trial; they were partisans of Socrates. Both were convinced of his innocence. Xenophon's *Apology* does not pretend to be a verbatim account of what Socrates said at his trial. Plato's *Apology* does, but it may instead be Plato's attempt to say what he thought Socrates should have said. We are not in a position to know how much of Plato's *Apology* is reportage and how much is Platonic invention. This is a problem we have with all those of Plato's works that feature Socrates. From the time of the trial to the present day the conviction of Socrates has been controversial. Were the official charges against Socrates the real reasons for his trial? Was he guilty of those charges? Did he deserve the death penalty? Was the entire trial a miscarriage of justice? In the remainder of this chapter I want to examine these questions.

Why was Socrates Tried?

The official charges against Socrates were impiety and corrupting the youth. Were these the real reasons he was brought to trial? To a contemporary reader it may seem implausible that so much could be made of the charge of impiety. We tend to think of piety and impiety today as matters of personal conviction, or lack of it. In ancient Greece matters were different. Religion was thought to be the foundation of the state. Athena, the goddess of wisdom, was the patron deity of Athens. Religion was not a matter of private belief, but of public observance. There were numerous occasions during the year where it was expected for Athenians to honor the gods, and in particular Athena, with prayer and sacrifice. Athena was part of a pantheon of gods, including twelve who were thought to have their homes on Mount Olympus. These Olympian gods had their own particular functions or domains of influence: Zeus was the god of justice and the leader of the gods, Aphrodite was the goddess of love, Ares the god of war, Hades the god of the underworld, and so on. From the time of Homer, the first and greatest of the ancient

Greek poets, this pantheon was commonly accepted or recognized. If one's city was at war, which was a common condition among Greek cities, one prayed and sacrificed to the gods, and especially to the patron deity of one's own state, for success. Not to do so would be suspicious: it would make people think that one did not wish for one's city to succeed, that one was disloyal to the state. Impiety, not believing in, recognizing or honoring the gods of the city, would be akin to treason. This is what the charge of impiety would have meant to the jurors. It would have been for them a most serious matter, especially if Socrates was thought to be trying to spread his disbelief in the city's gods.

What was meant by the phrase, "other new (strange) spiritual matters?" One hypothesis was that this referred to a "divine sign" that Socrates says appeared to him from time to time. According to Socrates, his divine sign only deterred him from actions he was about to perform; perhaps it consisted of the single word, "no" or "don't." Socrates was convinced that this sign was a communication with the divine. This should have been sufficient to show that he was not an atheist, a complete disbeliever in the gods; and traditional Greek religion allows for the possibility that the gods on occasion communicated with human beings. Still, Socrates' sign was not a common experience among his fellow Athenians. It may have seemed strange to them. Was Socrates claiming to have his own god or demigod who spoke only to him? Did he have a private cult, not a part of the state's religion? The Athenians were in general willing to introduce new divinities into the state religion. At the beginning of Plato's *Republic* Socrates says that he had gone to the Piraeus, the port city of Athens, to celebrate the inauguration of worship of the Thracian goddess Bendis. The Athenians, like other Greeks, were polytheists. They not only worshiped the twelve Olympian gods, but many other gods and demigods. There was always "room for one more" in the pantheon. But Socrates did not try to have his sign recognized as a new divinity.

Did a majority of the jury believe that Socrates rejected traditional Greek religion in favor of a personal divine voice unique to himself? To Xenophon this seemed preposterous. No one was more faithful in both public and private sacrifice to the gods, he argued, and Socrates' private divine voice was no different from other forms of divination. What arguments could the prosecution have made for impiety? Nor, he thought, was Socrates guilty of corrupting the youth. He showed by his own conduct the greatest self-control and this led his associates to follow his example. Xenophon mentions the fact, not mentioned in Plato's *Apology*, that Critias, the ring-leader of the Thirty, and Alcibiades, a brilliant but uncontroled Athenian democratic political and military leader, had been associates of Socrates, but he denies that Socrates was responsible for their corruption. Socrates "showed his companions that he was a gentleman[5] himself, and talked most excellently of goodness and of all things that concern man" (*Memorabilia* I.ii.17). Socrates restrained the bad impulses of these men, so long as they associated with him; they were corrupted by others.

Xenophon's mention of Critias and Alcibiades raises an interpretation of the trial that arose shortly after the event, and that has persisted to this day. According to this "political" interpretation the charge of impiety was just a smokescreen for the real reason that Socrates was tried: his opposition to the democracy.[6] Socrates criticized the Athenian practice of electing most public officials by lot, and this, it was thought, "led the young to despise the established constitution" (*Mem.* I.ii.9). This may have been the real source of the charge of "corrupting the youth." Critias and Alcibiades were examples of this corruption, though Critias was not a youth when Socrates knew him. Because of the amnesty, Socrates could not have been officially charged with corrupting either of them, but his prosecutors still may have mentioned their names during their speeches. Socrates was no friend of the government of the Thirty, but he had, as noted above, remained in the city during their reign of terror. Anytus, one of the prosecutors, was a prominent Athenian politician at the time of the trial. He may have thought that Socrates, as a critic of democracy, was a danger to the state. For all these reasons the jurors, or at least some of them, may have harbored resentment against Socrates.

Plato in his *Apology* does not specifically raise the political interpretation of Socrates' trial, but he also thought that there were reasons for the trial that were not stated in the official indictment. He distinguishes Socrates' current accusers – Meletus, Anytus, and Lycon – who charge him with impiety and corrupting the youth – from his "first accusers," who have been prejudicing the Athenians against him for decades, saying, "there is a man called Socrates, a wise man, a student of all things in the sky and below the earth, who makes the worse argument the stronger. Those who spread that rumor, gentlemen, are my dangerous accusers, for their hearers believe that those who study these things do not even believe in the gods" (18b–c). What Socrates is saying is that there is a long-standing prejudice against him, that he has already been convicted in the court of public opinion of being an atheist, and that given this longstanding prejudice it is impossible for him to get a fair trial.

Though these first accusers are the dangerous ones, in Socrates' view, they are largely anonymous. The one exception is the comic poet Aristophanes, whose play the *Clouds*, originally written in 423, is very probably the only work featuring Socrates written in Socrates' own lifetime. In the *Clouds* Aristophanes has Socrates tell his would-be student Strepsiades that the gods of the tradition do not exist, beginning with Zeus. The only gods worshiped in Socrates' school, he tells Strepsiades, are Chaos, the Clouds, and Tongue (i.e. the god of rhetoric). This disavowal of the traditional gods plus the introduction of strange or new divinities would have been a more serious matter than claiming to hear a private voice.

Though the *Clouds* was not successful when it was first performed in 423, many Athenians would have seen this play; Socrates assumes that his jurors are familiar with it. For some, it may have been the source of their ideas of who Socrates was. It was not the only source: Socrates must have been a public figure in 423 or Aristophanes would not have bothered to write a play about him, and Socrates says his first accusers were numerous. Still, Aristophanes' portrait of Socrates may well have been influential with many jurors, as Plato thought it was, and Aristophanes' Socrates is certainly a disbeliever in the gods of the state and an introducer of new divinities.

Plato believes that a major reason behind Socrates' prosecution was Socrates' philosophical activity. Socrates says that he has caused trouble for himself by examining the leading political figures in Athens. Not only did *they* come to dislike him, but so did many of their followers. "I realized," he states, "to my sorrow and alarm, that I was getting unpopular" (21e). A page later he restates the point: "as a result of this investigation, men of Athens, I acquired much unpopularity, of a kind that is hard to deal with and is a heavy burden" (22e–23a). Socrates' suggestion is that this unpopularity contributed to his trial. It may be that the leading politicians of the state, men like Anytus, felt that they had endured enough of his questions and decided to silence him. It was not just that Socrates was a critic of democracy; he was a critic of *them*.

How did this examination of others contribute to the charge of corrupting the youth? As Socrates notes, "young men who follow me around of their own free will, those who have most leisure, the sons of the very rich, take pleasure in hearing people questioned; they themselves often imitate me and try to question others" (23c).

Though Socrates denied that he was a teacher, he admits that these young men learned their practice of questioning others from him. One can only imagine the trouble these young people would have caused if they took their new-found Socratic techniques of investigation home to practice on their parents. To a proponent of traditional Athenian values, such young people might well seem to have been corrupted by Socrates. It is tempting to speculate that Anytus himself may have been one of the political leaders examined by Socrates and shown up in the presence of his followers. It is also tempting to speculate that his son, whom Socrates admits in Xenophon's *Apology* that he knew, may have brought Socrates' method of questioning into his own household. Anytus may have had personal reasons for holding a grudge against Socrates.

Was Socrates Guilty?

There is no reason to think that there were any procedural irregularities in the trial of Socrates. Socrates was convicted in accordance with Athenian law. There were several features of that law that would seem today to offer insufficient protection to defendants charged with capital crimes: the trial had to be completed in a single day, the scope of the charge of impiety was not specified precisely in Athenian law, and there was no appeal from the verdict of the jury. The defendant was not allowed to have legal counsel; he might hire a speechwriter, but he had to read his defense speech himself. There is a story that the speechwriter Lysias wrote a speech on Socrates' behalf, which he declined to give. The fact that a simple majority of the jury was sufficient to convict Socrates and put him to death seems unjust to us today. The jurors were not allowed to discuss the trial with each other before voting: they cast their votes after the prosecutors and the defendant made their speeches. These differences between Athenian law and ours make it extremely unlikely that Socrates would have been brought to trial, let alone convicted, in a modern court of justice, at least in a democracy. Be that as it may, however, Socrates' conviction was in accordance with the laws in place in Athens at the time.

If one were to look only at Aristophanes' *Clouds*, one would conclude that Socrates was guilty of the charge of impiety, for rejecting the traditional gods and introducing strange new ones. Since Socrates also in the play turns Strepsiades' son Pheidippides into a tradition-bashing scoffer who beats his father, one could conclude that he was guilty of the charge of corrupting the youth as well. Though the *Clouds* was not the only source of Socrates' bad reputation, it may have been an accurate portrait of how Socrates was seen by the majority of Athenians at the time of his trial. For Xenophon, on the other hand, the charges against Socrates were preposterous. He summarizes his view by asking:

> How then could he be guilty of the charges? For so far was he from "rejecting the gods," as charged in the indictment, that no man was more conspicuous for his devotion to the service of the gods: so far from "corrupting the youth," as his accuser actually charged against him, that if any among his companions had evil desires, he openly tried to reform them and exhorted them to desire the fairest and noblest virtue, by which men prosper in public life and in their homes. By this conduct did he not deserve high honour from the State? (*Mem.* I.ii.64)

For Plato, matters are not so simple. Unquestionably, Plato believed in Socrates' innocence, and wrote his *Apology* to show this. Still, the defense of Socrates that Plato attributes to him leaves two questions open. First, Socrates argues that he believes in the gods, "as none of my accusers do" (35d). There is no question that Socrates asserts his belief in "the gods"; but are they the gods the city believes in? Some recent interpreters have argued that they are not. Socrates' gods are not the gods of Homer and the Greek religious tradition, gods who quarreled with each other and who were not generally on friendly terms with humans. His gods agreed, especially about questions of value: they had the knowledge for which Socrates searched. They were also beneficial toward humans. Socrates' gods are morally perfect; the traditional gods are anything but that. Moreover, though Socrates describes himself as a servant of "the god" and on occasion "the god at Delphi," Apollo, he rarely refers to any god by name. This has made some interpreters question whether he believes in the gods of the city, as opposed to gods of his own devising. As one interpreter notes, Socrates "might almost be a monotheist."[7] Plato addresses this question of Socrates' religious beliefs in the *Euthyphro*, which we shall consider in Chapter 4.

Second, consider the charge of corrupting the youth. Suppose Socrates taught the young people who followed him around to believe in the kind of gods he believed in, who at least had different characteristics from the gods of traditional Greek theology. Would this have constituted corruption, in the eyes of the jury? Suppose Socrates had taught the youth, as Xenophon admits, to question the

Athenian principle of electing most officials by lot, which was a fundamental practice of Athenian democracy. Would this questioning have constituted corruption? Suppose Socrates had taught the youth to raise basic questions about the meaning of terms that ordinary Athenians thought they understood quite well, terms such as justice, courage, temperance, and wisdom. Suppose Socrates' inquiries had led, not to new conceptions of these terms, but to perplexity. Suppose Socrates taught the youth who followed him not to be good, loyal Athenians but skeptics. Would this have been corruption? Plato's dialogues raise a fundamental question about the aim of liberal education. Is it to produce good citizens, with faith in democracy and its institutions, or is it to produce critical minds? Plato was not a friend of democracy. One of the reasons for this is certainly that it was Athenian democracy that put Socrates to death. But Plato may have accepted and developed for his own purposes the Socratic view that the government of the state was best left not in the hands of the people but in the hands of an expert ruler, who becomes in Plato's *Republic* a philosopher-king, whose absolute power is based on absolute wisdom. Plato certainly approved of Socrates' attempt to make his young associates question the basic principles of democratic government. Practical democratic politicians like Anytus would have surely disapproved. They would have considered Socrates' raising of these questions to be corruption of the youth. The question of Socrates' political beliefs will be discussed in Chapter 7.

The Death Penalty

Socrates' trial had two phases, as do many trials today. In the first phase the guilt or innocence of the defendant is decided. In the second, if the defendant is found guilty, the prosecution and defense each get to propose a penalty, and the jury must decide between them. Socrates' accusers proposed death as the penalty for his impiety and corruption of the youth. To readers today this seems an impossibly severe penalty. It is sometimes said that his prosecutors did not desire Socrates' death, but rather hoped that he might propose exile as an alternative, which would have been within his rights. Socrates even mentions the possibility of exile when considering what punishment to propose. Yet this suggestion has problems, not the least of which is that, had the prosecutors wished to exile Socrates, they might simply have proposed that. Perhaps his accusers thought that death was the only way to silence Socrates' voice. But why would the jury agree to the death penalty? For one thing, as noted above, impiety was considered a very serious matter in ancient Athens, a threat to the foundation of the state, something akin to treason. To be impious was to risk the anger and disfavor of the gods, and the consequences of that could be disastrous. Socrates may have seemed to a majority of the jurors to be a serious threat to the well-being, even the survival, of the state.

In addition, Socrates no doubt angered the jurors by the way in which he dealt with the question of his penalty. According to Plato, Socrates' initial choice of a "penalty" is that he be given free meals in the Prytaneum, the city hall, a reward reserved for Olympic victors and other heroes. Socrates' reasoning is that he has done nothing wrong but, on the contrary, has devoted his life to the service of Athens by trying to persuade individual Athenians to care for virtue and wisdom above all else. "The Olympian victor," Socrates says, "makes you think yourself happy; I make you be happy" (36d–e). "Besides," he adds, "he does not need food, but I do." Eventually Socrates proposed a fine of thirty *minae*, a sizeable amount, funded by his associates, but the damage had been done. Xenophon had asked the rhetorical question whether Socrates did not deserve honor from the state in the passage from the *Memorabilia* quoted above; but it is one thing for a third party, a known follower of Socrates, to make this suggestion and another for Socrates himself to make it. Socrates' proposal would have seemed insufferably arrogant to many of the jurors. Nor was this the only occasion, according to Plato, in which he angered the jurors by what Xenophon called his haughty and arrogant remarks. He notes that the oracle of Apollo at Delphi declared that no one was wiser than he. He dismisses fear of death as unsuitable for him, and in the process he compares himself to the great heroes of Homer, including Homer's greatest hero, Achilles. He describes himself as the god's gift to Athens, like a stinging fly sent to arouse a "great and noble," but "somewhat sluggish" horse (30e). He refuses to bring his family before the jury to plead for mercy on their behalf, but instead lectures the jurors on their duty to judge his case in accordance with the law, following their oath as jurors. Throughout the trial Socrates refuses to do what jurors had been accustomed to see from a defendant: to show fear for what they might do to him. Near the very end of Plato's *Apology*, when Socrates is addressing the jurors who voted for his acquittal, he says that he believes that a good man cannot be harmed. Clearly, he thinks of himself as a good man. This complete lack of fear in the face of a guilty verdict would certainly have angered many jurors. This no doubt made it easier for them to vote for the death penalty.

The Trial: Conclusion

Socrates' trial was a "perfect storm" of circumstances that made his conviction seem inevitable. It occurred at a time when Athens was trying to recover from a devastating defeat, in a climate of recrimination concerning loss of the war, a loss for which some Athenians thought the leaders of the intellectual revolution were at least partially responsible. It followed the production of a play that made Socrates seem to be a denier of the traditional gods and a religious innovator. Socrates was a public figure, and his notoriety was enhanced by Aristophanes' play. Part of Socrates' reputation was that of a critic of Athenian democracy, which was in a fragile condition. Socrates' own practice of examining people who claimed to possess wisdom about what he called the "most important pursuits" made him unpopular with those in power. Finally, Socrates' own conduct at the trial was of such a nature as to anger members of the jury and enhance the likelihood of his conviction and death sentence.

The trial, conviction, and death of Socrates are major events in the history of philosophy and the history of Western civilization. The questions raised by the trial concerning, for instance, the nature of Socrates' religious belief and his relation to the city of Athens, reverberate through Plato's dialogues. When Plato thought of Socrates, which is constantly, he thought of him as a martyr who died for the sake of philosophy. Socrates' piety is a theme of the *Euthyphro*, which we shall examine in Chapter 4; his relation to Athens and its democratic government is a theme of the *Crito*, which we shall examine in Chapter 7. His defense of the philosophical life is a theme of the *Gorgias*, which we shall examine in Chapter 6. Even when Plato is not focusing directly on the issues that arise from the trial, however, his portrait of Socrates is influenced by Socrates' account of his practice of philosophy and by the character that he showed in his conduct at the trial. Plato's *Apology* may or may not be a historical document, an account of what Socrates said at the trial; but even if it is not it is a very important document for our understanding of Socrates as Plato saw him.

Socrates the Man: Conclusion

What emerges from these unfavorable circumstances is a portrait of a man who is less concerned with his own survival than prudence might dictate. But this fact is what makes Socrates a hero to his followers. Socrates pursued philosophical inquiry no matter what the cost. He saw himself, according to Plato, as a servant of "the god at Delphi," but he also saw himself as a pursuer of wisdom. In one of the most famous passages of Plato's *Apology*, Socrates states that "it is the greatest good for a man to discuss virtue every day and those other things about which you hear me conversing and testing myself and others, for the unexamined life is not worth living for men" (38a). He admits that those he is trying to convince won't believe this, but it is the code by which he lives. Earlier in the *Apology* he asks himself what he would say if the jury acquitted him on the condition that he give up the practice of philosophy, and he answers, "men of Athens, I am grateful and I am your friend, but I will obey the god rather than you, and as long as I draw breath and am able, I shall not cease to practice philosophy" (29d). The practice of philosophy was more important to Socrates than the continuation of his own life. At the very end of the *Apology*, when Socrates is considering his fate after death, he imagines himself in the underworld, examining the heroes of the Trojan War and the great poets, to discover who is wise and who merely thinks he is. This activity he describes as "extraordinary happiness" (41c). The practice of philosophical inquiry gave meaning to Socrates' life, made him happy. He thought that it would do the same for others who practiced it and that without it life was unworthy of human beings.

Plato and Xenophon see in Socrates a man of unequaled character. He was, as a character in Xenophon's *Symposium* states, "an admirable and good man" (IX.1: my translation).[8] At the conclusion of Plato's dialogue the *Phaedo* the narrator, Phaedo, describes Socrates as "of all those we knew the best, and also the wisest and most upright" (118a). Xenophon and Plato give us portraits of Socrates as they understand him. When we talk about Socrates' character, we are discussing his character as they understood it. For Plato and Xenophon, Socrates' character was not something that was separate from his practice of philosophy; it was in the practice of philosophy that Socrates showed his character. Socrates was, for Plato and Xenophon, in his essence a philosopher, a man who lived a philosophical life. His virtue, his wisdom, and uprightness, were the result of his philosophical inquiry, and it was displayed in the process of that inquiry. When we turn, as we shall in the next chapter, from an examination of Socrates the man to an examination of his philosophy, we need to remember that for Plato as for Xenophon Socrates was not just a practitioner of a certain philosophical method or a defender of certain philosophical views, but a man who lived by the philosophy he preached. Philosophy was, for Socrates, as for Plato, not just an intellectual discipline but a way of life. When we consider, as we shall, what Socrates says about virtue, we need to keep in mind the fact that for Plato as well as for Xenophon, Socrates was a virtuous man. Plato's dialogues do not simply offer us a set of abstract arguments; they put those arguments in the mouth of someone who exemplifies the virtue that he discusses. In Plato's *Laches* the title character describes himself as someone who both loves and hates discussion:

> Whenever I hear a man discussing virtue or some kind of wisdom, then, if he really is a man and worthy of the words he utters, I am completely delighted to see the appropriateness and harmony existing between the speaker and his words. And such a man seems to me to be genuinely musical, producing the most beautiful harmony, not on the lyre or some other pleasurable instrument, but actually rendering his own life harmonious by fitting his deeds to his words … The discourse of such a man gladdens my heart … (188c–e).

Plato's Socrates was such a man.

2

Socratic Method

The "Socratic Problem"

When we begin to inquire into Socrates' philosophical views, we face a problem that must be addressed, though I believe it cannot be solved. Though we know some things about Socrates the man, we have no direct evidence concerning Socrates the philosopher. Even in talking about Socrates the man, we have to rely on sources, such as the works of Xenophon and Plato, for information. The situation is the same when we discuss Socrates' philosophy. Socrates has left us no written evidence of his views or his methods. What we know or believe about Socrates we owe to the works of other authors. The first of these is Aristophanes, the second is Xenophon, and the third is Plato. All three of these knew Socrates personally. A fourth source is Aristotle, who was not an associate of Socrates because he was not born until fifteen years after Socrates' death. Aristotle was a member of Plato's Academy, the first institution of higher education in the West, during the last twenty years of Plato's life. He comments on occasion about Socrates in his own works, especially when offering an account of the historical background of the subject under consideration.

It would be convenient if these sources all coalesced to give us a single picture of Socrates, but they do not. Aristophanes portrays Socrates as an intellectual poseur and mountebank, head of a school called the *phrontistērion* or "think-tank," in which students learn all sorts of pseudo-science as well as "Unjust Argument," and in which they learn to despise the traditional gods. As we saw in Chapter 1,

Plato names Aristophanes in his *Apology* as one source of Socrates' bad reputation. Both Xenophon and Plato attempt to show that this Aristophanic portrait is a distortion of the truth. For both of these, Socrates was a noble man, a hero in fact, of the highest ethical standards and personal piety. They differed in their understanding of Socrates' philosophy, but they both understood him as a man who was, in the traditional Greek phrase for excellence of character, *kalos kagathos*, "admirable and good." Clearly, Socrates made a powerful impression on both men, with the result that they wrote about him extensively.

In the years following Socrates' death a genre of writing arose that Aristotle refers to as "the Socratic conversation" (*Poetics* 1447b10). A Socratic conversation shows Socrates in conversation with another individual or individuals on a variety of topics, usually of an ethical nature. Plato and Xenophon were not the first or the only associates of Socrates who wrote Socratic conversations, but their works are the ones that have survived intact. Xenophon wrote four "Socratic" works, an *Apology* and a *Symposium*, thought to be modeled on Plato's works of the same names, a set of memoirs of Socrates entitled the *Memorabilia*, and a work on estate management entitled the *Oeconomicus*. Plato wrote over twenty dialogues, the majority of which feature Socrates as the main speaker. It is chiefly thanks to these works that we have an abundance of "information" about Socrates. I put the word "information" in quotes because none of these works provide a straightforward set of biographical facts about Socrates. Both Plato and Xenophon use Socrates as a character in works that display a considerable amount of freedom in the topics they discuss and in the words they attribute to those who discuss them. Plato in particular wrote works of philosophy, works in which Socrates debates ethical subjects with various conversation partners, interlocutors. How much of these conversations was based on things that Socrates may actually have said and how much was Platonic invention is something that we cannot determine. Some interpreters have described these works as philosophical fictions. Much of Aristotle's interpretation of Socrates' philosophy is based on his reading of Plato's dialogues. Some scholars have therefore dismissed or downplayed Aristotle as a source.

This problem that we have with our sources is known as the "Socratic Problem," the problem of deciding which of our sources gives us the most accurate portrait of the historical Socrates. As I have said above, I believe this problem is unsolvable. It is similar to the problem of finding the historical Jesus in the Gospels. There is no question that the historical Socrates lies behind the various portraits of him in Plato, Xenophon, Aristotle, and even Aristophanes, but we have no way of knowing which portrait is closest to the truth. I do not wish to dismiss this problem as unimportant; many important problems are insoluble. I don't, however, attempt to propose a solution to this problem in this book. When it comes to the primary task of this work, which is the understanding of the philosophy of Socrates, we need not answer the question of what views the historical Socrates held and what methods he practiced. The philosophy of Socrates that has captivated interpreters in the past and continues to captivate them today is, by and large, the philosophy presented in the works of Plato. There have been moments in the history of Western culture when Xenophon's works were held in as high esteem as Plato's, or even higher, but for the most part it has been Plato's portrayal of Socrates that has been preeminent. The reasons for this are the artistic quality of Plato's works, which is unexcelled in ancient philosophy, and the richness of the philosophy they contain. This is not to say that Plato did not attempt to explain to his readers what his mentor and philosophical model Socrates was actually like. He did, but his portrayal of Socrates is enmeshed with Plato's own philosophical creativity in ways that make it impossible for us to separate them. In any case, when we discuss the philosophy of Socrates today, it is first and foremost the philosophy of *Plato's* Socrates that we discuss. The Socrates who primarily interests us is the character in those works. In this book, therefore, we shall investigate the philosophy of Socrates as it is presented in Plato's works. I shall mention at times the historical Socrates, but when I do I shall distinguish him from the Socrates of Plato's dialogues.

The Nature of Socrates' Philosophy

Plato portrays Socrates as a man whose life was dedicated to philosophy; but what does philosophy mean to Plato's Socrates? Is it primarily a method of inquiry, a particular approach to certain problems, or is it primarily a set of solutions to these problems? Is Socrates an investigator, searching for a truth he does not possess, or an expounder of a set of philosophical beliefs? In Plato's works we can find evidence for both answers to these questions. In some of his works Plato portrays Socrates as an inquirer, a man with questions and a method for exploring those questions, but without philosophical doctrines, that is without settled convictions that he has reached as a result of philosophical inquiry. A prime example of this portrait of Socrates can be found in Plato's *Apology*, which was a focus of the previous chapter. In other works Plato portrays Socrates as a man with answers to the questions he raises. A prime example of *this* portrait can be found in Plato's *Republic*. The *Republic* is one of Plato's longest works: it was divided in ancient times into ten "books." In the first book Socrates and several interlocutors discuss the nature of justice, but reach no definitive conclusions about it. In Books II–X Socrates presents a positive account of the nature of justice in both the city and the individual person, accompanied by accounts of the nature of the human soul, reality, and knowledge. These books contain the most comprehensive set of philosophical views found in the dialogues, and they are all expounded by the character Socrates.

Socratic vs. Platonic Philosophy

Does the philosophical system expounded in Books II–X of the *Republic* belong to Socrates? In one sense, the obvious answer is yes, since Socrates is the speaker of the dialogue who expounds them. The vast majority of interpreters, however, regard this system as Plato's, not Socrates'. They believe that Socrates in *Republic* II–X is a spokesman, a "mouthpiece," for Plato's own ideas. Whether the doctrines attributed to Socrates in the *Republic* are really Plato's and not Socrates' is a question that has been debated since antiquity. A doctrine that is of central importance in the *Republic* concerns the nature of reality, what Socrates calls "being." The view expressed there is that reality consists of a set of intelligible objects called "Forms" or "Ideas," which exist in separation from the world that we experience through our senses. The sensible world, according to this view, is only an image of the real world of the Forms. Aristotle thought that this doctrine of separately existing Forms was Plato's, not Socrates'; Socrates, he states, sought universal definitions of terms but "did not make the universals or the definitions exist apart" (*Metaphysics* M.4, 1078b30–31). Aristotle also attributes to Socrates a view that can be found in Plato's *Protagoras*, that moral weakness, knowing what is right but doing what is wrong, is impossible (*Nicomachean Ethics* VII.2, 1145b25–27). Aristotle is sometimes accused of deriving his knowledge of what Socrates thought solely from reading Plato's dialogues, but in these cases he seems certain that some of the doctrines attributed by Plato to Socrates are actually Socratic, whereas others (specifically the doctrine of separate Forms) are Platonic, despite the fact that both doctrines are attributed in the dialogues to Socrates. Plato in Book IV of the *Republic* divides the human soul into three parts – reason, spirit, and appetite – and allows the possibility that spirit or appetite might overpower reason on occasion, which would seem to make moral weakness possible. If so, then Plato allows for something that Socrates does not, though both views are attributed by Plato to Socrates.

Socratic Dialogues

Interpreters have attempted to distinguish among the Platonic works those which express Plato's philosophical views from those that express the views of Socrates. The *Republic* and *Phaedrus*, for instance, contain the theory of the tripartite soul; several dialogues – the *Cratylus*, *Symposium*, and *Phaedo* as well as the *Republic* and *Phaedrus* – espouse the separate existence of the Forms. Works that do not contain either theory but which still feature Socrates as the main speaker include the *Apology*, *Charmides*, *Crito*, *Euthydemus*, *Euthyphro*, *Gorgias*, *Hippias Major*, *Hippias Minor*, *Ion*, *Laches*, *Lysis*, *Menexenus*, *Meno*, *Protagoras*, and the first book of the *Republic*. These dialogues are often grouped together as "Socratic" dialogues. Apart from the fact that they do not contain either the theory of the tripartite soul or the theory of separate Forms, they have in common the fact that they were all written early in Plato's career. They are often therefore referred to as the "early" dialogues. This is a bit misleading, because the *Cratylus*, *Phaedo*, and *Symposium* also seem to have been written early in Plato's career; still, all of the above dialogues are in fact among Plato's early works.[1]

The Socratic Elenchus

What do these dialogues have in common, besides an early date and the absence of certain doctrines? Almost all of them describe or practice a certain method, known as the elenchus. "Elenchus" means "examination" or "test." Socrates uses this distinctive method to examine people, usually people who claim to have knowledge concerning a subject Socrates is interested in investigating. Because the result of this examination is almost always the proof that Socrates' interlocutor does *not* have the knowledge he claims to have, the word "elenchus" is often translated "refutation." As one interpreter notes, in these dialogues "we may almost say that Socrates never talks to anyone without refuting him."[2] It is the elenchus, more than an early date or the absence of certain doctrines, that marks these works as "Socratic." Socrates is, in essence, the philosopher who practices the elenchus. This method of argument is so closely associated with Socrates' name that a modern variation of it is still practiced in higher education, and in particular in law schools, as "the Socratic method." In the modern variation a questioner, usually the instructor, examines an answerer, usually a student, on a question, usually a point of law. In the modern variation the aim of the examination is to lead the student to the truth. Socrates' elenchus aims at the truth as well, but it nearly always results in the refutation of the person being examined.

The *Apology* and the Elenctic Dialogues

In this study we shall examine several works from the list above that are characterized by the Socratic elenchus. In most cases these will be dialogues in which Socrates uses the elenchus to examine various people. I shall refer to these works as "elenctic dialogues." The *Apology* is something of an exception. Though there is a relatively brief passage in which Socrates examines his chief accuser Meletus, most of the *Apology* is not made up of elenctic examination. The reason for this is that the *Apology*, though usually referred to as a dialogue, is not actually a dialogue but a speech. It is the speech in which, in addition to defending himself against the charges raised by his various accusers, Socrates defends his philosophical activity, which is to say his life. Since that activity consists in large part of examining others, the *Apology* gives Socrates' defense of his practice of the method of elenchus. The *Apology* is important because it is one of the few places in Plato's works where Socrates attempts to explain, and in fact to justify, his practice of elenchus.[3] The *Apology* gives a rationale for Socrates' elenctic activity, the activity that we see in the dialogues in the above list. This rationale is different from the rationale described in the *Meno*, as we shall see. The contrast between these two rationales provides a basis for the interpretation of Socratic philosophy found in this book.

Elenchus in the *Apology*

Interpreters often claim that in the dialogues listed above there is a single philosophy expressed. There is in fact a single method practiced in most of these dialogues (the *Menexenus*, like the *Apology*, is another exception; it is for the most part not a dialogue but a speech), but when it comes to the question of a single point of view or philosophical doctrine, matters are not so simple. Let us begin with the method of the elenchus, and specifically with Socrates' account of its nature in the *Apology*. Socrates describes his life in terms of a mission undertaken on behalf of the god Apollo, whose oracle is at Delphi. As Socrates tells the story, his associate Chaerephon went to Delphi to ask the priestess whether there was anyone wiser than Socrates. The priestess said, "no one," and Chaerephon transmitted that answer to Socrates. Now Socrates was puzzled at the oracle's pronouncement; he saw it as a riddle. (Oracles were well known for speaking in riddles; even today an "oracular utterance" may be thought of as one whose meaning is obscure.) "Whatever does the god mean?" he asked himself. "I am very conscious that I am not wise at all; what then does he mean by saying that I am the wisest?" (21b).

Socrates did not think the god would lie, but he could not work out his meaning. So, he set out to investigate the oracle's meaning, thinking that he might test (or refute) the oracle by finding someone wiser than himself. So he went, "very reluctantly," he says, to one of the "public men" of the city. "I thought that he appeared wise to many people and especially to himself, but that he was not," Socrates states (21c). Socrates then tried to show the man that he lacked wisdom, but only earned his dislike and that of those around him. "So I withdrew and thought to myself, 'I am wiser than this man; it is likely that neither of us knows anything worthwhile, but he thinks he knows something when he does not, whereas when I do not know, neither do I think I know; so I am likely to be wiser than he to this small extent, that I do not think I know what I do not know'" (21d). He then went to a second public figure, a man thought to be even wiser than the first, with the same result. As I noted in Chapter 1, Socrates describes this as the source of his unpopularity. Following his examination of the political leaders of the city, Socrates says he proceeded "systematically" (21e): he went next to the poets, where he reached the same conclusion as he had with the politicians. They thought they understood their own works, but almost anyone of the bystanders could have explained their poems better than they. They said fine things, but did not understand them. They composed not by knowledge but by inspiration. Moreover, they thought that they knew other things as well, but they did not. Socrates again concluded that he was wiser in this respect than those he had examined.

Finally, Socrates went to the artisans. He thought that they would know things he did not, and he was correct. Again, however, they thought that their knowledge of their crafts made them wise in "other most important pursuits, and this error of theirs overshadowed the wisdom they had" (22d–e). Again, Socrates thought he was better off than they. Finally, he reached the conclusion that the oracle was correct all along: "what is probable, gentlemen, is that in fact the god is wise and that his oracular response meant that human wisdom is worth little or nothing, and that when he says this man, Socrates, he is using my name as an example, as if he said: 'This man among you, mortals, is wisest who, like Socrates, understands that his wisdom is worthless'" (23a–b). Socrates had examined the leading candidates for wisdom in Athens, and discovered that he was wiser than all of them; but his wisdom consisted in the fact that he knew nothing about the "most important pursuits." He does not explain in this passage what those pursuits are; presumably they are the subjects that he later (29d–e) says he continually asks his fellow citizens to pursue above wealth, reputation, and honors: namely wisdom, truth, and the best possible state of their souls. What the Athenians don't know is how they ought to live. They ought to live in such a way as to perfect their souls, but they pursue other goals instead. They are ignorant about what really matters in life.

Why Pursue Philosophy?

Socrates says that he pursues this investigation in service to the god. It is, he believes, his mission. He continues to pursue it, "as the god bade me" (23b): he seeks out people who seem to be wise, and shows them that they are not. Those who hear his conversations believe he must know the answers to the questions he asks, but he insists he does not. No one does. He also says he pursues it because he believes "the unexamined life is not worth living," (38a) and that it is the greatest good for people to discuss "virtue … and those other things about which you hear me conversing and testing myself and others" (ibid.). It is natural to wonder why he thinks this. Does he think that, despite the fact that no one has yet answered his questions satisfactorily, someday someone might? Might Socrates meet someone with the wisdom that up to now he has believed only the god possesses? Does he think we might somehow *approximate* divine wisdom, even if we can't actually possess it? Does he think that it is not the attainment of wisdom, but the pursuit of it that is actually valuable? Socrates does not answer these questions. Perhaps the value of constantly searching for wisdom is just the humility that results from the awareness that one lacks it. Perhaps Socrates is a *skeptic* about the possibility of knowledge of the "most important pursuits." Perhaps he believes it is impossible for a human being to acquire this knowledge. If so, one might respond, why should one continually pursue questions that one cannot answer? Might it not be better to give up on the pursuit of wisdom and truth, and pursue wealth, reputation, and honors instead? This is not an idle question. In the *Gorgias*, Socrates encounters two figures, Polus and Callicles, who are proponents of the pursuit of pleasure and political power. Socrates argues for the pursuit of justice and in favor of the life of philosophical inquiry instead. This issue of what life one should pursue was on Plato's mind.

The Logic of the Elenchus

The issue of what life to pursue arises from what Socrates says in the *Apology* and elsewhere about his examination of others. What we have seen so far describes the *results* of this examination, namely the refutation of others and the resultant awareness of one's ignorance. The *Apology* does not tell us much about how those results are achieved. It does not tell us how Socratic examination, the elenchus, actually works. In order to understand the results of the elenchus, we must try to understand this. The elenchus starts with a question, the "primary question,"[4] asked by Socrates. The nature of this question varies from dialogue to dialogue, but in several dialogues it is a question about the definition of a term that has ethical significance. In the *Euthyphro* the question is, "what is piety?" In the *Charmides* it is, "what is temperance (moderation)?" In the *Laches* it is, "what is courage?" In the first book of the *Republic* it is, "what is justice?" In the *Meno* it is, "what is virtue?" Socrates never asks, "what is wisdom?" but in the *Protagoras* he attempts to show that all of the above virtues are in fact wisdom or knowledge.

Defining the virtues was a project to which Socrates was devoted. Not all of the questions Socrates asks are questions about the nature and correct definition of an ethical term, but all have some connection to ethical concerns.

The primary question is usually directed at someone who professes to have knowledge of the answer. Euthyphro is a self-proclaimed expert on piety; Charmides is praised by his mentor Critias as a young man who excels in temperance; Laches is a general and so is his fellow interlocutor, Nicias. Thrasymachus in the *Republic* has a theory about the nature of justice; Meno claims to have learned from the rhetorician Gorgias what virtue is; Protagoras claims to know, and be able to teach, personal and civic virtue. Usually this person regards answering Socrates' question as a simple matter, not requiring much deliberation, and as a result he responds confidently. Socrates then proceeds to refute his interlocutor's answer. Sometimes he says that the answer is not of the right sort: it describes an example or a part of the virtue in question, and not the virtue itself. Many other things exhibit the virtue as well. Once the interlocutor gets the point of the question, and responds appropriately, Socrates proceeds to show him that his answer conflicts with other beliefs that he has. He elicits from the interlocutor answers to these "secondary questions," and shows that his answers conflict with his primary answer. The interlocutor has a choice as to which statement to withdraw, but he always withdraws his answer to the primary question. It is not clear why the interlocutor prefers to retain his answers to Socrates' secondary questions, but he does. At this point Socrates repeats the primary question, and the interlocutor makes a new attempt to answer it, at which point again Socrates elicits from him answers to secondary questions that conflict with it, again refuting the attempted answer. This process repeats until the interlocutor expresses perplexity and admits that he does not know the answer. Eventually the dialogue ends in a state of perplexity; both Socrates and the interlocutor admit that they do not know the answer to Socrates' primary question.

Elenchus in the *Sophist*

This is the way the elenchus works, at least in theory. The elenchus, thus understood, is a method of refutation. It shows an interlocutor that he is mistaken in his attempt to answer Socrates' primary question. It does not prove that the interlocutor's primary answer is actually incorrect; it only shows that this answer conflicts with other statements that the interlocutor prefers to retain. It shows that his answer is inconsistent with other statements he believes. This point is made very clearly in a passage from Plato's dialogue the *Sophist*. Like the *Apology*, the *Sophist* contains one of the few places in which Plato attempts to explain and justify the elenchus. The *Sophist* is not an early dialogue, nor is it a Socratic dialogue: the main role in the conversation is taken, not by Socrates, but by an "Eleatic Visitor." The method of elenchus is not even attributed to Socrates in the passage in which the method is explained. The Eleatic Visitor attributes it to certain unnamed practitioners of what he calls "noble sophistry" (231b). What these noble Sophists try to do is to remove people's false beliefs in their own wisdom:

> They cross-examine someone when he thinks he's saying something though he's saying nothing. Then, since his opinions will vary inconsistently, these people will easily scrutinize them. They collect his opinions together during the discussion, put them side by side, and show that they conflict with each other at the same time on the same subjects in relation to the same things and in the same respects. The people who are being examined see this, get angry at themselves, and become calmer toward others. They lose their inflated and rigid beliefs about themselves that way, and no loss is pleasanter to hear or has a more lasting effect on them. (230b–c)

Though this method is not attributed to Socrates, it is clearly the method of elenchus, and it is clearly described as a method of bringing out inconsistencies in the beliefs of someone who falsely believes that he has knowledge. Since no genuine expert will hold inconsistent beliefs about his or her area of expertise, this method proves that the interlocutor is no expert.

The Structure of the Elenctic Dialogue: The *Charmides*

The elenchus thus described is, as I have said, an engine of refutation. It can show an alleged expert that he does not know what he is talking about. The repeated application of the elenchus produces a dialogue with a certain structure: Socrates asks his primary question, the interlocutor makes several attempts to answer it, all of which fail, the interlocutor admits perplexity and the dialogue ultimately ends inconclusively. Several of the dialogues listed above

follow this pattern, with variations. Sometimes there is more than
one interlocutor. Sometimes the interlocutor does not admit perplexity, but only frustration. Still, the pattern is there. Consider, for
example, the *Charmides*. Socrates has just returned from the battlefield at Potidaea, where many Athenians have been killed. He
passes briefly over the war, however, because what he really wants
to discuss is the state of philosophy at Athens. At this point a youth
named Charmides arrives, whom Critias introduces as his cousin.
(Charmides and Critias, incidentally, are both relatives of Plato.)
Charmides is distinguished for his beauty, but also for the state
of his soul, which Critias praises. Eventually, after some badinage
about a headache remedy and a question about whether Charmides
possesses the virtue of temperance, Socrates gets down to business,
asking Charmides what temperance is. "If temperance is present
in you," Socrates states, "you have some opinion about it" (159a).
Charmides offers a couple of attempted definitions of temperance
– temperance is quietness and temperance is modesty – each of
which Socrates quickly refutes. Charmides then states that "I have
just remembered having heard someone say that temperance is
minding one's own business" (161b; this is close to the definition
of justice as doing one's own work given by Socrates in *Republic*
IV, at 433a–b). Socrates suggests that he must have heard this from
Critias; and, though Critias initially denies it, it turns out that this
is the case. Socrates initially attempts to refute this definition too,
at which point Charmides admits that he is "at a total loss" (162b)
and Critias takes over the argument.

Critias at first attempts to defend his definition, but then he
switches to the claim that temperance is self-knowledge. He looks
to Socrates for agreement, but Socrates replies, "You are talking to
me as though I professed to know the answers to my own questions
and as though I could agree with you if I really wished. This is not
the case – rather, because of my own ignorance, I am continually
investigating in your company whatever is put forward" (165b–c).
A little later he asks Critias, "how could you possibly think that
even if I were to refute everything you say, I would be doing it for
any other reasons than the one I would give for a thorough investigation of my own statements – the fear of unconsciously thinking
I know something when I do not?" (166c–d). Socrates asks Critias
two basic questions about temperance, as Critias defines it. His first
question is, "If temperance is knowledge, what is it knowledge of?"
His second question is, "Of what benefit is temperance, if it is as
he defines it?" Critias proves unable to answer either question. The

other arts, argues Socrates, have objects different from themselves; medicine is knowledge of health, and its benefit is that it produces health. What is the object of temperance? Critias answers that, unlike the other arts, temperance is the knowledge of knowledge. (This shift from temperance as knowledge of oneself to temperance as knowledge of knowledge leads Critias into all sorts of trouble, but it may not be as strange as it sounds. The temperate person, on Critias' account, is one who knows what he knows and what he does not know. He won't attempt to act beyond his limitations: he won't attempt to cure a serious disease, if he knows that he doesn't know medicine, but will leave that to a doctor.)

Socrates argues against Critias' definition. There are no other psychological properties that have themselves as objects: there is no vision of vison, no hearing of hearing, no desire of desire, and so on. By analogy, it would seem that there can be no knowledge of knowledge. When Critias seems unable to handle this objection, Socrates says, suppose we just accept that such a thing as knowledge of knowledge is possible; how will it benefit us? The temperate person will know what subjects are kinds of knowledge, but won't be able to tell whether another person has that knowledge or not. The temperate person will know *that* medicine is a science, but will not know *what* the doctor knows. It is the art of medicine that benefits people, not temperance. (In this respect temperance seems to be like a branch of philosophy known today as the philosophy of science. The philosopher of science investigates what science is, and whether a supposed science is really a science, but it does not follow that the philosopher of science knows what the actual scientist knows.) But let us concede even that. Let us suppose, says Socrates, that we can know not merely what a doctor is, but how to distinguish a genuine doctor from a quack, and so on with the other arts and sciences. Still, all the sciences are not equally important.

What we really want to know is the science that will make us happy, and that, says Critias, is the science of good and evil. Even if we organize our lives as scientifically as possible, if we don't know what is good and what is evil we will not benefit from our organization. Temperance, as Critias has defined it, will not benefit us. Socrates concludes: we couldn't show that the knowledge of knowledge was even possible, or that the temperate person could pick out genuine experts, but we conceded both points; yet we still couldn't show that temperance, defined as the knowledge of knowledge, was beneficial. And yet, he says to Charmides, "I think that temperance is a great good, and if you truly have it, that you are blessed" (176a). Charmides says he doesn't know whether he is temperate or not; he asks, "how would I know the nature of a thing when neither you nor Critias is able to discover it?" (176a–b), but he promises Critias that he will continue to associate with Socrates every day, even if he must do so by force, and Socrates says he will not oppose him.

The arguments in this dialogue are fiendishly difficult at times, but the structure of the dialogue is clear. There is the primary question, "What is temperance?" and a series of attempts to answer it, each of which is refuted. Charmides at one point expresses his perplexity, and so does Socrates. Critias never does, though he is unable to answer Socrates' objections to his definition of temperance as knowledge of knowledge. It certainly seems as though that definition, like the previous ones, has been refuted. The dialogue ends in perplexity. It is hard to see what positive results might be drawn from it. We don't know whether Charmides fulfilled his pledge to Critias to associate with Socrates daily. We do know that he ended up badly, as an associate of Critias who died with him in the battle to restore the democracy. Whatever high promise he had was not fulfilled.

Other elenctic dialogues closely resemble the *Charmides* in this respect: the *Euthyphro, Hippias Major, Hippias Minor, Ion, Laches, Lysis, Protagoras,* and *Republic* I all end in perplexity after several rounds of elenctic argument. This is what we would expect from the method as described in the *Apology*, whose purpose is to display the ignorance of the interlocutors. There are variations in the pattern: in the *Hippias Major* Hippias never seems to understand the kind of answer Socrates wants. In the *Lysis* the young interlocutors, Lysis and Menexenus, are not experts in the nature of friendship; they are just friends, as Charmides is not said to be an expert in temperance, but temperate. Some dialogues do not fit the pattern: The *Euthydemus* contains two elenctic passages between Socrates and a youth named Clinias, but they are sandwiched in between the clowning performance of two self-proclaimed experts in dialectic, Euthydemus and Dionysodorus, who won't sit still to be examined by Socrates. Not all dialogues in which the elenchus is featured end in perplexity: the *Meno* does not, nor does the *Crito* or the *Gorgias*. I shall have more to say about these three dialogues.

Two Questions about the Elenchus

These dialogues raise two serious questions about the elenchus. The first is whether an interlocutor has to have certain characteristics in order to be a candidate for the elenchus. If an interlocutor refuses to "play Socrates' game," so to speak, can the elenchus get off the ground? Can someone be, by temperament or conviction, impervious to Socrates' method of examination? Euthydemus and Dionysodorus seem to be so; so, ultimately, is Callicles in the *Gorgias*. The second question is whether the elenchus can be put to a positive use. We have seen that it can play a negative role in refuting hypotheses; can it play a positive role in supporting them? There are two passages that indicate that it can. In a passage in the *Sophist* at the end of the excerpt quoted above, the Eleatic Visitor says that

> Doctors who work on the body think it can't benefit from any food that's offered to it until what's interfering with it from inside is removed. The people who cleanse the soul, my young friend, likewise think the soul, too, won't get any advantage from any learning that's offered to it until someone shames it by refuting it, removes the opinions that interfere with learning, and exhibits it cleansed, believing that it knows only those things that it does know, and nothing more. (230b–c)

If treatment of the soul is like treatment of the body in illness, it would seem to be a two-stage process. In the first stage of healing the body, what is harmful to it within must be removed. In the second stage, the cleansed body can benefit from food offered to it. If the treatment of the soul is parallel to treatment of the body, then there would be a first, destructive phase of treatment in which the elenchus is at work, cleansing the soul of its false beliefs. Once this first stage is completed, then the soul can be offered true beliefs. If this is so, then learning is possible. The soul's best hope is not just to have its false beliefs illuminated and removed by the elenchus, and to be left in a cleansed state, but to somehow acquire true beliefs in place of the false ones. This passage does not indicate how that second stage of learning is accomplished.

Elenchus in the *Meno*

The *Meno* does. At the beginning of this dialogue Meno asks Socrates if he knows how virtue is acquired. Socrates says that he is so far from knowing how virtue is acquired that he does not know what virtue is, and further that he never has met anyone who did. Meno, shocked at this admission, offers to explain the nature of virtue to Socrates, but fails in repeated attempts. In the process of refuting

Meno Socrates gives a brief tutorial on what a good definition should look like. Finally, Meno gives up in disgust, stating his perplexity:

> Socrates, before I even met you I used to hear that you were always in a state of perplexity and that you bring others to the same state, and now I think you are bewitching and beguiling me, simply putting me under a spell, so that I am quite perplexed. Indeed, if a joke is in order, you seem, in appearance and in every other way, to be like the broad torpedo fish, for it too makes anyone who comes close and touches it feel numb, and you now seem to have had that kind of effect on me, for both my mind and my tongue are numb, and I have no answer to give you. Yet I have made many speeches about virtue before large audiences on a thousand occasions, very good speeches as I thought, but now I cannot even say what it is. I think you are wise not to sail away from Athens to go and stay elsewhere, for if you were to behave like this as a stranger in another city, you would be driven away for practising sorcery. (80a–b)

Meno's expression of frustration makes several interesting points. The first is that he believes that Socrates, like himself, is perplexed. Socrates reinforces this statement in his reply to Meno: "If the torpedo fish is itself numb and so makes others numb, then I resemble it, but not otherwise, for I myself do not have the answer when I perplex others, but I am more perplexed than anyone when I cause perplexity in others" (80c). The second point is that Meno admits that he is perplexed, but he does not draw the inference that he does not know what virtue is. Instead, and this is the third point, he accuses Socrates of somehow playing a trick on him, of numbing him so that he cannot define virtue. Socrates, he states, is like a magician. The implication is that Meno's perplexity is the result, not of his ignorance, but of Socrates' trickery. Were it not for Socrates, he would be able to speak well about virtue before large audiences, as he has many times in the past. So far two familiar features of the elenctic dialogue have been found: Socrates admits his ignorance, and his interlocutor admits his (though in this case grudgingly and with a qualification). So far the dialogue has been a perfect example of an elenctic dialogue, with repeated refutations of attempted answers to the Socratic question, what is virtue? If the dialogue ended at this point, with both characters expressing their own ignorance, it would not be surprising. The *Meno* would be one more example of an elenctic dialogue ending in perplexity.

The Doctrine of Recollection

What happens next, however, *is* surprising. Socrates asks Meno to try again to explain the nature of virtue and Meno asks Socrates how he would know the nature of virtue if he actually encountered it. Socrates first compares Meno's question to a debater's argument, which states that one cannot search either for what one knows (because one already knows it) or what one does not know (because one will not know what to look for). He then offers an account of the possibility of learning, which he attributes to "priests and priestesses whose care it is to be able to give an account of their practices" (81a–b). What they say is that

> ... the human soul is immortal, at times it comes to an end, which they call dying, at times it is reborn, but it is never destroyed ... As the soul is immortal; has been born often and has seen all things here and in the underworld, there is nothing which it has not learned; so it is in no way surprising that it can recollect the things it knew before, both about virtue and other things. As the whole of nature is akin, and the soul has learned everything, nothing prevents a man, after recalling one thing only – a process men call learning – discovering everything else for himself, if he is brave and does not tire of the search, for searching and learning are, as a whole, recollection. (81b–d)

The Examination of the Slave

Socrates illustrates this theory by examining a slave of Meno's. Meno assures Socrates that the slave has not been taught geometry. Socrates asks the slave how to construct a square double the size of an original square. The slave gives two answers, first that the new square should have a side twice as long as the original one, and second, that it should have a side one and a half times as long. Socrates refutes both answers, and the slave admits that he does not know the answer. Socrates comments to Meno that the slave is now aware of his ignorance. "He thought he knew, and answered confidently as if he did know, and he did not think himself at a loss, but now he does think himself at a loss, and as he does not know, neither does he think he knows" (84a–b). Socrates then asks Meno whether the slave has been harmed by being questioned, made perplexed and numbed, as by a torpedo fish, and Meno answers that he does not think so. Socrates continues: "Indeed, we have probably achieved something relevant to finding out how matters stand, for now, as he does not know, he would be glad to find out, whereas before he thought he could easily make many fine speeches to large audiences about the square of double size and said that it must have a base twice as long" (84b–c).

Up to this point the Socratic examination of the slave has the structure of a typical Socratic elenchus. But the examination doesn't end there. Socrates leads the slave, through a series of further questions, to see that it is the square drawn on the diagonal of the original square that is double its area. Though Socrates' questions are indeed "leading," Meno agrees that the opinions expressed by the slave are all his own. The conclusion Socrates draws is that "the man who does not know has within himself true opinions about the things that he does not know" (85c). These opinions must have always been in his soul, needing only the right questions to be awakened. Further, "These opinions have now just been stirred up like a dream, but if he were repeatedly asked these same questions in various ways, you know that in the end his knowledge about these things would be as accurate as anyone's" (85c–d).

Are the questions that Socrates asks the slave, which lead him to the correct conclusion part of the elenchus of the slave? This is a difficult question to answer. They are part of the continued examination of the slave, and they do elicit from the slave answers to Socratic questions, answers that express what the slave believes; but it is not the slave who puts forward the key to the answer to the problem. It is Socrates who introduces the concept of the diagonal, and shows the slave how to construct a square on that diagonal. The hypothesis that solves the problem comes from Socrates and not from the slave, though the slave agrees with Socrates when he presents it. It is not typical for Socrates to put forward his own answers to his questions in the elenchus. It is also not typical – in fact this is the only case we find in the elenctic dialogues – for any character, whether Socrates or an interlocutor, to put forward an answer that survives the elenchus and is regarded by everyone involved as true. However we decide this question whether the continued examination is a case of the elenchus, though, it is clear that the first part of the examination, in which the slave puts forward answers to the geometric problem that Socrates refutes, is an example of the elenchus. The justification of the elenchus that this discussion gives is that the elenchus identifies the false beliefs of the interlocutor, the beliefs that make it impossible for him to discover the truth, and leave the way open for the true answer to be recollected. The elenchus thus has a positive, as well as a negative function. The doctrine of recollection does not explain how we are to know which answers are false and, perhaps more importantly, which answers are true. It does justify faith, however, that repeated applications of the elenchus may lead eventually to the discovery of truth.

The *Apology* vs. the *Meno*

Thus we have, in the *Apology* and the *Meno*, two very different justifications of the elenchus. According to the *Apology*, the elenchus shows people that they do not know what they think they know, because no one knows the answers to Socrates' questions. According to the *Meno*, the elenchus helps in the process of eliciting the correct answers to Socrates' questions, which everyone knows, at least implicitly. The account of the elenchus given in the *Apology* explains the structure of the typical Socratic dialogue, in which repeated applications of the elenchus lead to perplexity. It is an explanation that accounts for the fact that Socrates, like the people he examines, does not know the answers to his questions. The justification of the elenchus given in the *Meno* explains something that I have not commented on until now. Along with the constant refutation in the typical Socratic dialogue, there are, on occasion, hints dropped by Socrates that suggest certain answers to his questions. Socrates does not explain where these hints come from; at times he seems unaware that he is dropping them. Sometimes it is not clear whether they are intended as positive contributions to the answers to his questions or not. The doctrine of recollection in the *Meno* explains how Socrates might have answers, or partial answers, to his questions.

Two Faces of Socrates in the Elenctic Dialogues

Socrates thus behaves in the elenctic dialogues in two different ways. On the one hand, he behaves like an ignorant inquirer, seeking answers he does not have. On the other, he behaves like a philosopher with a positive account of the answers to his questions. Many interpreters prefer the first Socrates; they like to see him as an ignorant inquirer. But the other Socrates is present, too. He is not just present in the *Republic* and *Phaedrus*, where he expounds a theory of the tripartite soul, or in those dialogues wherein he expounds the theory of separate Forms. He is present, as we shall see in later chapters, in the *Protagoras*, where he has a theory of virtue that identifies it with knowledge, and in the *Gorgias*, where he defends the philosophical life. He is present too, though less obviously, in the *Euthydemus, Euthyphro, Laches, Meno*, and the first book of the *Republic*, and perhaps in other dialogues as well. In all of these works Socrates not only refutes his interlocutors, but suggests possible ways of going right where his interlocutors go wrong. How can he do this, if he is as ignorant as he professes to be? That is a question I shall address in the next chapter.

Recollection and the Elenctic Dialogues

As I have said, many interpreters prefer Socrates the ignorant inquirer to Socrates the philosopher with answers to his questions. They are especially suspicious of doctrines, such as the theory of the tripartite soul and the theory of separate Forms, that present rather grand explanations. This is part of the reason they are happy to follow Aristotle in assigning the theory of separate Forms to Plato rather than to Socrates. They are apt to assign the doctrine of recollection to Plato as well, with some reason. In the *Phaedo* Socrates connects the doctrine of recollection to the theory of separate Forms. Socrates identifies the objects of knowledge for which he is searching with Forms, and recollection explains how it is possible to have knowledge of them. One interpreter described the "two pillars" of Platonism as "the immortality and divinity of the rational soul, and the real existence of the objects of its knowledge – a world of intelligible 'Forms' separate from the things our senses perceive."[5] To which a later interpreter added that the architrave connecting these two pillars is the doctrine of recollection.[6] It is surely correct that the doctrine of recollection becomes a feature of Plato's theory of knowledge; but it is also true that the doctrine of recollection answers a question which is suggested by the elenctic dialogues: how can the elenchus, which is a method of refutation, have a positive use in the discovery of truth? The answer expected from the *Apology* is, it can't. The *Meno* argues that it can. And the doctrine of recollection is introduced in an elenctic dialogue. If it becomes Platonic doctrine, it is nonetheless introduced to answer a question which is elicited by the Socratic method itself, the question raised by Meno: how can one search for something one doesn't know?

3

Knowledge and Ignorance

In the last chapter we saw that Socrates presents two faces to the reader of Plato's works. The first face is that of an ignorant inquirer. The second is that of a man who seems to have answers to the questions he asks. In this chapter we shall discuss this contrast further. In the *Apology* Socrates concluded as a result of his examination of people who were thought wise that only the god was wise concerning "the most important pursuits," and that human wisdom was limited to awareness of one's ignorance. We saw Socrates in the *Charmides* insist on his ignorance when Critias looked to him for agreement about the nature of temperance. In the *Meno* Socrates said that he was even more perplexed than other people concerning the answers to his questions. Many more examples could be given of this Socratic profession of ignorance; we shall see some in later chapters.

Socrates' Profession of Ignorance

What is it that Socrates means by this profession of ignorance? First of all, Socrates means to deny that he possesses wisdom or knowledge. We would distinguish between these two terms, but the ancient Greek philosophers, and in particular Socrates, tended to use them interchangeably. When Socrates denies that he possesses wisdom, he does not mean to deny that he possesses what we might call "garden variety" knowledge. He knows his way home from the gymnasium or the market-place. He knows whether it is night or day. The wisdom that he denies having concerns what in the *Apology* he called the most important pursuits. This includes knowledge of how to live. In the *Apology* he encourages the Athenians to pursue, not wealth, power, and honors, but wisdom, truth, and the best state of their souls. The best human life would be the life in which one's soul was in its best state. The name given to that state in Greek philosophy is *eudaimonia*. The word is often translated "happiness," but this translation, though useful, is somewhat misleading. The Greek philosophers did not mean by *eudaimonia* a life that was merely subjectively pleasing, but a life that was objectively good as well. In Chapter 1 I mentioned the Greek phrase *kalos kagathos*, "admirable and good," as a brief description of the best human life. To say that a life was *eudaimōn* was to say not just that it was pleasant, but that it was admirable and good as well. But what was *eudaimonia*? What made a life admirable and good? This is one of the things that Socrates said he did not know. We also saw that Socrates was especially concerned with virtue and with the individual virtues: piety, justice, temperance, courage, and wisdom. As Socrates understands virtue, it is a trait of character that contributes to the *eudaimonia* of a person. But if one does not know what *eudaimonia* consists in, how can one know what virtue is?

The Nature of Knowledge

When Socrates says that he lacks knowledge or wisdom concerning the best human life, he means that he is not in the highest possible cognitive state with respect to that life. By a "cognitive state" I mean a mental condition that concerns one's attitude toward the truth of a given proposition or set of propositions. Consider, for example, my cognitive state with respect to the location of my favorite pen. I am, as an absent-minded professor, always mislaying this pen. Sometimes my cognitive state with respect to its location is ignorance: I don't know where it is. Sometimes, when I don't know where my pen is, I may have an idea about where it might be, and sometimes this idea may produce the cognitive state of belief or conviction. But my belief may be mistaken; I may go to the place where I believe my pen is, only to find that it is not there. Sometimes my cognitive state may be only a guess, a hypothesis, about the location of my pen, but at other times I may be (subjectively) certain of its location. Even this subjective certainty may turn out to be mistaken, however: I may end up saying, "I was just *certain* that my pen was on my dresser, but when I looked it wasn't there." If I have *knowledge* of the location of my pen, on the other hand, it is not just that I am subjectively certain of its location; the location is *objectively* certain. Knowledge is *infallible*; if I know I can't be wrong. It happens that, as I write this, my pen is beside me on my desktop, in plain sight. Philosophers have developed scenarios to indicate that even such a state is not infallible, but practically speaking, I know where my pen is when I see it before me. There is no higher cognitive state than knowledge, and knowledge entails truth.

Socrates contrasts this infallible state with his own. One feature of knowledge, which accompanies infallibility, is finality. If I know something, the discussion concerning it is over. If I know the location of my pen, then there is no further debate about its location. Socrates regards the questions he raises, however, as always subject to further discussion. They are open issues, not closed. Someone may always raise a new point that may lead him to revise his opinions. As he says at *Gorgias* 506a: "the things I say I certainly don't say with any knowledge at all; no, I'm searching together with you so that if my opponent clearly has a point, I'll be the first to concede it." If he had knowledge, this would not be so. In addition, Socrates thought of knowledge not as having an isolated proposition or two as its object, but rather an entire body of propositions and practices. He often compared the knowledge of ethics that he sought to the various arts and sciences, such as mathematics. The mathematician does not know just some individual propositions, such as that $2 + 2 = 4$ or that a square has four sides; he or she knows arithmetic or geometry. Nor does the mathematician know just a body of facts; he or she knows how to perform certain actions, such as how to add or subtract, or how to construct a square double the area of a given square. It is the existence of a body of mutually supporting propositions and practices that gives each individual proposition the status of knowledge. If Socrates had knowledge of the highest principles in ethics, he would not only know the definition of *eudaimonia*, but the definition of virtue and each of the individual virtues, and he would know how the other properties of the virtues followed from these definitions. In terms of the question raised by Meno at the start of the *Meno*, if Socrates knew what virtue was, he would know, and be able to explain to Meno, how virtue was acquired. Lacking knowledge of virtue, he says, he cannot explain to Meno whether virtue can be taught, or is acquired in some other way.

Definition

Socrates believed that knowledge began with definitions. He was not seeking what are called "nominal definitions," definitions such as "a bachelor is an unmarried man," which explain the meaning of words, but what are called "real definitions," definitions that express the real nature of a thing, what it is essentially. As Aristotle says, Socrates "was seeking to deduce, and the essence is the starting point of deductions" (*Metaph.* M.4, 1078b24–5). This is why so many of the elenctic dialogues are directed toward definitions. What Socrates is looking for is a set of definitions that do not merely state that something is the case, but explain why it is the case. Socrates wants an account of *eudaimonia* that explains not just what *eudaimonia* is, but why it is the first principle that he is seeking. The kind of definition of virtue that he is seeking will not just state the nature of virtue; it will explain how virtue is relevant to *eudaimonia*. Some interpreters have suggested that a better term than "knowledge" for the object of Socrates' search is "understanding." Another term that is sometimes used is "science." What Socrates wants is a science of ethics, something like geometry, which will enable him to understand how all the parts of the subject are interrelated.

The "Priority of Definition" Principle

Such a science is hard, if not impossible, to obtain. Today, over 2,400 years after Socrates, we have several rival ethical theories that attempt to explain the difference between right and wrong, good and evil, but no single theory that is accepted by everyone. Mathematics has been a science since the time of Socrates, but ethics is still not a science. It is no wonder that Socrates professed his ignorance, his perplexity, concerning the subject. Socrates may have accepted a principle that made the discovery of such a science especially difficult. In the *Meno*, Socrates asks Meno how he could know anything about virtue if he did not know the definition of virtue: "if I do not know what something is, how could I know what qualities it possesses?" (71b) In other places he suggests that if one does not know the definition of a term, one cannot know whether an alleged example is really an example of the term. These two principles together generate what has been called the "priority of definition" principle: until one knows the definition of something, one cannot know anything at all about that thing. This principle has been called the "Socratic fallacy." It is what gives rise to Meno's question to Socrates: if you don't know anything about a subject, how will you look for it? If one cannot at least identify examples of some term such as "water," how will one ever be able to discover the nature of water? This problem may not be as difficult to solve as it sounds – after all, it does seem to be the case that whether a given action is courageous or pious might depend on the definition of courage or piety, and so might the answer to the question whether courage or piety is advantageous or capable of being learned. It does, however, make knowledge difficult to obtain. Most people think they know, in the sense of being able to identify, instances of courage and piety, even if they can't define those terms. The priority of definition principle says that they are mistaken. It is not clear that Socrates accepts the priority of definition principle, but he says things in various places in the dialogues that suggest that he does.[1]

Belief and Perplexity

Socrates, as I have said, repeatedly denies that he has knowledge of the first truths of ethics. He does not know how he ought to live; he does not know the nature of virtue. Interpreters have noted that this does not mean that Socrates does not have beliefs, even very strong beliefs, about these matters. If he does, this might explain how Socrates can claim ignorance about these matters and yet express beliefs, including strong beliefs, about them. This point is, as far as it goes, correct. But when Socrates pleads ignorance he on occasion says things that go beyond the mere disavowal of knowledge: he says he is *perplexed* about the answers to his questions. Perplexity involves uncertainty: it involves not knowing what to believe about the answer to his questions. When Socrates says he is perplexed he is saying that he does not have a fixed belief about the answer. As he says at the end of the *Hippias Minor*, "I waver back and forth and never believe the same thing" (376c). Socrates may disavow knowledge and still have strong beliefs about some question, but he cannot admit perplexity and still have strong beliefs. The two perspectives are strictly incompatible.

Socrates as Midwife

Socrates on occasion uses his lack of knowledge as a reason for refusing to answer his own questions. As Aristotle put it, "This was why Socrates used to ask questions and not to answer them – for he used to confess that he did not know" (*De Sophisticis Elenchis* 183b7–8). We find a striking explanation of this refusal to answer in Plato's *Theaetetus*. Socrates is introducing his method of philosophizing to Theaetetus, a young student of the mathematician Theodorus. He compares his method to his mother Phainarete's practice of the midwife's art. "One thing which I have in common with the ordinary midwives," he says, "is that I myself am barren of wisdom. The common reproach against me is that I am always asking questions of other people but never express my own views about anything, because there is no wisdom in me; and that is true enough … I am not in any sense a wise man; I cannot claim as the child of my own soul any discovery worth the name of wisdom" (150c–d).

Now the *Theaetetus* is not usually considered a Socratic dialogue, because it is not among the dialogues written early in Plato's career; still, as has been noted, it has the structure of one: it is "a dialogue in which a confessedly ignorant Socrates asks for a definition of a problematic item, dialectically examines a series of candidate answers, and at the end admits failure."[2] That is, it fits the description of what I have called an elenctic dialogue. The comparison between Socrates and a midwife, it has been argued, is a Platonic invention rather than something traceable to Socrates himself;[3] but the structure of the dialogue and the midwife analogy indicate that Plato, later in his life, returned to the figure of the Socrates of his earlier works and offered us a commentary on him as a philosopher, a reflection on the nature of his philosophical activity.

The "Barren" Socrates

In light of this comparison I shall refer to the portrait of the Socrates who examines others but who refrains from attempting to answer his own questions as the "barren" Socrates. I contrast this portrait with that of the Socrates who does not refrain from stating his opinions; sometimes he states them tentatively, in the form of a suggestion, and sometimes he states them with great passion and conviction. Only on rare occasions, as at *Apology* 29b, where he says that he knows that it is wicked and shameful to do wrong, to disobey one's superior, does Socrates state his view as something he *knows*. In the *Gorgias*, after having described his views as "held down and bound by arguments of iron and adamant," (508e) Socrates says, "yet for my part, my account is ever the same: I don't know how these things are" (509a). Though he does not know them, he says, "I set it down that these things are so." In other words, Socrates claims true belief, not knowledge. The contrast I am drawing is not between a Socrates who has, and one who disavows, knowledge; it is the contrast between a Socrates who refuses to state his opinions and one who states them.

The "Fertile" Socrates

The Socrates who does not refrain from stating his opinions, who believes that these opinions are true, I refer to as the "fertile" Socrates. In the *Theaetetus* Socrates contrasts himself with his followers in this respect. Though he is barren, Socrates says, and therefore never expresses his opinion about anything, some of those who associate with him express their opinions; and, though some of these opinions are errors, "phantoms," some of them are fertile truths: "they discover within themselves a multitude of beautiful things, which they bring forth into the light" (150d). Socrates' role, that of an intellectual midwife, is to "deliver them of this offspring" (150e) and to test it in in all possible ways to determine whether it is a phantom or a fertile truth. Though Socrates does not possess such truths himself, he is able to determine what kind of offspring his followers produce. It seems clear that what Socrates is talking about is his practice of the elenchus, understood in light of the doctrine of recollection. Though the doctrine of recollection is not referred to directly, it seems to be part of the background assumed in this passage. The only example in the elenctic dialogues of a Socratic interlocutor bringing forth a "fertile truth" is the slave in the *Meno*; Socrates' other interlocutors produce only phantoms. Despite what Socrates says about having fertile companions, it is Socrates who proves to be fertile.

The Socrates who refuses to express his opinion, because he says he lacks wisdom, is barren; the Socrates who expresses his opinion, though he may also say that he lacks wisdom, is fertile. The fertile Socrates puts forward his opinion, however tentatively or forcefully he may state it, not necessarily as something he knows, but as the truth. When we ask whether the Socrates of the elenctic dialogues is barren or fertile, the answer seems to be that he is both. He frequently disavows knowledge and expresses perplexity, and the elenchus is designed to examine the beliefs of the interlocutor, not Socrates' beliefs; but he also on occasion expresses his own opinion. But Socrates cannot be both barren and fertile: he cannot refuse to state his opinion and state it. He cannot be perplexed and at the same time have strong convictions about what he says perplexes him. Can this inconsistency be resolved?

The Ironic Solution: Thrasymachus

One solution to the tension between the barren and the fertile Socrates can be found in book I of the *Republic*. As in a typical Socratic dialogue, Socrates has been examining the views of his interlocutors, in this case about the nature of justice. He has refuted the claim of Cephalus that justice is telling the truth and paying one's debts and the claim of Cephalus' son and heir Polemarchus that justice is helping one's friends and harming one's enemies. At this point, Thrasymachus breaks into the discussion with a challenge to Socrates: "if you truly want to know what justice is, don't just ask questions and then refute the answers … Give an answer yourself, and tell us what you say the just is" (336c). When Socrates responds that he is seeking an answer to the question, but is incapable of finding it, Thrasymachus responds with "a loud, sarcastic laugh. By Heracles, he said, that's just Socrates' usual irony. I knew, and I said so to these people earlier, that you'd be unwilling to answer and that, if someone questioned *you*, you'd be ironical and do anything rather than give an answer" (337a). According to Thrasymachus, Socrates' refusal to answer his own question is ironic; Thrasymachus believes that Socrates is pretending not to have an answer but that he has one that he refuses to give. In other words, Socrates is dissembling. Thrasymachus does not, of course, think that Socrates has the *correct* answer; he thinks that he, Thrasymachus, has that. He does not explain why Socrates refuses to answer; perhaps it is a ploy to lure others into the conversation, perhaps it is simply due to reluctance on Socrates' part to subject himself to questioning. Moreover, Thrasymachus thinks that this Socratic coyness is a well-known trait: he refers to it as Socrates' "usual" irony. Socrates, thinks Thrasymachus, is a known dissembler, a hypocrite. His pretence of ignorance is just a mask that he wears to keep others from criticizing views that he pretends he does not have, but that others know he does have.[4]

The Ironic Solution: Alcibiades

Thrasymachus is no friend of Socrates, and his charge that Socrates is being ironic in concealing his own answer to the question, what is justice, is intended as a criticism. In Plato's *Symposium*, however, Alcibiades, who is favorably disposed toward Socrates – in love with him, in fact – makes the same charge. Plato's *Symposium* is one of the best-known Platonic dialogues. It is not considered a Socratic dialogue, because it contains an exposition of the Platonic theory of separate Forms, but it is among those dialogues that are considered stylistically early. Like the *Theaetetus*, it seems to contain a Platonic reflection on the nature of Socrates, but it is a reflection that is radically opposed to the *Theaetetus* portrait of Socrates as barren. The *Symposium* is set in 416; the poet Agathon is celebrating his first victory in a competition of tragic plays and several guests, including Socrates, assemble at his house for drinks and a meal. (A year later Alcibiades would end up in Sparta, having escaped from emissaries sent to recall him from Sicily to stand trial for profaning the Eleusinian mysteries.) The guests decide to give a series of speeches in behalf of Love. The kind of love that they are particularly interested in is a form of homosexual love in which men in mid-adulthood pursue youths, who trade sexual favors for an introduction into Athenian adult life. The series of speeches culminates in a speech given by Socrates, which describes his introduction into the nature of love by a priestess of Mantinea, Diotima, who describes a ladder of ascent from the love of a single beautiful body through several stages to the experience of the separate, Platonic, Form of Beauty itself.

At this point a very drunk Alcibiades, accompanied by several other revelers, breaks into this hitherto solemn and sober affair and completely disrupts it. He is invited to offer a speech of his own on behalf of Love, but he says he will only speak in praise of Socrates, whom he has discovered sitting next to Agathon. Now Socrates and Alcibiades are described in several places in the dialogues as being in a relationship of the sort just described, and the normal assumption would be that Socrates is the pursuer of Alcibiades. It turns out, ironically, however, that it is Alcibiades who is the one who is in love with Socrates, as he states at 213b. Alcibiades compares Socrates to a statue of Silenus, a satyr, a comical figure from Greek mythology, half human and half horse. This kind of statue is "split right down the middle, and inside it's full of tiny statues of the gods" (215b). Alcibiades also compares Socrates to the satyr Marsyas, who enchanted people with his flute. Unlike Marsyas, however, Alcibiades says Socrates needs no instruments to enchant people; he does it with words alone. Even a poor, second-hand account of Socrates' words leaves people "transported, completely possessed" (215d). Socrates tries to convince Alcibiades that his "political career is a waste of time" (216a), just as he tried to convince the citizens of Athens not to pursue wealth, power, and honors, but the best state of their souls; but Alcibiades' response is to cover his ears and flee: "the moment I leave his side, I go back to my old ways: I cave in to my desire to please the crowd" (216b).

The key feature of the Silenus is the contrast between its ugly, comical exterior and the divine images within. Likewise, the key feature of Socrates is the contrast between his outward appearance and his inner reality. His appearance is that of a pursuer of handsome youths: "to begin with, he's crazy about beautiful boys; he constantly follows them around in a perpetual daze" (216d). The reality, however, is quite different: "I wonder, my fellow drinkers," Alcibiades asks

> … if you have any idea what a sober and temperate man he proves to be once you have looked inside. Believe me, it couldn't matter less to him whether a boy is beautiful. You can't imagine how little he cares whether a person is beautiful, or rich, or famous in any other way that most people admire. He considers all these possessions beneath contempt, and that's exactly how he considers all of us as well. In public, I tell you, his whole life is one big game – a game of irony. (216d–e)

To this Alcibiades adds, "also, he likes to say he's ignorant and knows nothing" (216d). In reality, however, things are once again different: "I don't know if any of you have seen him when he's really serious. But I once caught him when he was open like Silenus' statues, and I had a glimpse of the figures he keeps hidden within: they were so godlike – so bright and beautiful, so utterly amazing – that I no longer had a choice – I just had to do whatever he told me" (216e–217a). The figures Socrates keeps within, concealed from the outer world, are his virtues: "his natural character, his moderation, his fortitude – here was a man whose strength and wisdom went beyond my wildest dreams!" (219d). The occasion on which Socrates revealed himself, Alcibiades relates, was that of his failed seduction attempt. Alcibiades is, on the one hand, angry that Socrates had rejected this attempt; he describes Socrates as arrogant and insolent for refusing him ("he spurned my beauty, of which I was so proud," he says at 219c); but on the other hand he admires Socrates' virtue, including his wisdom.

In what does this wisdom consist? After describing Socrates' courage, self-control, and ability to concentrate while he was on military campaigns, Alcibiades offers this answer:

> … even his ideas and arguments are just like those hollow statues of Silenus. If you were to listen to his arguments, at first they'd strike you as totally ridiculous; they're clothed in words as coarse as the hides worn by the most vulgar satyrs. He's always going on about pack asses, or blacksmiths, or cobblers, or tanners; he's always making the same tired old points in the same tired old words. If you are foolish, or simply unfamiliar with him, you'd find it impossible not to laugh at his arguments. But if you see them when they open up like the statues, if you go behind their surface, you'll realize that no other arguments make any sense. They're truly worthy of a god, bursting with figures of virtue inside. They're of great – no, of the greatest – importance for anyone who wants to become a truly good [*kalos kagathos*] man. (221d–222a)

This is the most positive appreciation in Plato's works of the power of Socrates' speech to transform the character of those who hear it, or read it. Alcibiades, ultimately, was not transformed by Socrates. By his own admission, he refused to listen to Socrates' arguments; "I stop my ears and tear myself away from him" (216a–b), he says, because the allure of the crowd is too great. Plato, however, was; and I see in Alcibiades' praise of Socrates, drunken though it may be, an expression of Socrates' transformative effect on Plato's own life. Plato's encounter with Socrates made him into a philosopher. He saw the inner meaning beneath the surface of Socrates' arguments. These arguments, like Socrates himself, contain godlike wisdom. Alcibiades' speech, coming as it does hard on the heels of Socrates' speech, containing Diotima's account of the ascent of the soul to the Form of Beauty, suggests that Socrates, in Plato's eyes, may have achieved the highest wisdom. He was not the barren seeker after truth, but the fertile possessor of it. Alcibiades goes beyond the contrast between the Socrates who refuses to express his opinion and the Socrates who is willing to say what he thinks;

he goes beyond anything Socrates says in his own behalf about his own views. Alcibiades tells us that Socrates was wise, and that his profession of ignorance was as ironic as his profession of love for beautiful youths.

In the end, these two Platonic images of Socrates co-exist in Plato's dialogues. The appeal to irony in the *Symposium* suggests a way of reconciling them. As I noted in the previous chapter, interpreters have favored the barren inquirer over the fertile Socrates. They also tend to dismiss the speech of Alcibiades as the drunken comments of a spurned but still besotted lover. If we do not accept Alcibiades' ironic interpretation of Socrates, however, we are confronted with two images of Socrates that do not cohere. If we accept his claim that the portrait of the ignorant inquirer is merely an ironic mask concealing the Socrates who possesses divine images within himself this may help us to bridge the gap between the Socrates of the early or "Socratic" dialogues and the later, "Platonic" ones.

4

Piety

The *Euthyphro*

In the previous chapters I have discussed the cultural environment in which Socrates lived, and which led to his trial; the trial itself; the nature of the method of inquiry that Socrates practiced, the elenchus; the structure of the elenctic dialogue, which is based on that method; Socrates' profession of ignorance and the nature of the knowledge or wisdom that he disavowed; Socrates' desire for definitions and the priority of definition principle; the "barren" and the "fertile" Socrates and the tension between them; and finally, the use of irony as a possible way of resolving that tension. In this chapter I want to put these concepts to work in the examination of a single Platonic dialogue, the *Euthyphro*. The *Euthyphro* is set before Socrates' trial, at a preliminary hearing, and it discusses one of the key issues raised by the charges against Socrates, namely the nature of piety. Socrates practices the elenchus throughout the dialogue, and the dialogue displays the typical structure of an elenctic dialogue. Socrates professes his ignorance, and he offers to become Euthyphro's pupil so that he may learn what piety is. Euthyphro claims to be an expert on the subject, just the sort of person Socrates typically wants to examine. Socrates is looking for a definition of piety in the dialogue. Some interpreters have seen in the *Euthyphro* a commitment to the priority of definition principle.[1] Socrates offers a brief account of what he is looking for in a definition. Socrates initially appears as barren, but eventually he offers an opinion of his own concerning the nature of piety. This opinion may provide a basis for constructing a positive Socratic conception of piety and thus, religion. The tension between the barren and the fertile Socrates is not discussed in the dialogue, but one can see the distinction present there. The *Euthyphro* is a nearly perfect example of the ideas developed so far.

The *Euthyphro* is important for other reasons as well. In his discussion of definition Socrates introduces the concept of a Form, a precursor of the Platonic theory of separate Forms. The *Euthyphro* raises a version of a question that is still debated by philosophers of religion today. In Socrates' version, the question is, is the pious pious because the gods love it, or do they love it because it is pious? The modern version asks, is what is right right because God commands it, or does God command it because it is right? Is morality subjective, based on God's will, or objective? This is sometimes called "the *Euthyphro* problem." Finally, the *Euthyphro* is a miniature masterpiece, a delight to read in its own right. For all these reasons the dialogue deserves our attention.

The Setting of the Dialogue

The *Euthyphro* is set at the porch, the portico, of the "king-archon," an Athenian official whose job was to review court cases involving religious matters, to determine if they should go to trial. Socrates explains to Euthyphro that he is there to answer an indictment. He is being charged by an unknown young man named Meletus with corrupting the youth. Socrates says that Meletus "is likely to be wise, and when he sees my ignorance corrupting his contemporaries, he proceeds to accuse me to the city as to their mother. I think he is the only one of our public men to start out the right way, for it is right to care first that the young should be as good as possible" (2c–d). Socrates' reference to Meletus as wise is certainly ironic; we see from the *Apology* that Socrates thinks Meletus has never given any thought to the education of the youth (25c). His statement that the right way to care for the state is to care for the youth first, however, is not ironic; it is Socrates' own view. When Euthyphro asks Socrates how Meletus says he corrupts the youth, Socrates replies, "he says that I am a maker of gods, and on the ground that I create new gods while not believing in the old gods, he has indicted me" (3b).

Euthyphro

Socrates and Euthyphro know each other. Euthyphro greets Socrates in a familiar way, asking him why he has come to the porch of the king-archon, and Socrates responds in kind. Moreover, Euthyphro is favorably disposed toward Socrates: when Socrates says that Meletus is proceeding in the right way in indicting him for corruption, Euthyphro responds, "I could wish this were true, Socrates, but I fear the opposite may happen. He seems to me to start out by harming the very heart of the city by attempting to wrong you" (3a). He shows his familiarity with Socrates by saying, when Socrates recites the charge that he is a maker of gods, that "this is because you say that the divine sign keeps coming to you" (3b).

Euthyphro is a religious prophet, but an unsuccessful one. "Whenever I speak of divine matters in the assembly and foretell the future, they laugh me down as if I were crazy," he complains; "and yet I have foretold nothing that did not happen" (3c). Euthyphro has not fared well with interpreters. One refers to his "monumental conceit and stupidity,"[2] while another calls him "prodigiously conceited."[3] This judgment may be somewhat harsh. Granted, Euthyphro is very confident at the start of the discussion of his own knowledge of religious matters. Granted, he never admits that he has been shown to lack wisdom by Socrates (though his sudden departure at the end of the dialogue may be an implicit recognition of this fact). Granted, he is not up to the rigors of the Socratic elenchus. Yes, Euthyphro is conceited and stupid, or perhaps ignorant, but is he more so than many of Socrates' other interlocutors? Many of them are embarrassed in the same way Euthyphro is and fare no better in the face of Socratic questioning. In fact the *Euthyphro* is a rather typical elenctic dialogue in these respects. Socrates makes virtually all of his interlocutors look foolish in these dialogues.

One recent interpreter has appealed to a distinction from ancient comedy to understand the relation between Socrates and his interlocutors.[4] In ancient comedy, of the sort that Aristophanes, for instance, wrote, there is a pair of stock characters, the *alazōn* and the *eirōn*. The *alazōn* is an imposter, someone who pretends to have some ability or experience he actually lacks. The *eirōn*, on the other hand, is just the opposite. He knows more than he lets on, and especially more than the *alazōn*. In comedy the *eirōn* gets the better of the *alazōn*; he exposes him and chases him from the stage, usually with a beating. We do not know the degree to which these two comic models may have been in Plato's mind when he wrote his elenctic dialogues. I am not suggesting that every one of the interlocutors in these dialogues is described for comic effect (though some are, including, I believe, Euthyphro). Nor am I suggesting that the claim to knowledge of every one of Socrates' interlocutors is regarded with irony by Socrates (though Euthyphro's claim to knowledge is certainly so regarded). Plato wrote dialogues, not comic plays. Nonetheless, the interlocutors in the elenctic dialogues have several key features in common with the *alazones* of Greek comedy. First, they usually pretend or claim to have knowledge of, expertise in, some subject of interest to Socrates. Second, Socrates often treats them with irony, which they usually do not detect. Third, he bests them in dialectical conversation, revealing (to the reader, and perhaps to those in the audience, if not always to the interlocutor himself) that they are ignorant. The "beating" that Socrates administers is not a physical but a philosophical, dialectical, one. Fourth, though most of them do not leave in haste at the end of the dialogue as does Euthyphro, they are left in a state of confusion, a confusion Socrates often says he shares. Fifth, Socrates, on the other hand, gets the upper hand in the argument; as an *eirōn* he disclaims knowledge, but he seems at the end of the dialogue to know more than the alleged experts he defeats in argument. Exactly what he knows is not revealed, but as Socrates points out in the *Apology* (23a) people think he must have the answers to the questions he asks others. Though he denies this, in the *Apology* and elsewhere, the fact that Socrates resembles the *eirōn* of Greek comedy suggests that this disclaimer may be ironic. As we saw in the last chapter, both Thrasymachus and Alcibiades make this claim.

Euthyphro is an *alazōn*: he claims to be an expert in religious matters. He does so in response to Socrates' astonished statement when Euthyphro announces that he is prosecuting his father on a charge of murder. Socrates exclaims, "Good heavens! Certainly, Euthyphro, most men would not know how they could do this and be right. It is not the part of anyone to do this, but of one who is far advanced in wisdom" (4a–b). Euthyphro agrees. A little later, when Socrates says to Euthyphro, "by Zeus, Euthyphro, you think that your knowledge of the divine, and of piety and impiety, is so accurate that ... you have no fear of having acted impiously in bringing your father to trial?" (4e), Euthyphro replies, "I should be of no use, Socrates, and Euthyphro would not be superior to the majority of men, if I did not have accurate knowledge of all such things" (4e–5a). Clearly, Euthyphro makes a claim to knowledge that most people do not have. Again, when he cites two examples of gods punishing their fathers for unjust acts, and Socrates asks him whether he believes the stories are true, Euthyphro replies, "yes, Socrates, and so are even more surprising things, of which the majority has no knowledge" (6b). This answer gives us a clue to Euthyphro's conception of knowledge, the basis for his belief that he is an expert on piety. What Euthyphro has is *lore*, a collection of stories about the gods, some of which are arcane. What he lacks is a critical understanding of the nature of piety, as the subsequent discussion reveals. It is this critical understanding, expressed in the ability to answer Socrates' questions about the nature of piety, that Socrates is looking for.

Euthyphro's Case and its Justification

Euthyphro is in court to prosecute his father on a charge of murder. He explains to Socrates the details of his case: the victim was a dependent of his. This man had killed one of the household slaves while drunk and Euthyphro's father had him tied up and thrown into a ditch until a priest could be consulted (homicide being one of the crimes that had religious implications). The dependent died of hunger and exposure before the messenger sent to the priest returned. Now, Euthyphro says, "both my father and my other relatives are angry that I am prosecuting my father for murder on behalf of a murderer when he hadn't even killed him, they say, and even if he had, the dead man does not deserve a thought, since he was a killer. For, they say, it is impious for a son to prosecute his father for murder" (4d–e). Euthyphro states two reasons for his prosecution. One sounds modern; the other was ancient even in Euthyphro's time. "It is ridiculous, Socrates," he states, "for you to think that it makes any difference whether the victim is a stranger or a relative. One should only watch whether the killer acted justly or not; if he acted justly, let him go, but if not, one should prosecute, [even] if, that is to say, the killer shares your hearth and table" (4b–c). Justice is impartial, and takes precedence over family relations. This sounds modern, but the next part of his reasoning comes from the archaic past of Greek religion: "the pollution is the same if you knowingly keep company with such a man and do not cleanse yourself and him by bringing him to justice" (4c). The Greek word translated "pollution" is *miasma*, and it gives an idea of the concept involved. A murderer brings a cloud into the house he inhabits, something like an illness, and with it the anger of the gods. Someone sheltering a murderer invites disaster, in the form of divine vengeance, for himself and all who live with him. It is essential for this pollution to be cleansed from the house, and this can only be done by bringing the murderer to justice. It is not clear what is needed to remove the pollution: perhaps the death or exile of the murderer, perhaps only a ritual cleansing of the murderer and the home. Euthyphro believes this can only be produced by a judicial proceeding. It has been argued that Euthyphro is wrong about the law, that this is not an appropriate case to bring to trial, and that if tried it would have been likely to bring about his father's acquittal.[5] Socrates does not, however, tell Euthyphro that he is wrong to prosecute his father. He does not take a stand on the substantive issue of his father's guilt. What he says is that Euthyphro must be "far advanced in wisdom" to prosecute his father. As we have seen, Euthyphro agrees with Socrates' assessment. It is Euthyphro's claim of expert knowledge that arouses Socrates' interest in examining him, and that leads to Euthyphro's downfall. The dialogue turns on the question whether Euthyphro has the accurate knowledge he claims to have; and as it turns out, he is shown not to have it. (Whether Euthyphro realizes this is not so clear.)

One thing we might see in Euthyphro's prosecution of his father is a conflict of duties. On the one hand, Euthyphro's father and other relatives insist, it is impious for a son to prosecute his father for murder. Respect for one's parents was a religious obligation in Euthyphro's day, much as it is regarded by those who accept the Ten Commandments, including the commandment to honor one's father and mother, as religious obligations today. On the other, Euthyphro argues, not only does impartial justice override filial piety, but it may be the only way to see that impiety is removed from Euthyphro's household. We recognize today that there might be a conflict of duties within a family if a family member believes that another has committed a serious crime. We might face something like the dilemma that Euthyphro faces if we found ourselves in his position. Euthyphro does not see himself as in a dilemma because he does not accept the principle that it is impious for a son to prosecute his father, even if he thinks his father is guilty. Still, this principle is accepted by Euthyphro's father and other relatives. On the surface at least, the two virtues of justice and piety seem to conflict. Justice requires that Euthyphro prosecute his father (as he thinks); filial piety requires that he not prosecute him (as his relatives think). Can filial piety be reconciled with impartial justice?

Can virtues conflict with one another? These are questions raised by Euthyphro's prosecution of his father. The relation between piety and justice will be pursued by Socrates later in the dialogue. Socrates will attempt to integrate the two virtues, to show that they are compatible. To this extent, though perhaps only to this extent, he supports Euthyphro's point of view.

What Socrates wants from Euthyphro: Forms

Socrates pretends to be impressed by Euthyphro's claim of expert knowledge. We know from the *Apology* that his expectation is that Euthyphro will turn out to be unwise, as all of his other inter-locutors have. When he says that he wants to become Euthyphro's pupil, his offer is surely ironic. What he wants, he says, is to learn the nature of piety so that he can answer the charge of Meletus and deflect Meletus' attention to Euthyphro instead of himself, something Euthyphro says he would welcome. Socrates begins his questioning of Euthyphro where he begins the questioning of several alleged experts, with a request for a definition of the subject matter of the expert's area of expertise, in this case the nature of piety. "So tell me now, by Zeus," he asks, "what you just now maintained you clearly knew: what kind of thing do you say that godliness and ungodliness are, both as regards murder and other things; or is not the pious the same and alike in every action, and the impious the opposite of all that is pious and like itself, and everything that is to be impious presents us with one form ... in so far as it is impious?" (5c–d). When Euthyphro, as we shall see, fails to understand initially what Socrates wants, he repeats the request: "I did not bid you tell me one or two of the many pious actions but that form itself that makes all pious actions pious, for you agreed that all impious actions are impious and all pious actions pious through one form ... Tell me then what this form itself is, so that I may look upon it, and using it as a model, say that any action of yours or another's that is of that kind is pious, and if it is not that it is not" (6d–e). What Socrates tells Euthyphro he wants is a Form. He uses the terms *eidos*, *idea* and *paradeigma* to identify what he wants. All of these are terms used to describe the separate Forms attributed to Plato by Aristotle. Why should we not see Socrates' request in terms of that Platonic theory? Why should we not attribute that theory to Socrates, though it occurs in an elenctic dialogue?

It is sometimes said that, though Socrates uses the language of the theory of Forms, we should not see in these passages any commitment to the actual theory itself. This is unconvincing; if we did not know that these passages occurred in an elenctic dialogue we would without question say that they concerned Platonic Forms. The Forms are described by Socrates as what philosophers call *universals:* entities that are not, like particulars such as Socrates and his actions, restricted to a single place and time. Socrates can only exist in one place at a time: he can't be in the gymnasium and at the same time in the market-place. His actions, too, are limited in space and time: if Socrates is carrying on a conversation with Euthyphro at the porch of the king-archon he can't be carrying on that very same conversation at the same time with Meno in another location. Socrates' conversation with Euthyphro is a single, locatable and datable event. A universal, on the other hand, can have multiple locations. Consider a prayer. In one sense this can be thought of as a single thing, but the same prayer can be spoken, or silently recited, by many different people at the same time or at different times. Or consider the color green. We may talk of a "particular" shade of green, but even this particular shade can be present in many different particular things at the same time or at different times. A universal, philosophers say, has, or can have, *multiple instances.* Socrates makes this point about piety when he says that it is "the same and alike in every action" (5d) and when he says that "all pious actions [are] pious through one form" (6d–e). To say that universals exist is to commit oneself to a bit of metaphysics, of ontology: it is to offer a part of an account of the kinds or categories of things that exist in the universe. It is not a particularly obscure or arcane bit of metaphysics – Euthyphro eventually gets what Socrates wants – but it is metaphysics nonetheless.[6]

Socrates does not merely get Euthyphro to understand that he is looking for a universal. This universal, piety, he says, is what "makes" all pious actions pious. It is a *cause* of the piety of those actions. It is because of piety that those actions are called pious. It should be clear from this that we are not talking simply about the word "pious" but about a thing, a characteristic, that pious things have. This thing also is, or provides, a paradigm, a standard or a model, that can be used to determine whether a given action is pious or impious. Socrates does not explain precisely how this works, but suppose we come to see that piety is a characteristic of a certain sort, perhaps because we identify this characteristic in a particular example. Consider, for example, the characteristic, "tartness." Suppose we learn to identify what tartness is by having a particular experience, which we get, let us say, by tasting an apple. Using the experience of the taste of some particular apple to identify what tartness is, using it as a paradigm, we can extend our understanding of tartness to other cases. If Euthyphro's prosecution of his father is truly pious, and we discern that characteristic of piety in this particular example, we can use our understanding of that characteristic in applying it to other cases of piety. These characteristics of Forms, that they are universals, causes and paradigms, standards or models, are also characteristics of the separate Platonic Forms.

What is missing from the Forms in the *Euthyphro* is the claim that the Forms exist in separation from the things they characterize. According to Aristotle, Plato thought that knowledge of phenomenal things, the things we experience in the world around us, was impossible, because these things were always changing and knowledge required stable objects. He thought there could be knowledge of Forms – Socrates was right about that – but he thought that Forms could not be part of the world we experience through our senses. He posited therefore a separate world in which these Forms, these objects of knowledge, existed (*Metaph.* A.6, 987a29–b10). This world Plato refers to as the world of "being"; he refers to the phenomenal world of changing objects as "becoming." Socrates does not refer to this doctrine of two worlds in the *Euthyphro*. The Form of piety is not said to exist in a separate world, but rather "in" every action (5d). Socrates thus has Forms, but not separate Forms. He is searching for a real, not a nominal definition, as I noted in Chapter 3; and the objects he is searching for are Forms. This Socratic conception of Form appears in other dialogues as well: in the *Meno*, at 72c, in the *Protagoras*, at 330c–331c, and in the *Hippias Major*, at 286d. This conception of Form is not prominent in the elenctic dialogues, but it is present there.

There is a practical as well as a theoretical aspect to Socrates' search for real definitions of ethical terms. Consider the immediate cases. Socrates is about to face the charge of impiety brought against him by Meletus. If he can acquire *knowledge* of the true nature of piety, he might be able to explain to Meletus, or more importantly to the jurors, why his particular religious views are not impious. He could thus obtain acquittal on this charge. Euthyphro is about to prosecute his father on a charge of murder. If he actually knows that this act is pious, then well and good; but if, as the subsequent dialogue shows, he does not know this, then he may be embarking on a disastrously mistaken course of action, as his relatives think. Even if Euthyphro happens to be right about his prosecution of his father, if he only has correct opinion about what is pious and not knowledge, he will be unable to explain to the jurors why he is right. If he cannot explain the nature of piety, he may be unable to convince the jurors of the rightness of his case.

This may help us to understand why Socrates is interested in acquiring knowledge, and in particular definitional knowledge, of the terms he investigates. It is sometimes said that we know things we cannot define, and in the "garden variety" sense of knowledge this may be true. But the moral terms Socrates wants to define are controversial: what seems pious or just to one person may seem impious or unjust to another. Without a definition that can be applied to particular cases as a standard or paradigm we won't be able to resolve those controversies. We literally will not know what we are talking about when we use these controversial terms. Socrates' assumption is that these terms refer to something definite, a Form, a characteristic of things. It is only our understanding of the nature of these Forms that is inadequate. If we could but grasp the nature of the Forms we would not only acquire knowledge of how to use the controversial terms of our language; we would acquire understanding of the way things work.

Euthyphro's Attempts to Define Piety.
Their Refutation

Euthyphro's initial attempt to answer Socrates is based on his own case: "the pious is to do what I am doing now, to prosecute the wrongdoer, be it about murder or temple robbery or anything else, whether the wrongdoer is your father or your mother or anyone else; not to prosecute is impious" (5d–e). Euthyphro doesn't simply say, piety is what I am doing now, prosecuting my father for murder; his answer is general, but not general enough to cover all instances of piety. This is what Socrates reminds him of at 6d–e, quoted above. Euthyphro's second attempt to define piety is an improvement on the first. This time Euthyphro responds succinctly: "what is dear to the gods is pious, what is not is impious" (7a). Socrates responds that this is the sort of definition he is looking for, but there is a problem. Suppose the gods disagree about what is pious. (This is something that Socrates does not believe, but Euthyphro does.) If so, then one and the same action may be loved by one god and hated by another. The same action will thus be both pious and impious. Socrates leads Euthyphro to modify his definition to state that "what all the gods hate is impious, and what they all love is pious, and that what some gods love and others hate is neither or both" (9d).

This definition states a significant view about the nature of piety. It describes piety as a universal characteristic, the state of being loved by all the gods. It gives no other criteria for an action's being pious than this. If all the gods love an action, it is pious, and that is that. There is no appeal from the love of the gods. The gods do not have or need any reason to love or hate an action; it is solely their love of it that matters. If the gods love it when everyone to eats a certain food, then eating that food is a pious act. Call this view subjectivism. Subjectivism is similar in nature to a view often discussed in ethics about what makes right actions right: this view claims that what makes right actions right is the fact that God commands those actions. This view is referred to as "the divine command theory." The weakness of this theory lies in the fact that if God commands an action which we think of as morally wrong, such as human sacrifice, the fact that God commands the action would make it right. This seems unacceptable to most people today; the result is that the divine command theory has few contemporary proponents, at least in this simple version. (There are more complex versions of the theory that attempt to answer this objection.) Euthyphro's answer has the same problem: if all the gods hate his prosecution of his father, then it is impious, whatever Euthyphro may think and however well he may defend his action; and if they all love what he is doing, then it is pious, whatever his relatives think. The way to determine whether an action is pious or impious is simple (if impractical): take a poll among the gods and find out what they all love. These two similar positions seem altogether too subjective to many people. We like to think that we have come a long way from the moral acceptance of human sacrifice, and we like to think that we have found a basis of morality that is sounder and more objective than what may seem right to a group of gods who, at least in Greek mythology, do not generally have the best interests of human beings at heart.

Though Euthyphro's account of piety may seem to us unacceptably subjective, however, it has something about it that would have seemed obvious to a religious prophet such as Euthyphro, steeped as he was in the lore of Greek mythology. It is a fact, or it would have seemed to Euthyphro to be a fact, that whether the gods approve of an action is at least *relevant* to the question whether the action is pious. If there are no gods, an action could not be pious or impious. An action might be just, or admirable or good, but if there are no gods to approve of it it cannot be pious, because piety is what is loved by the gods. Piety is not a matter of human intention, of the desire to please gods that human beings *believe* exist; as Euthyphro defines piety, it is a matter of actually pleasing gods who *actually* exist. Therefore, if there are no gods, there can be no pleasing the gods, and thus no piety. (The same holds true for the divine command theory. If there is no God, there can be no divine commands, and right and wrong cannot exist, at least according to the theory.)

Euthyphro is not necessarily wrong, therefore, to think that some reference to what pleases the gods is essential to defining piety. But what role does it play? Socrates tries to lead Euthyphro to a recognition of the weakness of his subjectivist position. He tries to get Euthyphro to admit that if all the gods love an action, they must do so for a reason. Euthyphro does admit this, but he undermines his own view in doing so. What Socrates asks Euthyphro is whether what is loved by all the gods is loved by them because it is pious, and Euthyphro answers affirmatively. But now we have statements that are at odds with each other: according to the first, what causes an action to be pious is the fact that all the gods love it, but according to the second, what causes the gods to love it is the fact that it is pious. Both can't be true. Ordinarily, when A is the cause of B, B can't be the cause of A. Consider two statements: "it is raining" and "the street is wet." I may say "the street is wet because it is raining," but not "it is raining because the street is wet." It may be true that actions that are pious are loved by all the gods. It may be true, in other words, that "loved by all the gods" and "pious" pick out the same objects. It may be that "being loved by the gods" is what Socrates calls at 11a "an affect or quality" of piety, that the pious has the quality of being loved by all the gods. But this does not explain the *nature* of piety; that will only be explained, Socrates thinks, if we give an objective reason that explains why all the gods love it. Recall that a Form, according to Socrates, is what *makes* an action pious; and Socrates thinks that Euthyphro has not explained this.

Euthyphro could have avoided the problem raised for him by Socrates if he had just stuck to his subjectivist position and, when Socrates asked for a reason why the gods loved pious actions, had just said, "for no reason." He might also have avoided the problem if, when asked for a reason, he had mentioned some other characteristic, if he had said for instance that the gods love pious acts because they are just, or courageous, or wise. Of course, that would only have led to a further investigation into the meaning of those terms, and thus into the heart of the Socratic search for the definitions of ethical terms, but it would have avoided the tight little circle that Euthyphro gets himself into by defining piety as what all the gods love and then explaining what all the gods love in terms of piety.

Euthyphro's Perplexity

At this point Euthyphro admits his perplexity: "Socrates, I have no way of telling you what I have in mind, for whatever proposition we put forward goes around and refuses to stay put where we establish it" (11b). Euthyphro's remark gives rise to a Socratic comparison between Euthyphro's attempted definitions and the statues of Daedalus in Greek mythology, which were so lifelike they could move on their own. Euthyphro complains to Socrates that it is not he who makes his statements move, but Socrates: "as far as I am concerned they would remain as they were" (11d). Euthyphro does not exactly admit that the argument has shown that he is mistaken in his definitions; he may still think that he has something in mind, but that he no longer is able to express it. After that complicated argument concerning piety and what is loved by the gods, it is perhaps no wonder that Euthyphro is confused. So far in the dialogue we have seen the elenchus work in its typical manner, as an engine of refutation. Euthyphro has put forward three definitions of piety, and Socrates has refuted all three. Euthyphro has no more definitions to offer and, given Euthyphro's perplexity and Socrates' professed ignorance, we might expect the dialogue to end at this point. If Socrates were purely the barren character described in the *Theaetetus*, perhaps it would.

Socrates' Constructive Contribution

The dialogue, however, does not end at this point. Socrates now offers a constructive suggestion: that "all that is pious is of necessity just" (11e), but not all of justice is pious. Piety is a *part* of justice, that part which concerns "care" of the gods (12e). This point about care is Euthyphro's contribution, and Socrates says, "you seem to me to put that very well." There remains, however, a problem with the definition of the term "care." We care for horses, dogs, and cattle in order to benefit and improve the objects of our care, but we do not care for the gods in an attempt to improve them. (The unstated reason for this, on which Euthyphro and Socrates must agree, is that the gods are already perfect, or at least unimprovable by us.) Euthyphro, faced with this problem, says that the kind of care involved in pious action is "the kind of care, Socrates, that slaves take of their masters" (13d). Socrates describes this kind of care as "service." Now, however, another problem arises. Socrates asks, "to the achievement of what aim does service to the gods tend ... what is the excellent aim that the gods achieve, using us as their servants?" (13e) Euthyphro's answer is that "if a man knows how to say and do what is pleasing to the gods at prayer and sacrifice, those are pious actions such as preserve both private houses and public affairs of state. The opposite of these pleasing actions are impious and overturn and destroy everything" (14b). It would seem from Euthyphro's answer that the "excellent aim," the "altogether fine work" (13e9) at which our service to the gods aims is the preservation of private homes and "affairs of state." Socrates does not refute this suggestion of Euthyphro, but neither does he endorse it. Rather, he focuses on the means by which Euthyphro believes that this end is achieved: prayer and sacrifice, which he describes as a "sort of trading skill between gods and men" (14e). But what benefit do the gods receive from these trades? "What they give us is obvious to all. There is for us no good that we do not receive from them, but how are they benefited by what they receive from us?" Socrates asks (14e–15a). Euthyphro replies that our gifts to the gods are "honor, reverence, and ... gratitude" (15a).[7] These gifts do not benefit the gods, except by pleasing them, Euthyphro admits; but to say this is just to return to the view that had been rejected earlier, that piety is what pleases the gods, or what they all love. As Socrates points out to Euthyphro, this is to move in a circle again. "Either we were wrong when we agreed before, or, if we were right then, we are wrong now" (15c).

The Conclusion of the Dialogue

Socrates says that

> ... we must investigate again from the beginning what piety is ...
> For you know it, if any man does ... If you had no clear knowledge

of piety and impiety you would never have ventured to prosecute your old father for murder on behalf of a servant. For fear of the gods you would have been afraid to take the risk lest you should not be acting rightly, and would have been ashamed before men, but I know well that you believe you have clear knowledge of piety and impiety. (15c–e)

At this point, however, Euthyphro has had enough. He throws in the towel, beating a hasty retreat with the excuse that he is in a hurry and it is time for him to leave. Socrates protests that Euthyphro has dashed his "great hope" (16a) that he might learn what piety and impiety are and so escape Meletus' indictment, and so the dialogue ends.

It is clear by now, as it was in all likelihood clear at the beginning of the dialogue, that Socrates' praise of Euthyphro as one who knows what piety and impiety are is ironic. The preceding dialogue has shown that Euthyphro does not know what the nature of piety is. If Socrates ever held out hope that Euthyphro might actually teach him the nature of piety, it is surely gone at this point in the dialogue. It is unlikely that Socrates' offer to become Euthyphro's pupil was ever seriously intended. What, then, did Socrates hope to attain by engaging in conversation with Euthyphro? Was his aim to dissuade him from prosecuting his father? Socrates never quite says that Euthyphro's prosecution of his father is wrong; he just states that only one who was "far advanced in wisdom" could be right in doing it. Euthyphro has shown that he is not far advanced in wisdom. Therefore, in Socrates' eyes at least, he ought not to continue his prosecution. Perhaps Euthyphro realizes this; perhaps that is the reason that he departs hastily. There is an ancient statement that Socrates saved Euthyphro from prosecuting his father by his refutation of him (Diogenes Laertius 2.29).[8] Perhaps, however, Euthyphro is simply ashamed of his performance in argument with Socrates and seeks the only escape from shame he can find. We cannot tell from his brief excuse at the end of the conversation what his state of mind is. Perhaps Socrates' aim in examining Euthyphro is simply to perform what he describes in the *Apology* as his service to the god, and to show that Euthyphro is not wise. But is that his only aim? If so, why does he offer Euthyphro his constructive suggestion concerning the nature of piety? Does Socrates perhaps aim to teach Euthyphro something about the nature of piety?

Why do Euthyphro and Socrates Disagree?

Socrates and Euthyphro cannot agree on a definition of piety, I think, in part because they are trying to define different terms. The Greek word *hosiotēs*, which we translate, "piety," is in fact ambiguous. It might mean "piety," but it might mean "holiness." Euthyphro thinks Socrates is asking him to define holiness. If asked what makes something holy, a Greek of Euthyphro's time might well have said, like Euthyphro, that holiness was the state of being loved by the gods. A great variety of things might be considered holy: an altar, a code of laws, or a book. "Holy" is roughly synonymous with "sacred." A grove of trees, for instance, might be considered holy, sacred, to the goddess Athena. If asked to give an account of why this was so, Euthyphro might have a complicated story to tell about the history of the grove and its relation to the goddess, but in the end the account would come down to the fact that the goddess loved this particular grove of trees. The idea of holiness is subjective, just as Euthyphro thinks: it involves a relation to a subject, a god. Piety, on the other hand, differs from holiness, though it overlaps with it. Though a great number of different kinds of things might be considered holy, it is primarily actions of persons and the persons who perform them that are considered pious. It would not make sense to say that a grove of trees could be pious. The concept of piety involves a relation to a person as well, but in the case of holiness the relation is to the persons, the gods, who appreciate the object, whereas in the case of piety the relation is to the person who performs the action. An action is pious if it is performed by a person with a certain attitude, and a person is pious if he or she performs certain actions with this attitude. The gods are pleased when persons display this attitude in their actions. They judge, correctly, that such persons and their actions are pious. But the piety of the person or action does not consist in the fact that it pleases the gods. It consists in the fact that the person or action possesses the appropriate attitude.

Is Progress toward a Definition of Piety made in the Dialogue?

What is that attitude? The *Euthyphro* does not tell us. The dialogue ends inconclusively. Still, there are indications in the *Euthyphro* that lead toward a positive account, a definition of piety. The chief indication is the suggestion that Socrates makes, that piety is a part of justice, the part concerned with the care of the gods. It is true that Socrates and Euthyphro prove unable to define this care, but the proposal itself is not refuted. If we want to understand piety, the proposal is that we must understand what justice is. Unfortunately, there is no account of justice in the elenctic dialogues that explains what justice is, not even in the first book of the *Republic*, which is devoted to the topic. All we know from Socrates' suggestion is that one part of justice is concerned with human beings, whereas the other part is concerned with divine beings. How does one behave justly toward the gods? I would suggest that it is by treating them in accordance with their natures. In order to behave justly, then, one must know the nature of the being under consideration. Socrates does not tell us much in the *Euthyphro* about the nature of the gods. It is clear from other works, however, beginning with the *Apology*, that he regards them as superior in knowledge and virtue to human beings. "Only the god is wise," Socrates concludes from his examination of the leading candidates for wisdom among the citizens of Athens. At the end of the *Apology*, when Socrates is considering the possibility that he might continue to exist in the underworld, he expresses confidence that he will be judged by just judges there. In the *Euthyphro*, when confronted with Euthyphro's stories of how Zeus overthrew his father and how Zeus's father in turn castrated his father, Socrates says "I find it hard to accept things like that being said about the gods" (6a). Such stories are unworthy of the gods; they are not part of a just understanding of them. Socrates' gods are wise and virtuous; they don't behave badly toward each other or toward us. Our attitude toward the gods should be one that respects their superior wisdom and virtue. A name for this attitude might be "reverence" (15a).

Euthyphro suggests that piety, reverence toward the gods, has the effect of preserving "private houses and public affairs of state" (14b). This explains how piety benefits us, but it does not answer the question how it benefits the gods. It is Euthyphro's failure to answer this question that scuttles the argument. Euthyphro cannot do more than say that our piety pleases the gods. If piety is a matter of justice, however, and if justice is treating something with the attitude appropriate to it, perhaps we can say just a bit more than that reverence is pleasing to the gods. In the first book of the *Republic* Polemarchus says that justice is "to give to each what is owed to him" (331e), to render to each thing its due. Polemarchus has the wrong idea of what is owed to each thing – he thinks it is helping one's friends and harming one's enemies – but the idea that justice is something we *owe* others may not be mistaken. When we treat someone justly, giving to that person what is owed, it is true that this may be pleasing to that person. When we treat the gods with the reverence due to them, we please them. We do more than this, however. We acknowledge, by our actions, that the gods are owed treatment of a certain sort. We recognize that it is just to treat the gods reverentially. The benefit the gods receive from this is the recognition that is due to them because of the kind of beings they are. That may be what justice toward the gods consists in. Consider, as a possible parallel case, honors paid to the dead, in particular to those who have died in battle. Unlike honors paid to those who are still alive, the dead cannot be benefitted by those honors, either because they no longer exist or because they exist after death in a place, Hades according to Greek mythology, where our actions cannot affect them. Nonetheless, many people believe that we have a moral obligation to honor the dead, that it is something we owe to them, that it is simply the right thing to do. Perhaps revering the gods is in this respect like revering the dead: a matter of justice.

The *Euthyphro* and other Elenctic Dialogues

The *Euthyphro* is one dialogue among several that are devoted to the project of defining virtue. One prominent claim that is entertained in three of these dialogues, the *Laches*, *Meno*, and *Protagoras*, is that virtue might best be understood as knowledge or, as the *Meno* ultimately suggests, right belief. The *Euthyphro* does not make this claim, but the claim that Socrates does make, that piety is part of justice, seems to be compatible with it. If piety consists in performing actions with a certain attitude in mind, and that attitude is reverence toward the gods, reverence is a response to knowledge of the nature of those gods. If virtue is practical wisdom, and if practical wisdom is knowledge of what to do in each situation that one faces, then the knowledge of what to do in our interactions with the gods will depend on our knowledge of those gods. If the gods are immoral, angry, and in general not well-disposed toward human beings, as the theological tradition of which Euthyphro is a part says they are, right action toward them will be to try to placate them, to "win them over" with gifts and sacrifices. If the gods, on the other hand, are wise, moral, and in general well-disposed toward human beings, as Socrates believes, right action will consist at least in part in expressions of gratitude toward the gods for their wise beneficence. Knowing the nature of the gods will be crucial to piety. Socrates' view of the gods, as some interpreters have claimed, is significantly different from the view of people such as Euthyphro. Euthyphro may be eccentric, but he is a believer in the Greek theological tradition. If Socrates is right and Euthyphro is wrong about the nature of the gods, then Socrates will have, and Euthyphro will lack, genuine piety. Piety in the end will turn out to be reverence, and reverence will turn out to be, if not identical to knowledge or right belief, then at least rooted in it.

5

Virtue

We have now identified a particular method, the elenchus, and a particular set of dialogues, those making extensive use of the elenchus, as Socratic. Several of the elenctic dialogues are devoted to a project that Aristotle identified as Socratic: the definition of ethical terms. In several of these dialogues Socrates defines virtue in terms of knowledge, specifically knowledge of good and evil. In this chapter we shall examine this view of virtue as it is put forward in three dialogues, the *Laches*, *Protagoras*, and *Meno*. (The *Meno* first proposes, then criticizes and modifies this claim. It concludes that virtue is not knowledge but right opinion.) This claim is associated with two others: that vice is ignorance and that moral weakness is impossible. These three claims together are referred to as the "Socratic paradoxes." They are paradoxes in the sense that they are counter to (*para*) common or popular opinion (*doxa*). These claims together constitute a position known as "intellectualism." In this chapter we shall examine these claims, to see what they mean and how Socrates argues for them. Finally, we shall look at his criticism of the claim that virtue is knowledge at the end of the *Meno*. If Socrates were simply the practitioner of the elenchus, if he were the barren Socrates of the *Theaetetus*, he would not present his own, constructive answers to the questions he raises for others.

Two of the three dialogues we shall examine, the *Laches* and *Protagoras*, have the structure of a typical elenctic dialogue; yet Socrates manages to insert into these dialogues his own suggestions concerning the nature of virtue, as he does also in the *Euthyphro*. In these dialogues he is not simply barren, but fertile. The third dialogue, the *Meno*, makes extensive use of the elenchus, but it does not have the expected negative conclusion. We shall have to consider whether this conclusion represents a change of view on Socrates' part. It is in general very difficult, if not impossible, to determine the order in which Plato composed his elenctic dialogues. The *Laches, Protagoras*, and *Meno*, however, are related to each other in such a way that it seems possible to place them in a linear sequence. The *Laches* first articulates the view that virtue is knowledge, but in a general way. The *Protagoras* makes the view a good deal more specific: it offers an account of the kind of knowledge that virtue is. The *Meno* first defends, then criticizes this view, and finally offers a modification of it.

The *Laches*: What is Courage?

The *Laches* is in most respects a typical elenctic dialogue. It discusses the nature of courage; a series of definitions are proposed; each is refuted, and the dialogue ends in perplexity. What is unusual about the dialogue is the amount of space (about half the dialogue) that it devotes to introducing the main discussion. The first half of the dialogue sets the scene and introduces the characters. Two Athenians, Lysimachus and Melesias, are sons of distinguished Athenian statesmen, Aristides "the Just" and Thucydides (not the historian). They have enlisted the aid of two generals, Laches and Nicias, to assist them in determining how their children should be educated. They want the children to attain the level of excellence of their grandparents, a level that Lysimachus and Melesias have fallen short of. (The problem is a familiar one from the Socratic dialogues: why do illustrious Athenians not succeed in passing on their own excellence to their sons?) They have invited the generals to observe a demonstration of a man fighting in armor, and they want Laches and Nicias to advise them as to whether it would be worthwhile for their children to learn the art. Laches suggests that they include Socrates, who is also present, in their deliberations, as he "is always spending his time in places where the young men engage in any study or noble pursuit" (180c). When the generals disagree on the value of learning this particular skill, Lysimachus turns to Socrates to "cast the deciding vote" (184d). Socrates objects that this is not the right way to proceed: "it is by knowledge that one ought to make decisions, if one is to make them well, and not by majority rule" (184e; here we have Socrates' critique of Athenian democracy in a nutshell). We ought to ask whether any one of those present is an expert, and if we find one we ought to listen to him. Moreover, we ought to ask, not about this particular technique: "the question is really, I suppose, that of whether your sons turn out to be worthwhile persons or the opposite" (185a). Socrates, as we would expect, denies being an expert in the education of youth: "Socrates denies having any knowledge of the matter or being competent to decide which of you [Laches or Nicias] speaks the truth, because he denies having been a discoverer of such things or having been anyone's pupil in them" (186d–e). Lysimachus urges Socrates to examine Laches and Nicias to find out if they are experts, and this elicits two of the most salient comments on Socrates that we find in the dialogues. First Nicias says to Lysimachus,

> You don't appear to me to know that whoever comes into close contact with Socrates and associates with him in conversation must necessarily, even if he began by conversing about something quite different in the first place, keep on being led about by the man's arguments until he submits to answering questions about himself concerning both his present manner of life and the life he has lived hitherto. And when he does submit to this questioning, you don't realize that Socrates will not let him go before he has well and truly tested every last detail. (187e–188a)

This is followed by Laches' comment about being both a lover and a hater of discussion, which was quoted at the end of Chapter 1. When the man discussing wisdom or virtue lives in a way that is in harmony with his words, then Laches says he is delighted to converse with him. "Let Solon grant me this point, that the teacher should himself be good, so that I may not show myself a stupid pupil taking no delight in learning" (189a). Laches is happy to present himself to Socrates as a pupil because he knows, from shared experience on the battlefield, that Socrates is a good man.

The main discussion of the dialogue now begins. The question is "the manner in which virtue might be added to the souls of their [Lysimachus' and Melesias'] sons to make them better" (190b); but this presupposes that we must begin with the question what virtue is. Since this might be too large a question, however, Socrates proposes that they should begin by examining a part of virtue, the part closest to the technique of fighting in armor, namely, what is courage? Laches, a general, responds as we might expect a general to do: "good heavens, Socrates, there is no difficulty about that: if a man is willing to remain at his post and to defend himself against the enemy without running away, then you may rest assured that he is a man of courage" (190e). (We may be certain that when one of Socrates' interlocutors remarks that there is no difficulty in answering one of Socrates' questions that he will soon be embroiled in a host of difficulties.) As in the case of Euthyphro's first answer to Socrates' question, What is piety? Laches' answer is too narrow: what about the Scythians, who fight on horseback, Socrates objects, or "those who are brave in dangers at sea, and the ones who show courage in illness and poverty and affairs of state, and … not only those who are brave in the face of pain and fear but also those who are clever at fighting desire and pleasure?" (191d–e)

Laches sees the point. His next suggestion is that courage is "a sort of endurance of the soul" (192c). But courage is a fine thing, and only endurance accompanied by wisdom is fine, objects Socrates; endurance accompanied by folly is harmful. So it is wise endurance that is courage; but what kind of wisdom? Not that involved in spending money, or in medicine; and the man who endures in battle because the odds favor him seems actually to be less courageous than the man who endures against all odds. In general, the less skilled soldier who endures seems braver than the more skilled; but this person also seems more foolish. The argument has reached a point similar to that reached at about the midpoint of the *Euthyphro*, and Laches expresses a similar frustration, saying that he is annoyed with himself for being unable to say what he thinks he knows.

The *Laches*: Virtue is Knowledge

At this point Nicias enters the argument. Here Plato introduces a Socratic doctrine into the context of an elenctic dialogue. In the *Euthyphro* it had been Socrates who advanced the argument by suggesting that piety was a part of justice; now it is Nicias who does so:

> NICIAS: I have been thinking for some time that you are not defining courage in the right way, Socrates. And you are not employing the excellent observation I have heard you make before now.
>
> SOCRATES: What one was that, Nicias?
>
> NICIAS: I have often heard you say that every one of us is good with respect to that in which he is wise and bad in respect to that in which he is ignorant.

SOCRATES: By heaven, you are right, Nicias.

NICIAS: Therefore, if a man is really courageous, it is clear that he is wise.

SOCRATES: You hear that, Laches?

LACHES: I do, but I don't understand exactly what he means.

SOCRATES: Well, I think I understand him, and the man seems to me to be saying that courage is some kind of wisdom. (194c–d)

Nicias is able to make this suggestion because, as he has previously noted, he is familiar with Socrates. He goes on to say that courage is knowledge of "the fearful and the hopeful *in war and in every other situation*" (195a; my italics). To Laches, this is nonsense, for him, wisdom and courage are two different things. Are doctors courageous because they know what is to be feared in medicine? Are farmers, because they know what is fearful in farming? The courageous person, replies Nicias, knows for whom it is better to live than to die. This elicits the response from Laches that he must be speaking of seers, which Nicias denies. (Laches' objections to Nicias' position, which is really Socrates' position, are the objections of a man of common sense to a Socratic paradox.)

Socrates takes over the examination of Nicias from Laches (which is somewhat awkward, since it is his own thesis that he is examining). After having elicited from him the claim that animals are not courageous, since they lack understanding, Socrates argues that what Nicias has defined is not courage, but rather "virtue entire," as he puts it at 199e. Nicias has defined courage as knowledge of future evil, but there is not one kind of knowledge directed toward the past, another toward the present, and another toward the future; knowledge of past, present, and future evil is the same. So courage would be simply knowledge of good and evil; this is not a definition of courage, however, but of virtue in general. This contradicts our initial assumption that we were investigating a part of virtue. So we have not found out what courage is.

Nicias, it seems, has failed to define courage, but he has succeeded in defining virtue as knowledge of good and evil, the first of the Socratic paradoxes. But what does this definition mean? What kind of knowledge is he talking about? How can knowledge be virtue? Virtue is concerned with what I ought to do; how does knowledge of good and evil suffice to tell me that? These are questions that are clarified in the *Protagoras*.

The *Protagoras*: Protagoras' Conception of Virtue

The *Protagoras* is a confrontation between Socrates and the greatest of the Sophists. I mentioned in Chapter 1 that Plato had a rather low opinion of the Sophists in general. He seems to have had a higher opinion of Protagoras. In this dialogue Protagoras presents a theory of virtue that is an alternative to the conception of virtue that Socrates holds, that virtue is expert knowledge. Though he is ultimately defeated in argument, throughout most of the dialogue he defends his view ably, and his alternative conception of virtue is never really refuted. I discussed the opening of the *Protagoras* in Chapter 1. Socrates accompanies young Hippocrates, who wants to study with Protagoras, to Callias' house, where Protagoras is staying. Socrates asks Protagoras what Hippocrates will learn if he studies with him, and Protagoras responds, "sound deliberation, both in domestic matters – how best to manage one's household, and in public affairs – how to realize one's maximum potential for success in political debate and action" (319a); in Socrates' words, the art of citizenship. Socrates objects that he did not think that this could be taught. When the Athenians debate in the assembly some question involving expert knowledge, they only allow experts to speak, but when it comes to city management, they allow anyone to offer advice. This is evidence that they do not think there is an art of civic management that can be taught. Then he mentions the problem that Lysimachus and Melesias faced in the *Laches*: virtuous parents do not produce virtuous children. This too indicates that virtue cannot be taught. Socrates concludes:

> Looking at these things, Protagoras, I just don't think that virtue can be taught. But when I hear what you have to say, I waver; I think there must be something in what you are talking about. I consider you to be a person of enormous experience who has learned much from others and thought through a great many things for himself. So if you can clarify for us how virtue is teachable, please don't begrudge us your explanation. (320b)

Socrates has subtly modified the subject: we are not just talking about the art of civic management, but virtue. (Incidentally, I think that, for once, Socrates' praise of Protagoras is not ironic. Protagoras' account of virtue is one that is based on experience and Protagoras has thought matters through.)

Protagoras responds to Socrates' challenge in his "Great Speech," one of the longest speeches in the elenctic dialogues. The gist of his speech is that the political art, in the form of justice and a sense of shame, was given by Zeus to human beings so that they could live together in society. It is an art that all must possess, to some degree, if social life is to be possible. It is an art, but it is not an expert art, such as medicine, where one expert suffices for many persons. The political art is not expert knowledge, but common knowledge, like knowledge of Greek, which is taught by everyone. It is taught beginning at home, then in school, and finally in society at large, which teaches individuals to obey the law and punishes those who don't. "If there is someone who is the least bit more advanced in virtue than ourselves, he is to be cherished," says Protagoras, and he concludes, "I consider myself to be just such a person, uniquely qualified to assist others in becoming noble and good" (328a–b).

Socrates professes that he is persuaded by Protagoras, except for "one small obstacle" (328e). This small obstacle turns out to be the focus of most of the rest of the dialogue. Protagoras claimed in his speech that justice, temperance, and piety "were somehow collectively one thing: virtue" (329c). But how are they related to each other? "Is virtue a single thing, with justice and temperance its parts, or are the things I have just listed all names for a single entity?" Protagoras replies, "This is an easy question to answer, Socrates ... Virtue is a single entity, and the things you are asking about are its parts" (329d). When Socrates asks whether they are parts like the parts of a face, each with its own nature and function, or like the parts of gold, differing only in size, Protagoras answers that they are like the parts of a face. It is possible to have one of these parts and not others, as "many are courageous but unjust, and many again are just but not wise" (329e). This leads Socrates to ask whether courage and wisdom are also parts of virtue, along with justice, temperance, and piety, to which Protagoras responds, "absolutely, and wisdom is the greatest part" (330a). Protagoras' conception of virtue is rooted in ordinary understanding, which is just what we would expect from the Great Speech. Ordinarily, we think of the virtues as different from each other, and as separable, such that someone can have one of the virtues and lack others. When Protagoras says that wisdom is the greatest part of virtue, he may be expressing his own view as a Sophist and not the view of the ordinary person, but for the most part his conception of virtue is a common, popular one.

Socrates' Conception of Virtue:
Virtue is Knowledge

Socrates does not reveal at this point what his conception of virtue is. He is playing the role of questioner in the elenchus, not that of defender of a view. Very late in the dialogue, however, he gives an indication of the viewpoint behind his interrogation of Protagoras. He imagines the previous discussion criticizing him, saying that he had originally said that virtue could not be taught, but now he was arguing "the very opposite and [has] attempted to show that everything is knowledge – justice, temperance, courage – in which case, virtue would appear to be eminently teachable" (361b). What gives unity to the virtues is that all the parts of it have the same nature: they are all knowledge.

Socrates asks Protagoras a series of questions designed to show that the virtues are one and the same, or at least very similar. First he asks about justice and piety (recall his claim in the *Euthyphro* that piety was a part of justice), then about wisdom and temperance, then about temperance and justice. His aim is, by setting up a series of equivalences, to establish that piety=justice=temperance= wisdom. This would establish that all of the virtues that Protagoras has mentioned, except courage, are one and the same. Protagoras, however, resists Socrates' arguments at every stage. The argument breaks down completely at 334c, after Protagoras gives a short speech on the diversity of goodness. Socrates objects that he can't follow such speeches, because of his poor memory,[1] and threatens to leave. None of the spectators wants to see the discussion end, so it is finally agreed that Socrates and Protagoras will take turns examining each other. Protagoras examines Socrates on a poem of Simonides, of which Socrates gives a rather fanciful interpretation, after which Socrates recommends returning to the previous argument. Protagoras eventually agrees, reluctantly, to answer Socrates' questions.

Protagoras now modifies his previous position: he says that four of the five parts of virtue "are reasonably close to each other," but that "courage is completely different from all the rest. The proof that what I am saying is true is that you will find many people who are extremely unjust, impious, intemperate, and ignorant, and yet exceptionally courageous" (349d). It is a puzzle why Protagoras accepts the similarity of the other virtues when he had resisted Socrates' conclusions earlier in the dialogue, but now he stakes his entire position on the nature of courage, the one virtue that Socrates had not previously discussed. Once again, Protagoras is relying on a popular, common sense view of virtue. In this view courage is understood as a kind of intrepidity or daring in the face of danger, rather than as a kind of wisdom. Socrates makes two attempts to refute Protagoras' position. In the first argument Socrates tries to show that courage is wisdom by showing that the courageous are confident and that the more wisdom one has the more confident one is. Protagoras objects to the argument, and Socrates appears to drop it, but in the course of the argument Protagoras makes an admission that is fatal to his claim that one can be courageous and ignorant. Socrates asks Protagoras whether there are people who are confident without wisdom and Protagoras admits that there are. Are these people courageous, Socrates asks, to which Protagoras replies, "no ... These men are out of their minds" (350b). In other words, courage requires wisdom.

Hedonism and the Strength of Knowledge

The final argument is lengthy and complex. It involves two controversial premises, one of which Protagoras initially rejects. The premise he rejects is that the good for human beings is pleasure. This view is known as *hedonism*. Protagoras says that one must take pleasure in "honorable" (*kalois*, admirable) things. This is a view that Socrates accepts elsewhere, and it is surprising to see him arguing in the *Protagoras* that pleasure itself is the criterion of a good life. The second premise is one that Protagoras accepts enthusiastically, however, and it is crucial to Socrates' argument. Socrates contrasts this second premise with the view of the many:

> What do you think about knowledge? Do you go along with the majority or not? Most people think this way about it, that it is not a powerful thing, neither a leader nor a ruler. They do not think of it in that way at all; but rather in this way: while knowledge is often present in a man, what rules him is not knowledge but rather anything else – sometimes anger, sometimes pleasure, sometimes pain, at other times love, often fear; they think of his knowledge as being utterly dragged around by these other things as if it were a slave. Now, does the matter seem like that to you, or does it seem to you that *knowledge is a fine thing capable of ruling a person, and if someone*

were to know what is good and bad, then he would not be forced by anything to act otherwise than knowledge dictates, and intelligence would be sufficient to save a person? (352b–c; my italics)

This italicized principle states that, in a conflict between knowledge and other human psychological states, including pleasure, pain, anger, love and fear, knowledge of good and evil will always prevail. The previous argument had shown that knowledge was *necessary* for courage. This principle says that knowledge is *sufficient* for courage. Consider Laches' example of a soldier remaining at his post in battle. The view of the many is that, even if the soldier knows that it is best for him to remain, fear might overcome this knowledge and lead him to run away. If Socrates is correct, however, the knowledge that it is best to remain will always prevail: either it will prove stronger than fear, or it will banish fear completely. Given his acceptance of the strength of knowledge principle, Protagoras should accept that wisdom is sufficient for courage. When combined with his earlier acceptance of the claim that wisdom is necessary for courage, this should lead him to the conclusion that wisdom is practically equivalent to courage.

This strength of knowledge principle is at the heart of the Socratic view that virtue is knowledge. If knowledge were not sufficient for virtue, one would need something more to act correctly; will power, for instance. The strength of knowledge principle denies that this is the case. As mentioned above, Protagoras accepts this principle enthusiastically: "Not only does it seem just as you say, Socrates, but further, it would be shameful indeed for me above all people to say that wisdom and knowledge are anything but the most powerful forces in human activity" (352c–d). Socrates agrees, but notes that "most people are not going to be convinced by us. They maintain that most people are unwilling to do what is best, even though they know what it is and are able to do it. And when I have asked them the reason for this, they say that those who act that way do so because they are overcome by pleasure or pain or are being ruled by one of the things I referred to just now" (352d–e). In other words, most people believe in the existence of moral weakness, *akrasia*. Moral weakness is precisely acting in the face of knowledge that what one is doing is wrong, because one is overcome by pleasure or emotion. If the strength of knowledge principle is correct, moral weakness cannot exist.

The Argument with the Many: Moral Weakness vs. Cognitive Error

At this point Socrates does a strange thing. He launches into an argument designed to show that "the many" are wrong about moral weakness. This is strange because it violates the normal practice of the elenchus. Normally, when Socrates' interlocutor has agreed with him about the acceptability of a premise, that is sufficient for Socrates to continue the argument. Socrates does not normally bring in a third person or persons to the discussion. Protagoras asks why he does so in this case: "Socrates, why is it necessary for us to investigate the opinion of ordinary people, who will say whatever occurs to them?" (353a; this is a strange thing for the man who has defended the wisdom of ordinary people in his Great Speech to say.) Socrates' answer is that "this will help us find out about courage, how it is related to the other parts of virtue" (353b).

What ordinary people believe, according to Socrates, is that people choose immediate pleasures over long-term pleasures, though they know that the long-term pleasures are greater. To cite a common modern example, they choose to take drugs, in order to experience an immediate "high," though they are aware that doing so may ruin their lives and even kill them. But this phenomenon is in fact the result of an error of judgment. Ordinary people discount the consequences of their actions because they think of them as occurring in the distant future, and these future consequences appear smaller than they really are. Ordinary people, in misjudging the relative pleasure of the immediate over the long-term pleasure make an error in judgment, brought about by what Socrates calls "the power of appearance," which "makes us wander all over the place in confusion, often changing our minds about the same things and regretting our actions and choices with respect to things large and small" (356d). The antidote to the power of appearance is "the art of measurement," which "would make the appearances lose their power by showing us the truth, would give us peace of mind firmly rooted in the truth and would save our life" (356d–e). The art of measurement corrects for the distortion produced by the power of appearance. What the many think of as moral weakness is in fact cognitive error. Socrates calls this cognitive error ignorance. There is no such thing as moral weakness, choosing the lesser good over the greater in the face of knowledge of the greater. There *is* such a thing as choosing the lesser good when in fact there is a greater good available; but there is no such thing as choosing the lesser good in the face of *knowledge* of the greater good. Later in the argument Socrates extends the strength of knowledge principle to include belief:

> no one who knows or believes there is something else better than what he is doing, something possible, will go on doing what he had been doing when he could be doing what is better. To give in to oneself is nothing other than ignorance and to control oneself is nothing other than wisdom ... No one goes willingly toward the bad or what he believes to be bad; neither is it in human nature, so it seems, to want to go toward what one believes to be bad instead of to the good. (358c–d)

When this result is applied to the case of courage, it shows that no one knowingly and willingly goes toward what he believes to be bad. Courageous people who willingly go to war do so in the belief that this is "honorable and good" (360a); cowards, who don't willingly go to war, refuse to do so in the belief that it is not good. Assuming that the courageous are right and cowards are wrong, cowardice is the result of false belief, or ignorance, whereas courage is the result of wisdom. Wisdom is sufficient for courage; it is all the courageous person needs. There is no such thing as an ignorant courageous person, which is what Protagoras had asserted earlier. Protagoras has to admit that he has been defeated: "I think that you just want to win the argument, Socrates, and that is why you are forcing me to answer. So I will gratify you and say that, on the basis of what we have agreed upon, it seems to me to be impossible" (360e). It is at this point that Socrates says that the discussion has shown that both of them are "ridiculous" (361b). Socrates had earlier said that virtue could not be taught, but now he has been arguing that virtue is knowledge, in which case it could be taught; Protagoras had earlier stated that virtue could be taught, but now he has been arguing that "hardly any of the virtues turn out to be knowledge" (361c). He concludes that "we have gotten this topsy-turvy and terribly confused" (361c–d). Rather than continuing the discussion, however, Protagoras brings it to an end with praise of Socrates: "Socrates, I commend your enthusiasm and the way you find your way through an argument. I really don't think I am a bad man, certainly the last man to harbor ill will. Indeed, I have told many people that I admire you more than anyone I have met, certainly more than anyone in your generation. And I say that I would not be surprised if you gain among men high repute for wisdom" (361e).

Hedonism and Moral Weakness

As Socrates presents it, the argument with the many turns on the fact that the many are hedonists. Socrates asks the many, rhetorically, if they have any other theory of the good than hedonism, and at one point he says to them, "even now it is still possible to withdraw, if you are able to say that the good is anything other than pleasure or that the bad is anything other than pain" (355a). Now the strength of knowledge principle establishes that no one will knowingly choose a lesser good over a greater, whatever the good may be; but the problem is that the many do not accept this principle. Socrates' argument with the many is designed to show that, if they accept hedonism as their theory of the good, then their position is "ridiculous": knowingly to choose a lesser, immediate pleasure over a greater, but more distant pleasure, is to choose to do "what is bad, knowing it is bad, when it is not necessary to do it, having been overcome by the good" (355d). If the many are not hedonists, on the other hand, their position will not initially appear so ridiculous. They could argue that one might choose what one knows to be bad (less admirable, say, less *kalos*) because one is "overcome by pleasure." This seems intelligible; it seems, in fact, to be an everyday experience. But is it really so? If being "overcome by pleasure" refers to psychological compulsion, then the one who is overcome by pleasure does not really have a choice in the matter. Moral weakness is choosing the lesser good over the greater when one has, and knows that one has, the possibility of choosing the greater. Psychological compulsion is not the same as moral weakness. If, on the other hand, one does have a choice, is it really possible to choose a lesser good over a greater, whatever the good might be? Wouldn't such a choice inevitably be the result of cognitive distortion, brought on by the power of appearance? Does the person who chooses to become a drug addict really have a clear understanding of the future life he or she is giving up by this choice? Does he or she see the value of such a life? Knowledge, the result of the art of measurement, puts an end to cognitive distortion and enables us to see clearly what is good. In this case, too, knowingly choosing a lesser good would seem to be impossible. Socrates' argument may not depend on the many's acceptance of hedonism after all.

Virtue as Practical Wisdom

This argument, complex though it is, clarifies something left unclear in the *Laches*: the kind of knowledge that virtue is. It is what results from the use of the art of measurement. It is understandable that, if one chooses on the basis of the power of appearance, one might make a mistake and choose a lesser good that merely appears greater at the moment. If one does the necessary calculation, however, so that one has knowledge of the better course of action, then it is not so clear that one might choose the worse over the better course of action. The kind of knowledge that is involved here is not abstract, general knowledge of good and evil, but practical wisdom, *phronēsis*, knowledge of what to do in any given situation. It is this kind of knowledge that Socrates equates with virtue. Virtue is the psychological capacity to determine what one should do in any situation.

The *Meno*

This conception of virtue as practical wisdom is first defended, then criticized in the *Meno*. The Meno may be divided into three parts. The first part is a typical elenctic dialogue, like the *Charmides*, *Euthyphro* and *Laches*. In the middle part Socrates introduces the doctrine of recollection, discussed in Chapter 2. In the third part, Socrates puts forward the hypothesis that virtue is knowledge, then criticizes that hypothesis. The dialogue ends with the claim that virtue is right opinion. It is the third part of the dialogue that will primarily concern us in this chapter. In dramatic structure, the *Meno* is one of the simplest of the elenctic dialogues. It is a conversation between Socrates and Meno, with a brief appearance by Anytus, who later became one of Socrates' accusers. As noted above, I assume that the *Meno* was written after the *Laches* and *Protagoras*. The dialogue as a whole seems to provide a commentary on the elenctic dialogues, explaining the Socratic search for definitions and offering, as we saw in Chapter 2, a new justification for the elenchus, the doctrine of recollection, which gives to the elenchus a positive role in the discovery of truth.

What is Virtue?

The dialogue begins abruptly, without the usual introductory conversation, with Meno asking Socrates whether virtue can be taught, to which Socrates replies, "I am so far from knowing whether virtue can be taught or not that I do not even have any knowledge of what virtue itself is" (71a). He refers to his "complete ignorance about virtue," and adds, "If I do not know what something is, how could I know what qualities it possesses?" (71b) This question seems to be a particular case of the priority of definition principle, discussed in Chapter 3, which states that if one cannot define a thing, one cannot know anything about that thing. Socrates persuades Meno to explain to him the nature, that is the definition, of virtue. Meno tries three times and fails each time. His first definition, that there are distinctive virtues for a man, woman, child, a free man vs. a slave, is shown to be the wrong kind of definition, just as the initial attempts of Euthyphro and Laches had been mistaken. His next attempt, that virtue is the ability to rule over others, fails to apply to all cases of virtue. Both definitions fail to assert that what is done virtuously must be done justly.

Definition and Form

Throughout the discussion Socrates is carrying out a tutorial on the nature of definition. He begins the tutorial by making an analogy between the nature of virtue and the nature of bees, in which he says that, even if bees differ from each other in various respects, there is a single character in virtue of which they are all the same, a common nature in virtue of which we call them all "bees." He then says, "the same is true in the case of the virtues. Even if they are many and various, all of them have one and the same form which makes them virtues, and it is right to look to this when one is asked to make clear what virtue is" (72c–d). Socrates here uses the same language he used in the *Euthyphro* to explain the intended object of his definition. He wants a Form, the common nature that is the cause of all the many and various virtues being one. Socrates explicitly admits that the virtues may be "many and various," that is, that there may be differences among the virtues, in spite of which they have a common character that makes them all virtues. Socrates makes it clear that the unity of the virtues is a generic unity, one that allows for specific differences. Socrates continues the idea that virtue is a generic unity in the next two terms he shows Meno how to define: color and shape. Both are generic terms: there are many specific shapes and colors, but all have a common nature or Form that makes them all shapes or colors.

Meno proves unable to discern this common character of all the virtues. His third attempt to define virtue is "to desire beautiful things and have the power to acquire them" (77b). Once again the Greek word translated "beautiful" is *kalois*, and once again this term does not mean simply, "beautiful." Meno is not saying that virtue is simply having beautiful possessions, such as fine works of art. Rather, as in the phrase *kalos kagathos*, he regards such possessions as characteristic of a certain aristocratic lifestyle. Later in the argument he identifies what the virtuous person desires as "health and wealth ... gold and silver, also honors and offices in the city" (78c). Now Socrates does not think that these are the things that characterize a life as virtuous. One is reminded of Socrates' challenge to the Athenians in the *Apology* not to search for "wealth, reputation and honors," but rather wisdom, truth and "the best possible state of your soul" (29e). He first urges Meno to replace "admirable" with "good" (77b), and argues that everyone desires good things. Meno's initial response is that only some desire good things, but Socrates argues that no one wants bad things for himself, because bad things are harmful and make people miserable and unhappy, and no one wants to be unhappy. Those who want things that are actually bad, mistakenly believing them to be good, actually desire good things. So no one desires what is bad.

This introduces an important element of Socratic intellectualism, the claim that everyone desires the good. Even those people who desire things that are actually bad, do so in the false belief that they are good. If I desire to smoke cigarettes, which is harmful to my health, I do not so desire because I believe smoking is unhealthy, and thus bad for me, but in the mistaken belief that the pleasure produced by smoking will outweigh any pain smoking is likely to produce. The ultimate object of my desire, in this and in all cases, is not the specific object, in this case smoking, but the end I seek to obtain by smoking, namely the good, happiness. (Socrates makes a similar claim in the *Gorgias*, at 468b and c.) If people desire things that are in fact bad for them, therefore, we know that it is not because they desire something that they believe to be bad for them, but because they have false beliefs about what is good. The proper cure for this condition is the replacement of the false belief with a true belief, and the method for doing this is rational argument. This is an important aspect of intellectualism: the claim that the therapy for bad desires is cognitive change, the change of true beliefs for false.[2]

If everyone desires the good, then what distinguishes the virtuous person from others, according to Meno's account, must be the ability to acquire such things. But these must be acquired justly and piously; in cases where it would not be just to acquire these things, the failure to acquire them would be virtue. This once again breaks virtue up into parts, for it tells us that what is acquired with a part of virtue is virtue, which is not helpful if we do not know what virtue as a whole is. Socrates asks Meno, therefore, to "answer me again then from the beginning: What do you ... say that virtue is?" (79e)

Meno's Perplexity and Paradox; Recollection

It is at this point that Meno expresses his frustration and perplexity with his comparison of Socrates to the torpedo fish, which numbs those who touch it, as we saw in Chapter 2. Up to this point the *Meno* has proceeded like a typical elenctic dialogue. Meno has offered three definitions of virtue, and Socrates has refuted all three. Meno expresses perplexity, and if this were a typical elenctic dialogue it might end at this point, in perplexity. It is at this point, however, where Socrates introduces the doctrine of recollection and illustrates the doctrine with the examination of Meno's slave.

The Hypothesis that Virtue is Knowledge

At the end of the discussion of recollection Meno requests that Socrates return to his original question, whether "virtue is something teachable, or is a natural gift, or in whatever way it comes to men" (86d). Socrates now introduces the mathematical method of hypothesis and applies it to Meno's question: "let us investigate whether it is teachable or not by means of a hypothesis" (87b). The hypothesis he proposes is that virtue is knowledge: "is it plain to anyone that men cannot be taught anything but knowledge ... if virtue is a kind of knowledge, it is clear that it could be taught" (87c).

The next step in the investigation is to establish that virtue is knowledge.[3] Here is Socrates' argument:

(1) Virtue is something good
(2) If there is something good "different and separate from knowledge" (87d) then virtue may not be knowledge

(3) If, on the other hand, there is nothing good but knowledge, then "we would be right to suspect that" virtue is knowledge (ibid.)

(4) Virtue is beneficial

(5) Health, strength, beauty, wealth, and similar goods are sometimes harmful

(6) The same is true of "qualities of the soul" such as "moderation, and justice, courage, intelligence, memory, munificence, and all such things" (88a)

(7) Courage "when it is not wisdom" is a kind of recklessness, which is harmful; when "with understanding" it is beneficial (88b)

(8) Moderation and mental quickness "when they are learned and disciplined with understanding" (ibid.) are beneficial, but without understanding are harmful

(9) In general, "all that the soul undertakes and endures, if directed by wisdom, ends in happiness, but if directed by ignorance, it ends in the opposite" (88c)

(10) The conclusion is that "If then virtue is something in the soul and it must be beneficial, it must be knowledge, since all the qualities of the soul are in themselves neither beneficial nor harmful, but accompanied by wisdom or folly they become harmful or beneficial. This argument shows that virtue, being beneficial, must be a kind of wisdom" (88c–d)

Socrates extends the conclusion to all human activities, since these depend on the soul.

The argument starts out with the idea that there are several goods: health, strength, beauty, wealth, and various psychological traits, including moderation, justice, intelligence, memory, munificence, and the like. It ends with the conclusion that there is one good, which is knowledge or wisdom. How does this transformation take place? It results from the assumption that to be good a quality must be invariably, necessarily beneficial. The various goods mentioned initially are sometimes beneficial, sometimes harmful. So they are not genuine goods after all, but at most "goods."[4] What turns "goods" into genuine goods is the addition of knowledge or wisdom, in the role of director. Socrates does not say that knowledge alone is sufficient for a happy, successful life. Wisdom plays the role of director of natural "goods": it turns recklessness into courage, mental quickness into knowledge; wisdom "accompanies" all human activities, turning them into virtuous activities.

It is wisdom that creates virtue, but it does not create it out of nothing. Socrates had said in Plato's *Apology*, "Wealth does not bring about excellence, but excellence makes wealth and everything else good for men, both individually and collectively" (30b). There is no virtue without wisdom, but wisdom still requires a certain amount of "goods," whether material or psychological, on which to do its work.[5]

Objection: Where are the Teachers?

If virtue is knowledge, then we are not good by nature, but are made good by learning. If virtue is knowledge, therefore, it can be taught. (This would seem to resolve the predicament in which Socrates found himself at the end of the *Protagoras*.) But this leads to a problem. If virtue can be taught, then there ought to be teachers of it. But where are the teachers of virtue? Socrates proposes to Anytus, who has just joined the conversation, that the Sophists are teachers of virtue, and he gets Anytus' explosive dissent: any Athenian who is among those who are *kalos kagathos* would do a better job of educating a young man in civic virtue than a Sophist. Anytus challenges Socrates: doesn't he believe that there have many good men in the city? The problem, Socrates states, is not that there have not been good men in Athenian public life, but that they did not pass on their own virtue to their children. He cites Themistocles, Aristides, Thucydides (the grandparents of the children in the *Laches*), and Pericles as examples of parents who did not teach virtue to their children. His conclusion is that virtue cannot be taught. At this point Anytus leaves in a huff, warning Socrates that "it is easier to injure people than to benefit them" (94e).

Reply: Virtue as Right Opinion

Unable to find teachers of virtue, and yet with several examples of virtuous Athenian leaders, Socrates revisits his previous argument to see if there is a flaw in it. He discovers one, in the claim that only knowledge guides one correctly. Right opinion is as good a practical guide as knowledge. If someone has right opinion concerning the road to Larissa he or she will guide people to Larissa as successfully as one who has knowledge. The problem with right opinion is that it is not "tied down":

... true opinions, as long as they remain, are a fine thing and all they do is good, but they are not willing to remain long, and they escape from a man's mind, so that they are not worth much until one ties them down by (giving) an account of the reason why ... After they are tied down, in the first place they become knowledge, and they remain in place. That is why knowledge is prized higher than correct opinion, and knowledge differs from correct opinion in being tied down. (97e–98a)

The person with knowledge is not merely of the opinion that something is so; he or she has an account of the reason why this particular fact is so. Knowledge, on this account, is correct opinion plus a rational explanation of the matter in question.

Since there were no teachers for the virtuous men of Athens' past, their virtue was not acquired as knowledge. Their right opinions were akin to the sayings of soothsayers, prophets, and poets: "we should call no less divine and inspired those public men who are no less under the gods' influence and possession, as their speeches lead to success in many important matters, though they have no knowledge of what they are saying" (99d). It seems far-fetched to us to attribute to the influence of the gods all cases of right opinion, but it may not have seemed implausible to the Athenians to attribute to divine inspiration the judgments of their leading statesmen, especially those of Themistocles, which saved Athens at the Battle of Salamis. Whether or not we attribute divine influence to all right opinions, it seems that Socrates is making a serious revision to his claim that virtue is knowledge. It looks as though he is saying that virtue is right opinion, not knowledge. The conclusion of the *Meno*, however, suggests another possibility:

virtue would be neither an inborn quality nor taught, but comes to those who possess it as a gift from the gods which is not accompanied by understanding, *unless there is someone among our statesmen who can make another into a statesman. If there were one, he could be said to be among the living as Homer said Tiresias was among the dead, namely, that "he alone retained his wits while the others flitted about like shadows." In the same manner such a man would, as far as virtue is concerned, here also be the only true reality compared, as it were, with shadows.* (99e–100a; my italics)

Socrates does not identify the person whose virtue would be accompanied by understanding, and thus capable of being taught. Could Plato be thinking of Socrates himself as such a person? He certainly regarded Socrates as pre-eminently virtuous. It does not seem a stretch to describe the Socrates of Plato's dialogues as, "as far as virtue is concerned," the only reality among shadows. Plato's Socrates does describe himself in the *Gorgias* as "one of a few Athenians – so as not to say I'm the only one, but the only one among our contemporaries – to take up the true political craft and practice the true politics" (521d). Socrates did not create another statesman like himself, but he did, in Plato and perhaps others as well, create other philosophers like himself. Perhaps the passage is not a veiled reference to Socrates but an anticipatory reference to the philosopher-king of the *Republic*. The ability to teach virtue to others is a mark of the philosopher-king. In either case, perhaps the correct conclusion to take from the *Meno* is that virtue, in its common cases, is right opinion, but in an exceptional case could still be knowledge.

Even if we take the final argument of the *Meno* to be a serious revision of the claim that virtue is knowledge, the resulting account of virtue is as intellectualistic as the account containing the Socratic paradoxes. Right opinion is belief, and belief is a cognitive, rational state. Even if virtue is defined as right belief, moral weakness would still be impossible, since Socrates had said in the *Protagoras* that no one who knows "*or believes*" (358c) that there is a better alternative to an action he is performing will persist in doing that action rather than perform the other possible action, and that "no one goes willingly toward the bad or *what he believes to be bad*; neither is it in human nature, so it seems, to want to go toward *what one believes to be bad* instead of to the good" (358d; my italics). If virtue is true belief, then vice is false belief, and that is still considered ignorance.

Conclusion

For the bulk of this chapter we have seen Socrates, or his surrogate Nicias, argue that virtue is knowledge. This is first defined very generally, as knowledge of good and evil. In the *Protagoras* it is defined more precisely as practical wisdom, knowledge of what to do in every situation. Practical wisdom has two aspects: knowledge of what is good in general, and what is good in a particular situation. The knowledge of what is good in a particular situation results from the art of measurement. But what is good in general? The answer to this question is that the good is happiness, but what is happiness? The view on offer in the *Protagoras* is that the good is pleasure. Interpreters have differed over whether Socrates is himself committed to this view, or whether he only attributes it to the many. We shall consider this question in the next chapter. Whatever the nature of happiness, however, everyone desires to be happy. If people fail to be happy, it is either because they have an incorrect understanding of happiness or because they have failed to apply the art of measurement correctly. In either case the error is a cognitive one, an error in understanding. The correct remedy for errors of this kind is correction, the replacement of false belief or ignorance with knowledge or, as the conclusion of the *Meno* would have it, true belief. Socrates' account of virtue is paradoxical. If he is correct, the common sense views of ordinary people are confused. They lack an understanding of the fundamental nature of virtue.

6

Happiness

Virtue and Happiness

Socrates in Plato's elenctic dialogues is, as we have seen, a seeker of virtue. When he exhorts the Athenians to care for the best state of their souls, he is exhorting them to care for virtue rather than for wealth, reputation, and honors. The question arises, however, why seek virtue? It might seem that the answer to this question would be obvious: we seek virtue for its own sake. The life of virtue, the best state of the soul, just *is* preferable, for its own sake, to the life of vice. If virtue is knowledge or wisdom, as it is defined in the *Laches*, *Protagoras*, and most of the *Meno*, and if the alternative to virtue, vice, is ignorance, it might be thought self-evident that virtue would be preferable to vice. Who would choose to be ignorant if wisdom is possible? The key question would then become, whether wisdom or knowledge is possible. The logic of the elenchus, which leads to refutation, suggests that it is not. The *Meno*, however, through the introduction of the doctrine of recollection, holds out hope that wisdom may be possible. The barren Socrates denies that he has wisdom, and if *Socrates* lacks wisdom, where are we likely to find it? The fertile Socrates, in contrast, seems to be on a voyage of discovery that might lead in the end to wisdom, even if he is not quite there yet. There is a sense in which this answer, that the life we ought to pursue, the life devoted to the discovery of wisdom, is the only life worthy of a human being, just *is* the Socratic answer to the question why we ought to pursue virtue. When Socrates says in the *Apology* that the life without inquiry is not worth living, he is saying that the only life worth pursuing is that described in the elenctic dialogues.

For the most part, however, Socrates does not take this line in the elenctic dialogues. He argues that virtue, and in particular wisdom, is valuable for what it produces. What wisdom produces is *eudaimonia*, which is usually translated "happiness." As noted in Chapter 3, this is a somewhat misleading translation, however. Our concept of happiness is complex. One aspect of happiness is that of a pleasant, subjective, and intermittent mental state. When we ask people if they are happy, we may be asking them about their current mood. We also use "happiness" to describe a longer-lasting mental state, something akin to contentment or satisfaction, applicable perhaps to an entire life. People consider whether they are happy in their jobs, or in their marriages or families, or in their lives as a whole. This is closer to *eudaimonia*, but it is still more subjective than the Greek term. *Eudaimonia* does not exclude a sense of subjective satisfaction, but it also includes a sense of objective value. A life that is *eudaimōn* is a life that a rational person would choose to live, containing goods that make it objectively valuable. Sometimes Socrates uses the phrase "to do well" as a synonym for *eudaimonia*. The term has the connotation of success. If success in life consisted in amassing great wealth, reputation, and honors, which Socrates emphatically denies, then the one who succeeded in amassing these things would be *eudaimōn*. Socrates believes that the defining characteristic of a life that is *eudaimōn* is practical wisdom, *phronēsis*. All other characteristics that contribute to one's well-being are valuable if accompanied and directed by wisdom, but they are apt to be harmful otherwise. We saw this argument in the *Meno*, in the previous chapter, and a similar argument is to be found in the *Euthydemus* at 278e–282d. At one point in the argument Socrates states, "since we all wish to be happy, and since we appear to become so by using things and using them rightly, and since knowledge was the source of rightness and good fortune, it seems to be necessary that every man should prepare himself by every means to become as wise as possible" (282a).

The name for someone who believes that the end sought by virtue is happiness or *eudaimonia* is a eudaimonist. Socrates, like other Greek ethical theorists, is a eudaimonist. Eudaimonism just is the view that the ethical end is *eudaimonia*. What justifies the pursuit of virtue is the contribution of virtue to the attainment of *eudaimonia*. Moreover, like other Greek ethical theorists, Socrates believes that the *eudaimonia* one aims for is one's own. He is an ethical egoist.

One wants to be ethical because one wants to be *eudaimōn*, happy; one wants to live a good life. Ethical egoism is often associated with selfishness, however, as if one believed that one could attain the good life at the expense of others. Socrates, as we shall see, denies this. For Socrates, an essential component of a happy life is justice, and justice involves proper treatment of other persons.

The Problem: What Knowledge Produces Happiness?

What is it, though, that one needs to be wise about? What art must we learn to bring about our happiness? In the *Euthydemus* Socrates and his interlocutor Clinias consider several arts, and finally settle on what they call the "kingly art" (292a), but they prove to be unable to determine the nature of the wisdom with which this art is concerned, and the nature of the good that it produces. The kingly art makes people happy and it consists of a certain kind of wisdom, but what is that wisdom? The *Euthydemus* does not answer that question. The *Protagoras* offers an answer: the final argument, as we saw in the last chapter, defines happiness as pleasure, and describes the wisdom that produces a pleasant life as the art of measurement. We have reason, however, to think that this answer is not Socrates' considered judgment about the nature of happiness. Socrates usually refers to the kind of life that is desirable as *kalos kagathos*, admirable and good. But what kind of life is admirable and good? The ordinary Athenian of Socrates' time would have thought that the lives of the great Athenian political leaders – Pericles, for instance, or Themistocles – fit this description, but what made their lives admirable? They accomplished things for the apparent benefit of Athens – Themistocles, in particular, saved Athens at the battle of Salamis – but did they do so on the basis of knowledge? Socrates at the end of the *Meno* denies this and indicates that their achievements were based on true opinions, inspired by the gods. If true happiness results only from knowledge, these men cannot be examples of it.

There are two dialogues that offer an answer to this question, the *Crito* and the *Gorgias*. In the case of the *Crito*, the answer occurs in the course of an attempt to prove something else. It is a sidelight in Socrates' argument, though an important one. In the *Gorgias* the wisdom that constitutes happiness, though not the initial topic of the dialogue, turns out to be its central theme. The *Gorgias* defends the Socratic concern of the *Apology* that one ought to prefer wisdom, truth, and the best state of one's soul to the life spent in pursuit of wealth, reputation, and honors. The latter alternative, in rather cynical form, is defended by two characters in the dialogue, Polus and Callicles. Both the *Crito* and the *Gorgias* give the same answer to the question, what life should I pursue to obtain happiness? It is not the answer offered by the *Protagoras*.

The Problem of the *Crito*

The *Crito* is set in prison. Socrates' execution, which has been delayed while a ship is on a sacred voyage to Delos, is imminent. The matter Crito brings to Socrates is urgent. He has arranged for Socrates to escape from prison. (This was apparently something that occurred on occasion in the Athenian system of justice.) Crito and other friends of Socrates have bribed the prison guard and have enough money to deal with any informers who might turn them in. Crito suggests Thessaly as a possible destination for Socrates. He offers several reasons why Socrates should escape: he will be deprived of a friend if Socrates is executed; his friends will be thought too cheap to save him; it is unjust of Socrates not to save himself; he will be deserting his sons if he dies; he seems to be taking the easy way out, not the path of virtue. Time, however, is of the essence of Crito's plan: Socrates must escape on that very night. "Let me persuade you on every count, Socrates," he says, "and do not act otherwise" (46a).

The *Crito* as an Atypical Elenctic Dialogue

The *Crito* differs from other elenctic dialogues in that it does not deal with a theoretical question, such as the nature of temperance or piety, but with a practical one: should Socrates escape? This question is not an open-ended one, like the questions of definition we have considered. There are only two choices: Socrates should escape, or he should remain in prison. Here is one place where the elenchus can have a positive result: if one of the two alternatives is refuted, but the other is not, then the unrefuted alternative must be the correct choice. If the *Crito* is unusual in having this structure, it is also unusual in that Socrates does not play the role of the barren, ignorant inquirer. Rather, he plays the role of advocate, defending the view that he should remain in prison. Socrates does not, as he usually does in elenctic dialogues, profess his ignorance. He does not state that he is an expert on moral questions, but he tells Crito that one ought to listen to the expert and not to the many, and the principles that he puts forward on behalf of remaining in prison are his own. The *Crito* is an elenctic dialogue – the body of the dialogue is devoted to the elenctic examination of Crito's view that Socrates should escape – but it is not a typical one.

Socrates' Response to Crito

Socrates believes that he should remain in prison and await execution. He begins his argument against Crito by commenting on Crito's zeal: it would be valuable if Crito were right, but it is only harmful if he is wrong. "Not only now but at all times I am the kind of man who listens to nothing within me but the argument that on reflection seems best to me," Socrates says (46b).[1] We ought not to listen to the opinions of the ignorant many, but only to those of the wise. In the case of physical training, the wise person is the trainer. Failing to listen to the trainer harms the body. In the case of

> ... actions just and unjust, shameful and beautiful, good and bad, about which we are now deliberating, should we follow the opinion of the many and fear it, or that of the one, if there is one who has knowledge of these things and before whom we feel fear and shame more than before all the others. If we do not follow his directions, we shall harm and corrupt that part of ourselves that is improved by just actions and destroyed by unjust actions. (47c–d)

Crito agrees that we ought to follow the advice of the wise person, if one exists. The part of us that is improved by just actions and destroyed by unjust actions, though Socrates does not mention it by name, is the soul, or perhaps the character of the person.

Life is not worth living if one's body is "corrupted and in bad condition" (47e); likewise it is not worth living if the part of us that is concerned with just and unjust actions is corrupted. This part is more valuable than the body. The most important thing is not to live, but to live well. "And (to live) well is the same thing as to live admirably and justly" (48b; my translation). Here Socrates does not only endorse the ideal of the life that is *kalos kagathos*, admirable and good; he adds to ideals of the admirable and good the ideal of justice. The just life is the same as the admirable and good life. The admirable and good person is a just person. This triad of adverbs: to live well, admirably and justly, constitute Socrates' account of the happy life. *Eudaimonia* is not a matter of wealth, reputation, or honors, but of goodness, admirability, and justice.

The implication of this description is that if a just person has to die in order to avoid damaging his or her soul, then he or she should do so. We ought never to do wrong willingly, for that "is in every way harmful and shameful to the wrongdoer" (49b). This implies that we ought not to wrong or mistreat another, even in return for a wrong done to us: "one should never do wrong in return, nor mistreat any man, no matter how one has been mistreated by him," to which Socrates adds, "and Crito, see that you do not agree to this, contrary to your belief. For I know that only a few people hold this view or will hold it, and there is no common ground between those who hold this view and those who do not, but they inevitably despise each other's views" (49c–d).[2]

So far, Socrates has outlined a constructive account of an ethical theory. The aim of life is to live well, which is to live admirably and justly. The idea that the good life is the life of pleasure, the view put forward in the *Protagoras*, is not to be found here. Justice requires that one do no wrong. However pleasant it might be to wrong another person, that is absolutely forbidden by the *Crito*'s ethical code. There is no calculation of the pleasure or pain produced by a particular action, only a determination that an action does, or does not, wrong or mistreat someone. Socrates rejects the traditional Greek idea, defended by Polemarchus in *Republic* I, that justice is helping one's friends and harming one's enemies. There is no indication in the text that these principles, which are attributed to the wise, are tentative or uncertain. Socrates has in the discussion been careful to get Crito's agreement each step of the way as he lays out his ethical principles. He states that these are principles he has long held, and which he will not abandon now that he is threatened with death. The impression given is that Socrates and Crito have discussed these principles in the past and that Crito has agreed with them. Socrates wants to persuade Crito that he, like himself, should not abandon these principles under his current circumstances.

Socrates' next step is to ask Crito whether one ought to fulfill one's just agreements, and Crito again agrees that one should. If he were to escape, then, would he be in violation of a just agreement? Would he be "mistreating people whom we should least mistreat?" (50a) Crito is unable to answer this question; he says he does not know. The remainder of the dialogue is concerned with the speech of the laws, who persuade Socrates and Crito that he has an obligation not to escape but to remain in prison and await execution. It is not my purpose here to examine that speech. (I examine the speech in the next chapter.) What is important for our present purposes is the ethical theory just presented. The theory, though only presented in outline, states what is necessary to live a good life. It characterizes the good life as the just life, and it argues that one ought not to perform unjust actions, as they harm the soul. The argument creates an analogy between a healthy life, achieved by following the trainer who has expert knowledge, and a just life, achieved by following the one who is wise concerning justice. Justice is a virtue because it enables one to live a life that is mentally healthy, a life that is not ruined by acts of injustice. The good life, the happy or *eudaimōn* life, is the mentally healthy life.

Virtue and Happiness: The *Gorgias*

If the first defense of the just life as the happy, *eudaimōn* life, occurs in the *Crito*, the second, much longer defense, occurs in the *Gorgias*. In the *Crito* Socrates makes his case before Crito, an old and dear friend, who has agreed in the past to Socrates' principles. Crito does not contest the Socratic claim that the admirable and good life is the just life and that the just life is good because it is mentally healthy. What would happen, however, if those contentions were questioned? In the *Gorgias* we see Socrates' answer to that question. Plato provides Socrates with two interlocutors, Polus and Callicles, who reject Socrates' claims. They defend lives that are, on Socratic principles, unjust and therefore unhealthy. Callicles has a conception of justice that is quite different from and opposed to that of Socrates. The *Gorgias* is the greatest defense in the elenctic dialogues of the Socratic way of life, the pursuit of wisdom, truth, and the best state of the soul as opposed to wealth, reputation, and honors … and, most importantly, pleasure and power.

Socrates and Gorgias on Rhetoric

The setting of the *Gorgias* is the house of Callicles. The action occurs immediately following a speech, a rhetorical display, by Gorgias. The characters are Socrates and his associate Chaerephon, on the one side, and Gorgias, his student Polus, and Callicles, an aspiring Athenian politician, on the other. Callicles is otherwise unknown. Some have suspected that he is a Platonic invention. The opening conversation of the dialogue concerns the nature of rhetoric. What kind of a craft is it that Gorgias teaches? Gorgias tells Socrates that he teaches people to speak well on "the greatest good," (452d), which is the ability to persuade others in the law courts, council, and assembly. Socrates gets Gorgias to admit that this kind of persuasion does not involve knowledge, but only conviction. The orator persuades the ignorant, not the knowledgeable. Nor does the orator need to know the medical art to be able to persuade better than the doctor. Gorgias warns against the misuse of rhetoric, and claims that not he, but his students are to blame if they use it for unjust purposes. Gorgias admits to Socrates that he will teach his students justice, if they come to him not knowing what it is. Socrates then states that, since the just person will do just things, there is no point in Gorgias' warning against the unjust use of rhetoric.

Socrates and Polus

At this point Polus breaks into the conversation. Gorgias, he says, was ashamed to admit that one of his students might not know "what's just, what's admirable, and what's good" (461b) and said that he would teach him, which led to an inconsistency, "just the thing that gives you delight" (461c). Polus challenges Socrates to explain what kind of a craft he thinks rhetoric is, and Socrates says it is no craft at all, but a "knack … for producing a certain gratification and pleasure" (462c). He compares it to pastry baking and calls it a form of flattery. A legitimate art cares for the good of its subject, whereas a "knack" cares only for pleasure. Polus is shocked by this treatment of rhetoric as a knack: doesn't Socrates believe that orators are held in high regard in the city? Don't they possess power? Socrates responds that they are held in no regard at all, and, if power is the ability to accomplish something good, as opposed to pleasant, they have *no* power. They do what they *see fit* to do, but not what they *want*. What they want – what everyone wants – is what is good. As people want to be healthy and have their bodies in good condition, so they want to be happy and have their souls in a similar state. Orators do what they see fit to do: they put people to death, exile them, and confiscate their property; but unless they know that these things are done for the sake of what is good, they are not doing what they want.

Again, Polus is shocked. Wouldn't Socrates want the "power" to do what he sees fit? Socrates denies this: those who do what they see fit to do, but who are mistaken about whether it serves their good, are pitiable and miserable. If they put others to death unjustly, they do what is the worst thing they can do; doing injustice is worse than suffering it. Even a child could refute this, claims Polus. Consider Archelaus, the tyrant of Macedonia. He committed "the most heinous crimes" (471a) to become ruler, but now he is happy. You are trying to refute me rhetorically, replies Socrates. You offer witnesses in favor of your view, but "if I don't produce you as a single witness to agree with what I'm saying, then I suppose I've achieved nothing worth mentioning" (472b). The view on which they differ is whether one can be unjust but happy: Polus affirms that one can, and Socrates denies it. Moreover, Socrates holds that the person who is punished for unjust acts is better off than the one who escapes punishment, which Polus regards as laughable.

The Refutation of Polus

Polus is surely right to claim that his view is that held by almost everyone but Socrates. How does Socrates argue that he is mistaken? First of all, he gets Polus to admit that, while suffering injustice is worse than doing it, doing injustice is more shameful. Polus accepts a distinction between the pair "admirable" and "good," on the one hand, and "shameful" and "bad" on the other. If something is admirable, it must be either because it is pleasant or because it is useful (beneficial), and if something is shameful it must be so either because it is painful or bad. If acting unjustly is more shameful than suffering injustice, it must be either more painful or worse. It isn't more painful (to the agent, that is; it might be more painful to the recipient of injustice), so it must be worse. Acting unjustly, therefore, is both more shameful and worse than acting justly. "Submit yourself nobly to the argument, as you would to a doctor," Socrates tells Polus (475d). Polus agrees that "on this reasoning, anyhow," no one would prefer acting unjustly to suffering unjustly (475e).

Socrates now moves on to his second point, that for one who acts unjustly, not paying what is due ("getting away with" injustice, we might say) is a worse outcome than paying the just penalty. Justice involves being disciplined, punished, by someone. If the punishment is just, it is admirable. If it is admirable, it is either pleasant or beneficial. Being punished is not pleasant, so it must be beneficial, and thus good. This means that the soul which is punished justly is benefited, improved, and the person who is punished "gets rid of something bad in his soul" (477a). Socrates mentions three bad conditions of a human being: poverty, which affects one's financial condition; "weakness, disease, ugliness and the like" (477b), which affect one's body; and "injustice, ignorance, cowardice and the like" (in other words, vice), which affect one's soul. Corruption of the soul is the most shameful, and therefore the worst, of the three. (The argument here recalls Socrates' claims in the *Crito* that life is not worth living with a body that is ruined by illness or with a soul that is ruined by injustice, and that damage to one's soul is worse than damage to one's body.) It must therefore be more painful or more harmful than poverty or disease. It is not more painful; therefore it must be more harmful, and therefore "injustice, then, lack of discipline and all other forms of corruption of soul are the worst thing there is" (477e). Financial management gets rid of poverty, medicine gets rid of disease and justice gets rid of injustice. As injustice is the worst, most harmful condition one can have, justice is the most admirable of the three. Again, this means that it must be most pleasant or beneficial; but being punished is not pleasant; therefore, it must be most beneficial. The happiest person is not the person who gets rid of something bad but someone who does not have that condition in the first place. The second-best person is the one who gets rid of it; the least happy person is the one who retains it. This is the condition of the tyrant, such as Archelaus. The person who is unjust and who does not submit to just punishment is like the person who is ill and does not submit to a painful but beneficial medical procedure.

Socrates now sums up the argument: Polus had argued that someone like Archelaus, who was unjust without paying the penalty for it, was happy, whereas Socrates had denied this. He had held that to be unjust was worse than to suffer injustice, and that to escape punishment was worse than to be justly punished. Hasn't the argument proved Socrates correct? Polus answers, "apparently" (479e). Rhetoric would have a good use if it were used in the service of justice, not in the service of injustice. Now Polus, who has been going along with Socrates' argument, balks: "I think these statements are absurd, Socrates," he states, "though no doubt you think they agree with those expressed earlier" (480e). Socrates, having responded to

Polus that we must either abandon our earlier statements or accept their conclusion, now puts the icing on the cake: if we help ourselves and our friends and relations by seeing to it that we and they are brought to justice, we harm our enemies by seeing that they elude punishment, and so live as long as possible in corruption.

Critique of the Argument against Polus

The argument with Polus has been criticized.[3] It would seem that Polus dooms himself at the very start, when he admits that something may be admirable (*kalon*) in one of only two ways: by being pleasant or by being good (beneficial), and shameful by being painful or bad. By admitting that injustice is more shameful than justice he is forced to admit that it is worse. But this association between what is admirable and what is good and between what is shameful and what is bad would have seemed unproblematic for his Greek audience. Though the argument is complex, the Socratic points that underlie it are simple: the good condition of the soul is virtue – justice, courage, self-control, wisdom – and the bad condition of the soul is vice, including injustice. Virtue is the source of the health of the soul, and vice the source of its unhealthy, diseased condition. A healthy soul is a happy one, while a diseased soul is unhappy. As no one wishes to be unhappy, no one can wish, rationally, to be unjust. Injustice must be the result of ignorance about what is just or unjust. Virtue is knowledge, but in this case it is not knowledge of what is most pleasant, as it was in the *Protagoras*, but knowledge of what the healthy condition of the soul is. By noting that what is admirable may be either what is pleasant *or* what is good Socrates makes it clear, for purposes of this argument, at least, that the good life is not necessarily the most pleasant life. His argument relies on his rejection of hedonism as an account of the good. This argument, with its association between *eudaimonia* and the health of the soul recalls the analogy in the *Crito* between the health of the body and the health of the soul. This analogy will be important also in the final argument of the *Gorgias*, that against Callicles. As Polus' response to Socrates at 480e indicates, he is not convinced by Socrates' argument. No doubt he, like Meno at *Meno* 80a–b, feels that he has been tricked somehow by Socrates, though he can't say exactly how. If the elenchus aims at convincing Socrates' interlocutor that Socrates' view is correct, by enlisting the interlocutor as a witness on Socrates' behalf, this elenchus is a failure.

Callicles

At this point the third interlocutor, Callicles, enters the argument. As in *Republic* I, which it resembles in this respect, the three interlocutors exhibit increasing hostility toward Socrates and his line of argument. Gorgias is shocked by Socrates' disparagement of rhetoric, but he is interested in what Socrates has to say, and he encourages Callicles to continue his discussion with Socrates when Callicles wants to quit. Gorgias is not a proponent of injustice; he is not happy with the idea that rhetoric might be used for unjust ends. Polus, on the other hand, is. Polus is an advocate of injustice as a means to happiness, and he does not accept Socrates' argument to the contrary. Polus is an immoralist, an advocate of immorality as a means to happiness. The same is often said of Callicles. It seems, however, that Callicles has a morality, an ethics, but one which is different from both convention and Socrates' view. As noted above, we do not know anything about Callicles apart from what this dialogue tells us. He is described as a politician, and a democratic one: Socrates says he loves the *dēmos*, the Athenian people, and cannot contradict what they say. He shifts back and forth, whenever the people change their minds. Socrates says that he, on the other hand, is a lover of philosophy, which always says the same things.

Callicles' response to Socrates' final statement to Polus, and probably to his entire argument, is astonishment: "tell me, Socrates, are we to take you as being in earnest now, or joking? For if you *are* in earnest, and these things you're saying are really true, won't this human life of ours be turned upside down, and won't everything we do evidently be the opposite of what we should do?" (481b–c). Callicles is correct. Socrates' philosophy is a radical critique of the Athenian way of life, if not of the human way of life. As Socrates had charged in Plato's *Apology*, the Athenians spent their lives in the pursuit of wealth, honors, and reputation instead of wisdom, truth, and the best condition of their souls. What Socrates sought from the Athenians was a wholesale reorientation of their lives. He really did want to turn their lives upside down.

Conventional vs. Natural Justice

Callicles is correct also in his diagnosis of where Polus went wrong in his argument. Polus, like Gorgias before him, was undone by his sense of shame. It was shame that made Gorgias admit that he would teach justice to any of his students who were in need of it. It was shame that made Polus admit that doing injustice was more shameful than suffering it. Socrates claims to be pursuing the truth, says Callicles, but he is in fact appealing to conventional beliefs about what is admirable. But convention and nature are opposed to each other: by convention doing injustice is shameful, but by nature it is suffering injustice that is shameful: the truth, as Callicles sees it, is that doing injustice is more shameful according to law, which is based on convention, but suffering injustice is more shameful according to nature. "No man would put up with suffering what's unjust, only a slave would do so," he states (483b). What is just according to law is established by the weak majority, who band together to protect themselves from the few strong. They contend that wanting a larger share of good things is unjust, whereas it is just by nature for the strong to have a larger share than the weak:

> We mold the best and most powerful among us, taking them while they're still young, like lion cubs, and with charms and incantations we subdue them into slavery, telling them that one is supposed to get no more than his fair share, and that that's what's admirable and just. But surely, if man whose nature is equal to it arises, he will shake off, tear apart, and escape all this, he will trample underfoot our documents, our tricks and charms, and all our laws that violate nature. He, the slave, will rise up and be revealed as our master, and here the justice of nature will shine forth. (483e–484b)

Callicles' distinction between conventional and natural justice provides him with a powerful alternative to Socrates' vision of the best life for human beings. Callicles threatens the democratic outlook, which he claims to serve. He claims that what is just by nature is for the superior person to have a greater share than the inferior person. Is Callicles, like Polus before him, an immoralist? It would seem to depend on what we mean by a moralist. If a moralist defends conventional justice, then Callicles is certainly an immoralist. But if a moralist defends justice, though he may understand justice in an unconventional way, then Callicles may be considered a moralist, though with a very different view of morality than Socrates. Again, if a moralist is one who defends the equality of all human beings, as do such modern moral theories as Kantian deontology and utilitarianism, then Callicles is an enemy of morality. But it looks as though Callicles and Socrates have this in common: they defend the morality of the exceptional person, though they have different ideas of what the exceptional person stands for.[4] For Socrates, the virtuous person is the standard of morality; for Callicles it is the man of power.

Callicles' Critique of Philosophy

Callicles follows his defense of natural justice with a sneering attack on philosophy. It is all fine and good for a young boy to practice philosophy; it makes him well bred. "But when I see an older man still engaging in philosophy and not giving it up, I think such a man by this time needs a flogging" (485d). Such a man avoids the centers of the city, where men become prominent, but "instead lives the rest of his life in hiding, whispering in a corner with three or four boys, never uttering anything well-bred, important, or apt" (485d–e). Such a person could not defend himself in court if "some no good wretch of an accuser" (486b) brought charges against him; such a person could be knocked on the jaw with impunity. The allusion to Socrates' own trial and to his life is unmistakable, if somewhat unfair. Socrates spent a good portion of his life not whispering in a corner but in the public market-place. Socrates must respond to Callicles by defending the life devoted to the pursuit of virtue, the life of philosophy. Callicles claims to be saying all of this out of good will toward Socrates, whom he sees as a man of ability, and Socrates takes, or pretends to take, his remarks in the manner in which Callicles offers them. Socrates says Callicles has the three marks of a person who can test his views: "knowledge, good will, and frankness" (487a). Callicles has said the same thing to Socrates that Socrates has overheard him saying to his friends, so he is not afraid to say what he actually thinks. Callicles, Socrates says, is the only test he needs to establish the truth. If he and Callicles agree on something, he'll need no more proof that what they have agreed on is correct.

Socrates' Response to Callicles: Who is the Superior Person?

Socrates might attack Callicles by recalling a claim from his argument with Polus, that power must be good for its possessor, and arguing that the pursuit of political power does not make people happy. Callicles would be free to dismiss such an argument, however, as applying only to inferior people, who are incapable of achieving real power. Instead, Socrates attacks Callicles' notion of the superior person. Does Callicles mean the more powerful? If so, the many, who are collectively more powerful than the few, will be correct in legislating an equal share for all. Nonsense, replies Callicles: the superior are not the more powerful but the better: the more intelligent. Does this mean, asks Socrates, that the doctor, who is more intelligent concerning food and drink, should have a larger share of these goods? Or the weaver the larger share of clothes, or the cobbler the larger share of shoes, or the farmer the greater share of seed? "By the ones who are the superior I don't mean cobblers or cooks," replies Callicles, "but those who are intelligent about the affairs of the city, about the way it's to be well managed. And not only intelligent, but also brave, competent to accomplish whatever they have in mind, without slackening off because of softness of spirit" (491a–b).

Callicles' Hedonism

At this point the argument takes a strange turn. If asked, what is the end that this intelligent and brave individual is to seek, one would expect Callicles to state, political power. To rule is good, and the right of the superior person; to serve, bad, and the lot of the slave. Instead, Socrates asks Callicles whether the intelligent and brave ruler must be able to rule himself, to practice self-control over pleasure and the appetites. This directs the argument to the question, not of justice, but of self-control. The view that Callicles defends, at least at the start of his argument, is the view that pleasure, appetite satisfaction, is the good: "the man who'll live correctly ought to allow his own appetites to get as large as possible and not restrain them. And when they are as large as possible, he ought to be competent to devote himself to them by virtue of his bravery and intelligence, and to fill them with whatever he may have an appetite for at the time" (491e–492a). And a little later: "wantonness, lack of discipline, and freedom, if available in good supply, are excellence and happiness" (492c). It would seem that political power is not something to be sought for its own sake, but for the sake of satisfaction of one's appetites. The aim of life is appetite satisfaction, and the pleasure it brings. Callicles is a hedonist, and a rather vulgar one at that. It is not the refined pleasure of reading good books or listening to fine music that he has in mind; it is satisfying his physical appetites. It should be clear that this goal would even get in the way of the pursuit of political power as such: someone with enormous appetites would have to spend so much time satisfying them that he could not seek to rule over others.

Socratic Self-Control

Be that as it may, it is Callicles' hedonism that Socrates now attacks. The remainder of Socrates' argument is intended to show that self-control is essential to the good life. Self-control turns out, it seems, to be the chief virtue. His argument begins with a brief myth, which he attributes to "some clever man, a teller of stories, a Sicilian, perhaps, or perhaps an Italian" (493a), an apparent allusion to Pythagorean philosophy.[5] According to this myth, which consists of a number of virtually untranslatable puns, the soul is made of parts, in one of which the appetites reside. These appetites are imagined in terms of several jars: in the case of temperate persons these jars are sound and full of such things as wine and honey and milk and many other things, which are difficult to procure. The temperate person, "having filled up his jars, doesn't pour anything more into them and gives them no further thought. He can relax over them" (493e). The jars of the intemperate person, on the other hand, are "leaky and rotten. He's forced to keep on filling them, day and night, or else he suffers extreme pain" (494a). Does Callicles intend to say that the life of the intemperate person is actually happier than that of the temperate person?

It turns out that Callicles does. The temperate person, he claims, is living the life of a stone. The good life is that in which a maximum amount of such goods flow in. And out, says Socrates, comparing this life to that of a "stonecurlew", a bird famous for excreting as much and as often as it eats. But if pleasure is pain relief, isn't a life spent scratching pleasant? And what about the life of a catamite, the passive partner in homosexual intercourse? "Aren't you ashamed, Socrates, to bring our discussion to such matters," responds Callicles in disgust (494e). Such a life is about as far removed as he could imagine from the life of the superior person, the person of power. Does Callicles really want to say that all pleasures are equal? To be consistent, he does. Now Socrates asks Callicles whether pleasure, knowledge, and bravery are all different from each other. Callicles agrees that they are. But those who do well (that is, are happy), have the opposite experience of those who do badly. One cannot do well and do badly at the same time. But pleasure and pain *are* experienced simultaneously. Being hungry is painful, but eating while hungry is pleasant. When the pain of hunger ceases, so does the pleasure of satisfying one's appetite. It is the same with drinking when thirsty. But if doing well and doing badly are opposites that can't be experienced at the same time, while pleasure and pain can be, pleasure and pain can't be the same as doing well and doing badly. "The result," says Socrates at 497a, "is that what's pleasant turns out to be different from what's good." Callicles refuses to accept this; "I don't know what your clever remarks amount to," he replies. Gorgias has to intervene in the argument to get Callicles to continue. Though Socrates gets Callicles to answer his questions at several points from here on out, Callicles' willing participation in the elenchus ceases at this point. Now it is a necessary feature of the elenchus that one must say what one believes: if the interlocutor does not answer sincerely, stating his actual beliefs, Socrates will not be able to lead him into a contradiction. Callicles, however, no longer believes the answers he gives to Socrates. He explicitly says at one point, "I couldn't care less about anything you say … I gave you these answers just for Gorgias' sake" (505c; see also 501c). Increasingly, Socrates' questioning of Callicles becomes an interrogation of a hostile witness, and eventually, a monologue.

Rhetoric vs. Philosophy

For the present the two men carry on, and Socrates' arguments arise in quick succession. Callicles wants to call the wise and brave happy, but the ignorant and cowardly experience at least as much enjoyment as the wise and brave when a battle goes their way. Callicles now abandons the hedonism with which he had initially linked his view: "as though you really think that I or anybody else at all don't believe that some pleasures are better and others worse" he responds (499b). Socrates gets him to agree that we should "do all things for the sake of what's good" (499e). That includes pleasant things. It is not for everyone to pick out which kinds of pleasures are good and which are not; it requires a craftsman. But it is philosophy, not rhetoric, that is such a craft. Rhetoric is not the craft that seeks the good – it aims at what is pleasant – it is philosophy that aims at what is good. Rhetoric, like poetry, aims at pleasing the crowd, that is, at flattery. Socrates raises the possibility that there could be a kind of rhetoric that is aimed at "getting the souls of the citizens to be as good as possible and of striving valiantly to say what is best, whether the audience will find it more pleasant or more unpleasant" (503a), but that is not the kind of rhetoric practiced by Athenian politicians, including the great statesmen of Athens' past. Callicles mentions Themistocles, Cimon, Miltiades, and Pericles as statesmen who had the public good in mind, but Socrates denies that they were. A craftsman makes his product more organized and orderly, and in the case of the state, this means making the people more law-abiding. As Socrates had indicated in the *Crito*, if someone's body is in terrible condition then life for that person is not worth living, and the same goes for the soul. So the soul must be disciplined; and when Callicles again says, "I don't know what in the world you mean, Socrates, ask somebody else," Socrates responds, "this fellow won't put up with being benefited and with undergoing the very thing the discussion's about, with being disciplined" (505c).

Socrates' Defense of the Self-Controlled Life

At this point the elenchus breaks down. Callicles won't continue to answer, except for occasional perfunctory remarks, and Socrates must continue the discussion by himself. This is what he proceeds to do, with Gorgias' approval, asking the listeners to object if they think he makes a false step. He recapitulates the argument: the pleasant differs from the good, and we seek the pleasant for the sake of the good. It is due to organization and order that the soul becomes good, and order is produced by self-control. If a self-controlled soul is good, its opposite, an undisciplined and foolish soul is bad. The self-controlled soul would be just toward human beings and pious toward the gods, a remark reminiscent of the *Euthyphro*. Such a soul would also be brave; "so, it's necessarily very much the case, Callicles, that the self-controlled man, because he's just and brave and pious, as we've recounted, is a completely good man, that the good man does well and admirably whatever he does, and that the man who does well is blessed and happy, while the corrupt man, the one who does badly, is miserable. And this would be the one who's in the condition opposite to that of the self-controlled one, the undisciplined one whom you were praising" (507c). He continues: "a person who wants to be happy must evidently pursue and practice self-control. Each of us must flee away from lack of

discipline as quickly as his feet will carry him" (507c–d). He brings
the argument to a conclusion with the following remarks:

> Such a man could not be dear to another man or to a god, for he
> cannot be a partner, and where there's no partnership there's no
> friendship. Yes, Callicles, wise men claim that partnership and friend-
> ship, orderliness, self-control, and justice hold together heaven and
> earth, and gods and men, and that is why they call this universe a
> *world order*, my friend, and not an undisciplined world-disorder. I
> believe that you don't pay attention to these facts, even though you're
> a wise man in these matters. You've failed to notice that proportion-
> ate equality has great power among both gods and men, and you
> suppose that you ought to practice getting the greater share. That's
> because you neglect geometry. (507e–508a)[6]

Socrates' remarks give a cosmic dimension to self-control, and again
suggest a Pythagorean influence. Interestingly, though justice, piety,
and courage are listed alongside self-control as virtues, wisdom, the
crowning virtue of the *Laches* and *Protagoras*, is not mentioned.

Socrates now turns to Callicles' original challenge to him to
abandon philosophy and practice rhetoric. Socrates denies that
being knocked on the jaw or exiled or put to death are the worst
things that can happen to someone. Rather, "to commit any unjust
act at all against me and my possessions is both worse and more
shameful for the one who does these unjust acts than it is for me,
the one who suffers them" (508e). It is these conclusions that Socrates
says have been "held down and bound by arguments of iron and
adamant" (508e), though he once again denies that he knows them.
Still, "no one I've ever met … can say anything else without being
ridiculous. So once more I set it down that these things are so"
(509a-b). If one wants to protect oneself against suffering injustice,
one must either become a ruler or befriend the rulers of the city and
become like them (a sentiment of which Callicles approves); and
this is worse than being knocked on the jaw or exiled or even killed.
No one can escape death; one should not consider how long one
may live but "give consideration to how he might live the part of
his life still before him as well as possible" (512e–513a). To this Callicles replies, "I don't know, Socrates – in a way you seem to be
right, but the thing that happens to most people has happened to
me: I'm not really persuaded by you" (513c). Socrates says this is
because of his love of the people, but that "if we closely examine
these same matters often and in a better way, you'll be persuaded"
(513c–d). What that better way is he does not say. There follows a

critique of the statesmen and politicians of Athens' past and present. None of them, Socrates argues, aimed at the good of the city, but at what would please the citizens. Socrates says that only he is a practitioner of the true art of politics, which aims, not at the pleasant, but at the good.

The Myth of the After-Life

The dialogue concludes with the myth of judgment in the underworld. Socrates says that Callicles may think of it as "a mere tale" but, he says "I think it's an account, for what I'm about to say I will tell you as true" (523a). Those who have lived pious and just lives go to the Isles of the Blessed, while those who have lived in an unjust and godless way go to Tartarus for punishment. Death, as Socrates defines it, is "nothing but the separation of two things from each other, the soul and the body" (524b). After death the souls of the dead bear the marks of the lives they have led. Those who have led bad lives are either reformed by punishment or, if they are judged to be incorrigible, are set up as examples for others. Such a person would be Archelaus, whose life Polus had praised as happy. Most of the incorrigible bad come from the ranks of rulers, because their opportunity to do evil is greater than that of ordinary people. When the judges in the underworld see "one who has lived a pious life, one devoted to the truth ... a philosopher who has minded his own affairs and hasn't been meddlesome" (526c), they send him to the Isles of the Blessed. Clearly Socrates is anticipating his own fate, though whether his life could be described as not meddlesome might be debated. When someone who has lived a bad life comes before these judges he will be as disoriented, and will suffer the same fate as Socrates was to suffer before his earthly judges. Maybe Callicles will dismiss this myth as "an old wive's tale" (527a), but Socrates again refers to it as an account. He urges Callicles to follow it and practice "justice and the rest of excellence both in life and death ... and let's not follow the one that you believe in and call on me to follow. For that one is worthless, Callicles" (527e).

Is Callicles Refuted?

The main argument of Socrates against Callicles is certainly complete at 514d if not at 508a; at any rate before the final myth. Socrates' argument is in favor of the view that it is "the possession of justice and self-control that makes happy people happy and the possession of badness that makes miserable people miserable" (508b). Is the argument a success? Socrates says that his conclusion is "bound by arguments of iron and adamant," and that "anyone who says anything other than what I'm now saying cannot be speaking well" (508e–509a), so clearly he regards it as successful in that respect. On the other hand, the purpose of the elenchus is to convince Socrates' interlocutor, and Callicles, as we have seen, says he is not really persuaded. Judged by that standard, the elenchus of Callicles, like the elenchus of Polus, is a failure.

Does Socrates fail to persuade Callicles because Callicles is irrational, refusing to see the implications of his own admissions? The argument suggests that it is because Callicles and Socrates have radically different conceptions of the good life. For Callicles, the good life is one in which one has political power, so that one can preserve one's life at all costs. The extension of the argument to the underworld in the final myth may be necessary to establish that self-preservation is not the be-all and end-all of life. What does one do with political power, besides survive? Callicles' answer is that one pursues pleasure in the form of appetite satisfaction. Socrates' reply to this claim is twofold. First of all, the pursuit of appetite satisfaction is self-defeating: the more one expands one's appetites, the less able is one to satisfy them. But secondly, there must be more to life than the satisfaction of one's physical appetites. Socrates spoke at 493a–b of parts of the soul. The reference was brief, and the Greek does not in fact contain the word for "part"; it merely says, "that of the souls of fools where their appetites are" (493b1; my translation). Earlier, at 491d–e, he describes "being self-controlled and master of oneself" as "ruling the pleasures and appetites within oneself." Presumably, the part of the soul that rules the appetites, persuades them as 493a–b suggests, is reason. Socrates does not develop this picture of the soul, with its contrast between reason and appetite, or perhaps between the person or self and its appetites, in the *Gorgias*; for that development we need to look to Book IV of the *Republic*. Some such division of the self is needed, however, to make sense of self-control as something other than mere wisdom, which is how it was portrayed in the *Protagoras* (358c). Self-rule must mean something like the rule of one part of the soul over another. Discipline is this rule of the appetites by reason. It is this conception of discipline and proper order that creates the analogy between the health of the soul and the health of the body and that gives self-control the central role it plays in the *Gorgias*.

Conclusion: The *Crito* and *Gorgias* vs. the *Protagoras*

The *Crito* and the *Gorgias* present a different account of virtue and its relation to happiness than does the *Protagoras*. The *Protagoras* contains the clearest statement in Plato of the intellectualist position. The good is pleasure; wisdom is the essence of the virtues; wisdom consists in the art of measurement, which determines which of two pleasures is greater. The other virtues are identical to wisdom. Wrongdoing and vice are the result of ignorance, error, produced by the power of appearance. The *Gorgias* is opposed to all of these statements. The good is not pleasure, but psychic health. The central virtue, essential for establishing order within the psyche, is self-control. Self-control enables justice, but justice, piety, and courage are treated as distinct virtues. Socrates agrees with Callicles that the superior individual is wise – that is the basis for the political theory of the *Republic* – but wisdom consists, not in finding the action that maximizes pleasure but in knowing the value of psychological order. The intellectualist theory of the *Protagoras* may be a theory of the historical Socrates, but the theory of the *Crito* and *Gorgias* points the way toward the *Republic*. As Daniel Devereux states, "these different ways of understanding virtue do not fit together to form a unified conception. The presence of the two incompatible conceptions of virtue in the Socratic dialogues is just one of several inconsistencies and ambivalences ... The lesson to be drawn is that Plato is not setting out a systematic, unified, 'Socratic' theory of the virtues in these dialogues; rather, he is exploring and developing provocative claims and ideas of his mentor – claims and ideas that are not always consistent with each other."[7]

7

The State

In Chapter 1 we discussed briefly the "political" interpretation of Socrates' trial. Neither Plato in his *Apology* nor Xenophon in his brought up any specifically political charges against Socrates, but Xenophon, in his *Memorabilia*, responded to a couple of charges against Socrates of a political nature: that Socrates "taught his companions to despise the established laws by insisting on the folly of appointing public officials by lot" (I.ii.9) and that "among the associates of Socrates were Critias and Alcibiades; and none wrought so many evils to the state" (I.ii.12). It is thought that Xenophon is responding, not to the prosecution at the trial, but to a pamphlet circulated several years after the trial by a certain Polycrates (though Polycrates is thought in this pamphlet to have presented his charges in the form of a speech by Anytus, one of the three prosecutors). Xenophon tried to show that Socrates was innocent of these charges, but the suspicion has persisted among interpreters that Socrates may have harbored anti-democratic sentiments and transmitted those sentiments to his associates. In this chapter we shall return to the question of Socrates' political views, in relation to the trial but also in a broader context. We shall examine three questions: first, was Socrates disloyal to Athens? Second, was he a critic of Athenian democracy? Third, what were his views concerning the nature of the state? These questions have become a subject of debate, particularly in the last century.[1]

Plato was concerned to show that Socrates was a loyal Athenian citizen. His argument was grounded in the historical fact that Socrates remained in prison and faced execution. Plato wrote the

Crito to make a philosophical case for Socrates' loyalty to Athens. As we discussed in the previous chapter, the dialogue portrays Crito as coming to Socrates with a plea that he should escape from prison, and the dialogue attributes to Socrates a philosophical justification for his refusal to escape. How much of this philosophical justification is based on an actual Socratic conversation with Crito and how much is Platonic invention we cannot know. The dialogue, after all, describes a private conversation between the two men. Socrates, the character in the dialogue, bases his case, as we saw, on an account of justice. Justice is one of the essential features of the good life, and justice involves not doing wrong to another, even in retaliation. When the question arises whether it would be doing wrong to the state if Socrates should try to escape, Crito says he cannot answer.

The Speech of the Laws

It is at this point in the argument that Socrates imagines "the laws and the state" (50a) confronting them and asking whether Socrates intends to destroy the state: "or do you think it possible for a city not to be destroyed if the verdicts of the courts have no force but are nullified and set at naught by private individuals?" (50b). Socrates asks Crito, what should we say in response to this and other arguments, "for many things could be said, *especially by an orator* on behalf of this law we are destroying, which orders that the judgments of the courts shall be carried out" (50b–c; my italics). Some interpreters have been suspicious about the speech of the laws that follows, in part because it seems to be something an orator might say, and we know from the *Gorgias* that Socrates has no respect for orators.[2] Socrates' remark about what an orator might say does put the reader on notice that what follows is a rhetorical defense of the laws of the city; still, the speech as a whole is presented as a series of challenges to Socrates, to which he has no answer.

Shall we say, "the city wronged me, and its decision was not right ...," Socrates asks on Crito's behalf. The laws reply, "was that the agreement between us, or was it to respect the judgments that the city came to?" (50c). At this point the laws actually invoke Socrates' own method of elenchus on their behalf: "Socrates, do not wonder at what we say but answer, since you are accustomed to proceed by question and answer" (50c–d). The laws ask Socrates if he has any complaint against them. Is he dissatisfied with the laws on marriage, under which Socrates' mother and father brought him to birth? Does he have any complaint concerning the nurture of infants and education? Does he deny that he is as much their offspring as his parents', or that he is on an unequal footing with them, as he is on an unequal footing with his parents? Does he think that he has a right to retaliate against his country and its laws? If they attempt to destroy him does he think he can attempt on his part to destroy them? Doesn't he realize that "your country is to be honored more than your mother, your father and all your ancestors, that it is more to be revered and more sacred, and that it counts for more among the gods and sensible men, that you must worship it, yield to it and placate its anger more than your father's?" (51a–b). The laws continue:

> ... you must either persuade it or obey its orders, and endure in silence whatever it instructs you to endure, whether blows or bonds, and if it leads you into war to be wounded or killed, you must obey. To do so is right, and one must not give way or retreat or leave one's post, but both in war and in courts and everywhere else, one must obey the commands of one's city and country, or persuade it as to the nature of justice. It is impious to bring violence to bear against your mother or father; it is much more so to use it against your country. (51b–c)

Both Socrates and Crito accept these assertions of the laws. The laws here echo one of the few statements of Plato's *Apology* that Socrates professes to know: that it is wrong to disobey a superior, even in the face of death (29b).

The laws give everyone the right, if he is not pleased with them, to emigrate to another state, taking his property with him. "We say, however, that whoever of you remains, when he sees how we conduct our trials and manage the city in other ways, has in fact come to an agreement with us to obey our instructions ... We only propose things, we do not issue savage commands to do whatever we order; we give two alternatives, either to persuade us or to do what we say" (51e–52a). This is the third time that the "persuade or obey" alternative has occurred in the speech of the laws. Socrates, say the laws, is "among the Athenians who most definitely came to that agreement with them ... You have never left the city, even to see a festival, nor for any other reason except military service" (52a–b). Moreover, "you have had children in this city, thus showing that it was congenial to you" (52c). At his trial Socrates might have proposed exile as his penalty, but now he would be trying to do without the consent of the city what he might then have done with its consent. Again, Socrates and Crito both agree that Socrates has made a contract with the laws, to live in accordance with them.

Socrates has had all of his adult life to leave Athens if he so desired. He might have gone to Sparta or Crete, which he has often said are well governed. By remaining in the city he has shown that it and its laws are "outstandingly ... congenial" (53a) to him. If he leaves now he will become a laughingstock. If he goes to a well-governed city he will be perceived as a destroyer of the laws. If he goes to a city that is badly governed, "will your life be worth living?" (53c).[3] Will Socrates continue to say "that virtue and justice are man's most precious possession, along with lawful behavior and the laws?" (53c–d). Or will he adopt the uncivilized customs of those in Thessaly? "Will there be no one to say that you, likely to live but a short time more, were so greedy for life that you transgressed the most important laws?" (53d–e). What will become of his conversations about justice and virtue then? If Socrates cares for his children, he will not drag them off into exile. If they can survive in Athens in his absence, they will survive after his death; his friends will care for them. The laws urge Socrates not to value his life or his children more than goodness, "in order that when you arrive in Hades you may have all this as your defense before the rulers there" (54b). Socrates has not been wronged by the laws, but by men; "but if you depart after shamefully returning wrong for wrong and mistreatment for mistreatment, after breaking your agreements and commitments with us, after mistreating those you should mistreat least – yourself, your friends, your country and us – we shall be angry with you while you are still alive, and our brothers, the laws of the underworld, will not receive you kindly, knowing that you tried to destroy us as far as you could" (54c).

Despite the fact that Socrates has said that he wants only to consider the question of justice, the speech of the laws touches on other matters as well, such as Socrates' consistency and his concern for his children. The core of the speech is concerned with justice, however. The laws argue that the agreement with Socrates is a just one, that the relation between Socrates and the state is not an equal but an unequal one, that Socrates has contracted implicitly to obey the laws, and that he had the option to persuade the Athenians that their laws were wrong, unjust. He does not claim that, if this opportunity had been lacking, obedience to the laws would not have been required. It is simply a good feature of the laws of Athens that they add this opportunity to the contract. The essence of the case of the laws is that Socrates has made an agreement, that the agreement is just, and that therefore he must obey it. The agreement includes obeying the verdicts of the courts, and not only those verdicts he deems just. The laws admit, at 54b–c, that Socrates has been wronged; but they insist that he has been wronged not by them but by men, presumably by his accusers and the jurors. Socrates does not say that the law against impiety was unjust, or that his agreement to accept the verdict of the court was unjust. If he had attempted to persuade the Athenians that these laws were unjust, he failed, and as a result he must obey the laws as they stand.

The *Crito* and Civil Disobedience

Some interpreters have been disappointed in this argument. They have wanted Socrates to advocate a doctrine of civil disobedience, and they have thought that they might find a justification for civil disobedience in a remark of Socrates' in Plato's *Apology* that if the jury offered him acquittal on the condition that he stop practicing philosophy, he would continue to philosophize in service to the god (29d–30b). There are problems concerning the legitimacy of such an offer,[4] but even if it were a possibility, I do not see how the *Apology* remark applies in the case of the *Crito*. One traditional approach to the problem of civil disobedience is to invoke "higher laws," typically God's laws, as taking precedence over human laws. That is what Antigone does in Sophocles' play. It may be what Socrates does in the *Apology*. Socrates tells the jury there that he will continue to philosophize because it is part of his divine mission: Apollo has commanded it. A law, or a verdict, that forbade someone to follow a divine command would be an unjust law. But that is not what is at stake in the *Crito*. It is not Apollo who has come to Socrates with a plan for his escape, but Crito. There is no reason to think that a law is unjust, and might be disobeyed, because Crito, or even Socrates, thinks it unjust. There is no indication, moreover, that the laws in the case are unjust, or that Socrates thinks them so. Further, civil disobedience, as I understand it, is not the view that one may disobey the law with impunity. When Martin Luther King Jr. disobeyed the law during the civil rights movement, he expected to be punished for it, and was. Civil disobedience does not reject the right of the state to enforce its laws, even if it targets some of those laws as unjust. In any case, however, Socrates is not in prison awaiting execution because of disobedience to a law he believed to be unjust.

The Social Contract

The heart of the argument of the laws is that the individual has a contract with the state. The laws present what has been called a "social contract" theory of the law. In the social contract theory, the legitimacy of law is traced back to a contract among people to frame laws that protect their interests; the justification of law is that it is agreed to by people. In Book II of the *Republic* Glaucon presents a social contract theory of justice when he says that people make laws to protect themselves from being harmed by others. What legitimates the laws of Athens, according to their speech, is the benefits of the law in cases such as marriage and education. Laws are just because they benefit people. Nonetheless, the citizen's obligation to obey the law is a matter of agreement, an implicit contract between citizen and state. Consider a modern parallel. The benefit of the traffic laws is that they prevent accidents and ensure good order on the roads. Nonetheless, when one gets a driver's license the state insists that the licensed driver enters into an agreement with the state to obey the traffic laws.

Socrates' Response to the Speech of the Laws

Socrates ends the *Crito* with a comment that is unprecedented in the elenctic dialogues. He says the speech of the laws "resounds in me, and makes it impossible for me to hear anything else. As far as my present beliefs go, if you speak in opposition to them, *you will speak in vain*. However, if you think you can accomplish anything, speak" (54d; my italics). To this Crito responds that he has nothing to say. The uniqueness of this remark lies in Socrates' virtual refusal to hear further arguments. Crito may speak, but Socrates will not listen. His mind is made up. In any other context Socrates would, by inviting Crito to respond, be saying that he is willing to listen to further arguments. It would be a way of saying that he did not think he had attained final wisdom on the matter at hand. (See, for instance, *Gorgias* 506a.) Not here. Here, Socrates is permitting Crito to speak, but at the same time warning him that it would be futile to do so. Some interpreters, who reject the claim that the speech of the laws reflects Socrates' views, have thought that Socrates is saying that he has been overwhelmed by the rhetoric of the laws, not by the rationality of their arguments, that he has succumbed to a kind of madness, like the Corybants to whom he compares himself. My response to this is that it would be unprecedented for Socrates to admit to being so overwhelmed by rhetoric that he had no rational response. In the *Protagoras*, when he has heard Protagoras' Great Speech, when he confesses that he was entranced by it, Socrates still finds a response which permits the dialogue to continue. In *Republic* I, when Thrasymachus bursts into the conversation at 336c, Socrates admits to being almost dumbstruck, but he nonetheless manages a rational response. Socrates *always* manages a rational response, except here. I suggest that this is because Socrates is not just overwhelmed by the rhetoric of the laws' speech, but convinced by their arguments. The laws present their case like an orator, but they also ask Socrates at each point in the argument whether he has anything to respond. In each case he does not.

Why Treat Others Justly?

Socrates' obligation to obey the laws of Athens is a moral obligation. It derives from the ethical theory that Socrates had articulated in the pages preceding the speech of the laws. It is wrong to disobey the law because that would violate a just agreement, and violating a just agreement is something a just person will not do. To treat someone unjustly is to mistreat him or her, and this mistreatment corrupts the soul of the unjust person. The unjust person ignores this consequence of unjust action at his or her peril, for life is not worth living with a corrupt soul. Now as I have said in Chapter 6, Socrates is a eudaimonist, like all ancient ethical theorists. He thinks that ethical actions are justified by virtue of their contribution to one's *eudaimonia*, one's happiness or flourishing. It is the agent's own *eudaimonia* that is supposed to concern him or her, not the happiness of everyone. That means that an argument is needed to connect the happiness of the agent to the well-being of others. Why should not a person, like Polus' example of Archelaus in the *Gorgias*, seek his own happiness by trampling on the happiness of others? The major modern ethical theories, Kantian deontology and utilitarianism, take a notion of the moral equality of all persons for granted. The equal dignity of all persons for Kant and the equal susceptibility of all sentient beings to pleasure and pain for the classical utilitarians are for those theorists objective realities, one might say axioms of their systems, from which all moral reasoning begins. It is easy to see why, on both of these theories, mistreatment of others is wrong, and why a moral person would seek to avoid it. To ask, why should I care about the dignity of another person is to ask why I should adopt the Kantian framework of ethics at all. Similarly for utilitarianism. This is not obviously the case for ancient eudaimonism. The attractiveness of eudaimonism is that it seems that one can take it for granted that we all care for our own happiness or well-being or for the best quality of life that we can obtain. Whether this requires us to take interest in the happiness or well-being or the quality of life of another, however, is a question that requires an additional answer.

Part of the necessary argument is provided by the speech of the laws. They point out to Socrates that the agreement he has made with them is a just agreement. Why should Socrates care about honoring this agreement? The answer of the laws is that they have been beneficial to Socrates, to such a degree that he is in their debt. Though Socrates does not make anything of the following point, the laws of Athens are democratic laws. They accord to each citizen equal rights, equal standing as a citizen. If Socrates is to honor the just agreement with the laws, then he must treat his fellow citizens with respect. This provides a basis for just treatment of one's fellow citizens, but it is a legal argument. It is based on a particular form of government, a particular constitution. It does not provide a moral basis for treating other people, just as people, with respect. It does not tell Socrates how he should treat citizens of other city-states, who may be his enemies. He suggests an argument in favor of treating well those who live in proximity to him, his neighbors, in the *Apology*, when he asks Meletus, rhetorically, if he is so ignorant that he does not know that it is beneficial to himself to treat his neighbors well (25d–e); but this, again, does not explain how one is to treat those who are geographically or politically distant. Socrates needs a basis for such treatment if he is to extend justice beyond the scope of his immediate friends and neighbors, to human beings or rational agents as such.

Socrates has eudaimonist, egoist reasons for believing that he has an obligation to treat others justly. He believes that the good life is the admirable, the just life. He believes that in harming or wronging another person one damages one's own soul. As the myth at the end of the *Gorgias* points out, if one arrives in Hades with a soul that has been scarred by the commission of unjust acts, one will be judged accordingly. What is missing from Socrates' defense of justice in the *Crito* is something like an explicit formulation of the Kantian principle that all one's fellow human beings or all rational agents have an equal case for moral treatment, or the utilitarian principle that all sentient beings have an equal case for having their needs, interests, or preferences protected. I do not suggest that Socrates would oppose such a principle, were it proposed to him. I think it might even be implicit in his concept of justice. It is not, however, explicit, and it leaves a gap in his argument. The argument in the *Gorgias* with Polus and with Callicles would look different if Socrates could put forward the golden rule, or something like it, as a moral principle, even if Polus and Callicles should reject it. Socrates has to argue, however, for the just treatment of others on eudaimonistic and egoistic grounds, not on deontological, utilitarian, or other universalist grounds.

Socrates as Critic of Athenian Democracy

The fact that Socrates remained in prison and faced execution shows that he was a loyal citizen of Athens. The *Crito* provides a philosophical justification for his conduct by basing it on an account of justice and the social contract. Does that mean that Socrates was not also a critic of Athenian democracy? It does not. Socrates was such a critic. His critique of democracy was based on his philosophical preference for another conception of the state. What Socrates desired was a government, a state in which all of the citizens were dedicated to the pursuit of virtue. Socrates did not approve of the state of affairs in Athens, in which people pursued a variety of ends without state interference. (This is a point of which Pericles is particularly proud in his funeral oration; see Thucydides, *History of the Peloponnesian War*, II.37.) If democratic freedom is the freedom to pursue ends of one's own choice, Socrates did not value this sort of freedom. He thought that it was harmful to the state. What Socrates preferred was not Athenian democracy but what I shall call a "republic of moral inquiry."

Socrates was not principally concerned with the question whether the government in such a state was to be invested in a single person (monarchy), a small number of people (oligarchy) or a large number (democracy). He was interested in the principle that qualified a person or persons to rule. For Socrates that principle was knowledge of virtue and its relation to the good life. Now we have seen in the elenctic dialogues that Socrates' search for such a person has, time and time again, proved vain. The opinion Socrates expresses in the *Apology* is that such knowledge is reserved for the gods. The doctrine of recollection in the *Meno* is more optimistic: it indicates that such knowledge is implicit in the mind of each person, but that it needs questioning, elenctic examination, to be brought out. In any case, however, Socrates never encounters anyone in the elenctic dialogues who is in active possession of this knowledge, and he repeatedly denies that he has it himself. Given that, it is very unlikely that he thought that someday the active knowledge of the nature of virtue and the human good would be widely shared. In all of his discussions of political rule in the elenctic dialogues he assumes that at most one person in a given state would have such knowledge. Should it turn out otherwise, should it be that, as Protagoras states in his Great Speech, everyone in the state has the knowledge necessary to participate in ruling, Socrates would probably not be displeased, though he certainly would be surprised. But Socrates did *not* think that the ordinary citizen of Athenian democracy had that necessary knowledge; nor did he think that the oligarchs who made up the government of the Thirty had it. Socrates did not think that the necessary qualification for rule was free birth and citizenship (as in Athenian democracy), or a certain amount of property (as in the typical oligarchy), or hereditary right (as in traditional monarchy); he thought it was knowledge. What Socrates wanted to do was to find a person with the necessary knowledge and put him or her in absolute control over the state.

Interpreters sometimes argue that Socrates was democratic or "demophilic," a lover of the people, even in his criticism of democracy.[5] Socrates did think that the pursuit of virtue was something that ought to engage every man, woman, and child, whether young or old, free or slave, in the state. Socrates' desired republic of moral inquiry would not look much like Athenian democracy. It is sometimes said that, in the absence of a knowledgeable ruler, democracy would be Socrates' preferred form of government.[6] There is something to be said for this proposal. Until it betrayed its principles by convicting Socrates, the Athenian democracy had valued free speech as a fundamental social good, and free speech would seem to be necessary for philosophical inquiry. It is sometimes noted that a possible reason Socrates did not emigrate to Sparta or Crete, states which the laws claim in the *Crito* that Socrates had praised as well governed, is that they did not provide the freedom of speech necessary for philosophical inquiry. The problem with this proposal, however, is that it is speculative. There are no texts in the elenctic dialogues in which Socrates praises Athenian democracy for its freedom of speech, or in which he states that the government he prefers, as a matter of practice if not in theory, is democracy. In Socrates' preferred republic of moral inquiry, everyone would pursue moral knowledge by elenctic argument, and such a state would be democratic in the sense that this pursuit would be available to everyone. Such a state would be made up entirely of philosophers in the Socratic mold. Given the fact, however, that Socrates could not find one person who had the knowledge he was seeking and few who were even seeking it, the existence of such a state would seem to be extraordinarily unlikely.

Socrates' Political Views

Socrates' political views come out in several of the works we have examined. In the *Apology* Socrates explains to the Athenians why he has not taken an active role in the political life of the city. Such a role was expected for everyone in Athenian democracy: as Pericles states in his funeral oration, "we regard the citizen who takes no part in these duties not as unambitious but as useless" (Thucydides, II.40). Socrates gives two reasons for not participating actively in Athenian politics. The first is that his divine sign forbade him to do so (31d). The second is that he would not have lived long if he had: "if I had long ago attempted to take part in politics, I should have died long ago, and benefited neither you nor myself ... no man will survive who genuinely opposes you or any other crowd and prevents the occurrence of many unjust and illegal happenings in the city. A man who really fights for justice must lead a private, not a public, life if he is to survive for even a short time" (31d–32a). Socrates' complaint is that Athenian society is inherently and dangerously unjust. He offers two examples from his own history to illustrate his point. The first occurred when Socrates was a member of the presiding committee of the council, the body that set the legislative agenda for the assembly. There was great public support for a motion to try as a group the ten Athenian generals who had failed to recover the survivors after the Athenian naval victory at Arginusae in 406. (A storm had prevented recovery efforts.) "This was illegal," Socrates states, "as you all recognized later. I was the only member of the presiding committee to oppose your doing something contrary to the laws, and I voted against it. The orators were ready to prosecute me and take me away, and your shouts were egging them on, but I thought I should run any risk on the side of law and justice rather than join you, for fear of prison or death, when you were engaged in an unjust course" (32b–c). This occurred under the democracy. During the rule of the Thirty, Socrates was ordered to arrest Leon of Salamis, so that he might be executed. This was the sort of thing the Thirty did regularly: they murdered wealthy Athenians and confiscated their property. As Socrates says:

> They gave many such orders to many people, in order to implicate as many as possible in their guilt. Then I showed again, not in words but in action, that, if it were not rather vulgar to say so, death is something I couldn't care less about, but that my whole concern is not to do anything unjust or impious. That government, powerful as it was, did not frighten me into any wrongdoing. When we left the Hall, the other four went to Salamis and brought in Leon, but I went home. I might have been put to death for this, had not the government fallen shortly afterwards. (32d–e)

One can only imagine how the democratically inclined members of the jury reacted to having the injustice of the democratic government placed side by side with the injustice of the hated Thirty.

It was the injustice of both governments that convinced Socrates that he, as a just man, could play no role in the government of Athens. Still, Socrates did not withdraw altogether from the attempt to influence his fellow citizens to behave justly. He merely attempted to change the minds of his fellow citizens one by one, rather than *en masse*. The problem with the Athenians, he thought, was that they had the wrong conception of how they ought to live. In the language of the *Gorgias*, they did what they saw fit to do, but not what they wanted. What they wanted was to be happy, *eudaimōn*. They did not understand, however, how to achieve this condition. Socrates therefore urged them to pursue the genuine good, not the false idols they had been pursuing. He describes his activity as haranguing his fellow citizens, asking them:

> "are you not ashamed of your eagerness to possess as much wealth, reputation and honors as possible, while you do not care for nor give thought to wisdom or truth, or the best possible state of your soul?" Then, if one of you disputes this and says he does care, I shall not let him go at once or leave him, but I shall question him, examine him and test him, and if I do not think that he has attained the goodness

that he says he has, I shall reproach him because he attaches little importance to the most important things and greater importance to inferior things. (29e–30a)

What Socrates wants to do, first, is to reorient the Athenians away from the pursuit of wealth and power and toward the pursuit of wisdom, truth, and the best state of their souls. This is a point mentioned several times already in this book. Second, he wants to get them to argue elenctically about how to attain these goods. He wants to make all of the Athenians active pursuers of the good. That is his goal. That is why he describes himself in the *Gorgias* as the only Athenian of his generation to "take up the true political craft and practice the true politics" (521d). He doesn't flatter the Athenians by attempting to gratify their desire for the pleasant, in the manner of other Athenian political leaders, including men like Pericles, Cimon, Themistocles, and Miltiades – all considered among the greatest political leaders in Athenian history. Rather, he attempts to get his fellow citizens to pursue the good. The city that Socrates desires to create would not be a wealthy or a renowned city, for its citizens would not pursue wealth, reputation, and honors. It would, however, be a city in which all of the citizens were in active pursuit of virtue. It would be a city in which everyone behaved in the way Socrates behaves in the elenctic dialogues. Public debate about the best state of the soul would be the business of the city. It would be a city in which everyone pursued the examined life, the only life that Socrates thought worth living for a human being. It would be a city in which everyone was a philosopher. It would not look like Athens. Neither would it look much like Sparta or Crete.

The Moral Expert

What would happen in a republic of moral inquiry, a city in which everyone was actively pursuing wisdom, truth, and the best state of his or her soul? One possibility would be that different citizens would have different conceptions of virtue, and the republic would be occupied with intense philosophical debate. That, I suspect, was the actual situation in the Socratic circle, with some members, such as Antisthenes, advocating a life of moral strength and others, such as Aristippus, advocating a life devoted to the pursuit of pleasure.[7] I imagine, however, that Socrates has a different outcome in mind, which is that individual pursuers of wisdom and virtue will converge on a single understanding of those topics. The doctrine of recollection indicates that with repeated elenctic examination inquirers could eventually recover the wisdom latent in their souls. Someone who actually succeeded in the recovery of wisdom concerning the human good would meet Socrates' qualification for rule: knowledge of virtue and its relation to the good.

We get glimpses of such a person in several of the elenctic dialogues we have already examined. What Socrates is seeking is a moral expert, someone with ethical knowledge. In the *Apology* this seems to be an impossible ideal, as every interlocutor Socrates examines turns out to be ignorant and Socrates declares his own ignorance. Moreover, he states that genuine wisdom concerning the nature of virtue is in the domain of the gods; all human beings can be aware of is the extent of their ignorance. Still, he exhorts his fellow citizens to pursue this knowledge, and he even describes himself as continuing his elenctic examination with those in Hades. In the *Crito*, however, the moral expert seems to be more of a possibility. Socrates urges that we turn to such a moral expert, if one can be found, someone who plays a role analogous to that played by the physical trainer in the care of the body, and although he does not state that he is such an expert he presents a number of principles of ethical life that contrast with the views of the many. In the *Laches*, when asked to cast the deciding vote on the question whether the sons of Melesias and Lysimachus should learn the art of fighting in armor, Socrates replies that this is not a matter to be decided by a majority vote but by a moral expert, which he is quick to deny that he is.

In the *Protagoras* Socrates initially proposes that virtue cannot be taught. He challenges Protagoras with the fact that, when a technical issue is debated in the assembly, the Athenians only allow experts to speak, but "when it is a matter of deliberating on city management, anyone can stand up and advise them, carpenter, blacksmith, shoemaker, merchant, ship-captain, rich man, poor man, well-born, low-born – it doesn't matter – and nobody blasts him for presuming to give council without any prior training under a teacher. The reason for this is clear: They do not think that this can be taught" (319d–e). Socrates' point appears to be that he does not think virtue is a matter of expert knowledge: that is why he compares deliberation on technical issues with deliberation on public policy. To this Protagoras replies in his Great Speech with the claim that virtue is a different kind of knowledge, common to all people rather than the possession of a few experts.

As I stated in Chapter 5, Socrates never really responds to this defense of democracy. He does, however, argue for the claim that virtue is in fact a matter of expert knowledge, a claim he states finally at the end of the dialogue. Socrates also describes the art of measurement as an art that would give its possessor expert knowledge of good and evil and that would overcome the power of appearance.

In the *Gorgias* Socrates argues that it is not the business of every person to decide which pleasures are good, but that "it requires a craftsman" (500a). After having criticized some of the great heroes of Athenian democracy for having corrupted the city by teaching the citizens to pursue pleasure rather than the good, Socrates says, "I believe that I'm one of a few Athenians – so as not to say I'm the only one, but the only one among our contemporaries – to take up the true political craft and practice the true politics. This is because the speeches I make on each occasion do not aim at gratification but at what's best" (521d–e). Socrates does not claim to be a moral expert, only to be pursuing the same goal that a moral expert would achieve.

Finally, as stated in Chapter 5, Socrates qualifies the claim that virtue is not knowledge but right opinion, made at the end of the *Meno*, by holding out the hope that there might be a statesman who could make another like himself: such a person, he states, "could be said to be among the living as Homer said Tiresias was among the dead, ... the only true reality compared, as it were, with shadows" (100a). In discussing this passage we considered two possibilities: first, that Socrates himself might be such a person, that he might be the true reality among the shadows, and second, that Socrates is anticipating the philosopher-king of the *Republic*. The most explicit anticipation of the philosopher-king outside of the *Republic* is to be found in Socrates' second elenctic examination of Clinias in the *Euthydemus*. There Socrates argues that the kind of knowledge that is valuable is not that of the ordinary artisan or the rhetorician or the general but "the kingly art" (291b), which Socrates identifies with the art of the statesman and which he says makes people happy. The problem raised in the *Euthydemus* is of giving an account of this art. It is argued that knowledge makes people happy, but Socrates cannot identify the kind of knowledge that does this. This is a problem that is only solved in *Republic* IV, when Socrates identifies human happiness with psychological health, the position that we saw in Chapter 6 was stated in the *Crito* and developed in the *Gorgias*.

The Ruling Art in *Republic* I

The most explicit anticipation of the philosopher-king in the elenctic dialogues is in *Republic* I. This is no surprise, as the *Republic* as a whole is aimed at explaining who the philosopher-king is by way of explaining the nature of justice. Interpreters differ on the question whether the first book of the *Republic* was originally a separate dialogue, to which the rest of the *Republic* was later added.[8] Whether or not that is the case, *Republic* I has the form of an elenctic dialogue, similar to the *Euthyphro*, *Laches*, and *Charmides* in that it is a search for the definition of a particular virtue, in this case justice. As in the *Gorgias*, a succession of speakers, three in number, present ever more radical ideas of justice. As in most other elenctic dialogues, *Republic* I ends in an expression of perplexity on Socrates' part:

> Before finding the answer to our first inquiry about what justice is, I let that go and turned to investigate whether it is a kind of vice and ignorance or a kind of wisdom and virtue. Then an argument came up about injustice being more profitable than justice, and I couldn't refrain from abandoning the previous one and following up on that. Hence the result of the discussion, as far as I'm concerned, is that I know nothing, for when I don't know what justice is, I'll hardly know whether it is a kind of virtue or not, or whether a person who has it is happy or unhappy. (354b–c)[9]

This is a reasonable summary of the progress of the argument in the book, but although the dialogue does not succeed in defining justice, a task addressed in the rest of the *Republic*, it does display several of Socrates' assumptions about the nature of justice and the ruling art.

The first book of the *Republic* begins with a fairly elaborate *mise-en-scène*, in which Socrates describes his visit, accompanied by Plato's half-brother Glaucon, to the Piraeus, Athens' port, to see a festival honoring the Thracian goddess Bendis. The two are persuaded to go to the house of Cephalus, a rich metic (a resident alien), where there are several other people present. Socrates begins what initially appears to be an innocent conversation with Cephalus (recall the warning of Nicias in the *Laches* that no conversation with Socrates is innocent, but that all lead inevitably to a defense of the interlocutor's life) on the topic of old age and wealth. When Cephalus states that the greatest value of wealth is that it enables one to avoid injustice by paying one's debts and not cheating others, Socrates asks if that really can be the correct definition of justice: ought we to tell the truth or return borrowed weapons to someone who is out of his mind? At this point Polemarchus, Cephalus' son and heir, takes Cephalus' place as interlocutor. He offers a traditional definition of justice, borrowed from the poet Simonides, that justice is "to give to each what is owed to him" (331e). Polemarchus interprets this to mean that one should return good to one's friends and bad to one's enemies. Socrates launches a series of arguments against this view, the first of which compares justice to a craft. The doctor benefits friends in matters of medicine, and the ship's captain in a storm at sea, but when does the art of justice benefit people? Polemarchus suggests that justice is beneficial "in wars and alliances" (332e), but what about in peacetime? Polemarchus suggests that it is in partnerships, but Socrates argues that someone with particular knowledge is more beneficial than the just man in those arrangements: when buying a horse or a boat, one wants as a partner someone who is knowledgeable about horses and boats. (Of course one wants both, which is a possibility Socrates does not consider.) They reach the conclusion that justice is useful only for keeping things safe when they are not in use, in which case "justice isn't worth much, since it is only useful for useless things" (333e). Further, as the person who is skilled at helping one's friends, such as the doctor in the case of illness or the general in time of war, will be most skilled at harming his enemies, the just man, skilled at guarding money, will be most skilled at stealing it, so that "a just person has turned out, then, it seems, to be a kind of thief" (334a). At this point in the argument Polemarchus makes a remark familiar to us from other Socratic encounters: "I don't know any more what I did mean" (334b).The argument with Polemarchus continues through two more Socratic attacks: first, does Polemarchus mean that one should benefit those who are truly one's friends, or those who one believes, perhaps falsely, are one's friends? Second, is it the task of the just person to harm anyone? If justice is "human virtue" (335c, a point to which Socrates returns at the end of Book I), it must work to make people more just, not to harm them. "It is never just to harm anyone" (335e), he concludes, repeating a point made in the *Crito*.

Thrasymachus

At this point Thrasymachus, a teacher of rhetoric, bursts into the conversation with the comments about Socratic irony discussed in Chapter 3. He tries to get Socrates to answer his own question and explain what he thinks justice is, but he is eventually persuaded to give his own view, which is that "justice is nothing other than the advantage of the stronger"(338c). That is, in each state the rulers make laws to their own advantage: "democracy makes democratic laws, tyranny makes tyrannical laws, and so on with the others" (338d–e). When confronted by Socrates with a question similar to that he raised with Polemarchus about whether rulers seek what they believe is to their advantage or what is really to their advantage, Thrasymachus answers that the true ruler does not err: just as we don't call a doctor a doctor or an accountant an accountant when they make mistakes, we don't call a ruler a ruler when he formulates a law that is not to his advantage.

It is worth noting that Thrasymachus and Socrates agree on several points. They both see the question of justice as connected with ruling; they both see ruling as an art, and they both agree that the true ruler, the ideal ruler, the one with knowledge, will not make a mistake. What Socrates and Thrasymachus disagree about is the aim of the ruling art. For Thrasymachus, ruling is for the advantage of the ruler; for Socrates, it is for the advantage of the ruled. The doctor and the ship's captain do not seek their own advantage, but the advantage of their patients or crew. Socrates generalizes the point: "no one in any position of rule, insofar as he is a ruler, seeks or orders what is advantageous to himself, but what is advantageous to his subject, that on which he practices his craft" (342e). Thrasymachus responds with an insult – he asks Socrates whether he has a wet nurse – but also with his own account of the ruling art. Rulers are like shepherds or cowherds: they fatten the flock for their own ends, not those of the cows and sheep. Thrasymachus assumes that the law must be to the advantage of some and to the disadvantage of others, that it must make some happy and others unhappy. His assumption is that the happiness of one group must come at the expense of the happiness of the other – in other words, that legislation is a zero-sum game. Interestingly, Socrates seems to make a similar assumption. He assumes that the rulers benefit the subject population, not themselves, and that therefore they need to be compensated in some way for their activity as rulers. Actually, there is no necessity in either view. It does not follow from the fact that the rulers benefit from justice that the ruled should suffer. There is no reason why laws could not be made that benefit both ruler and ruled; indeed, this might be thought to be a feature of the account of a just law: that everyone benefits from it. That position would fit well with what the laws had argued in the *Crito*, when they claimed that Socrates benefited from their rule. Socrates and Thrasymachus look at the shepherd and his sheep from the perspective of their different notions of rule: Socrates thinks that the shepherd aims at the well-being of the sheep, whereas for Thrasymachus the shepherd is only preparing them to be sheared, or worse, slaughtered.

Now Thrasymachus says something that makes it seem as though he has changed his view: "Justice is really the good of another" (343c). As he follows this immediately by repeating the phrase, "the advantage of the stronger and the ruler," though, it seems clear that he does not mean to be changing his view, but at most his perspective. From the perspective of the rulers in the state, justice is self-interest, what is to their own advantage. From the perspective of the ruled, the subject population, justice is "the good of another," namely the rulers, and it is to their disadvantage. Justice makes the rulers happy, and the subject population unhappy. The same is true when Thrasymachus claims that "injustice, if it is on a large enough scale, is stronger, freer, and more masterly than justice." Again, immediately after saying this he repeats the claim that "justice is what is advantageous to the stronger" (344c), indicating that he does not think that he has changed the subject. When he praises injustice as "stronger, freer, and more masterly than justice," he is speaking of justice and injustice in the common, conventional sense, justice and injustice as seen from the perspective of the ruled. What he calls "injustice" in this passage is what he calls "justice" from the perspective of his own particular theory. A full statement of his position would be, "justice, which is the advantage of the stronger or the ruler, appears to be injustice from the perspective of the ruled."

Socrates' Defense of the Just Ruler

Socrates makes a variety of points in favor of his view of the just ruler and against Thrasymachus' conception. First of all, he reiterates the point that the practitioner in every art seeks the benefit of the object of the art, not his own advantage. The wage-earner's art is separate and distinct from the other arts.[10] The doctor acts as a doctor whether he gets paid or not. Second, he notes that rulers demand some form of compensation for their rule, which is proof that ruling is not to their advantage. Third, he presents a complex argument aimed to show that it is the just person who is good and clever, whereas the unjust person is ignorant and bad. Thrasymachus, in his praise of injustice, had said that the just person "always gets less than an unjust one" (343d). The just person never gets more than an unjust person in contracts, always pays more taxes, never gets refunds; his private finances always suffer when he holds office. The unjust person, if his injustice is on a grand enough scale, a tyrant – one who "kidnaps and enslaves the citizens ... is called happy and blessed, not only by the citizens themselves, but by all who learn that he has done the whole of injustice" (344b–c; one thinks here of Polus' celebration of Archelaus in the *Gorgias*). When Socrates asks Thrasymachus whether he regards justice as a virtue, he replies that injustice is a virtue (because it is profitable), whereas justice is, if not a vice, then "very high-minded simplicity" (348c). It is the unjust person, not the just one, Thrasymachus claims, who is clever and good. Socrates responds as follows: the just person tries to outdo the unjust person, but not another just person, whereas the unjust person tries to outdo everyone. (The notion of "outdo" is in need of some clarification. I think what Socrates means in the context of the argument is "exceed in virtue." What Thrasymachus means, in contrast, is "exceed in wealth or power," or perhaps simply in success.) The just person wants to exceed the unjust person in virtue, but not another just person. The unjust person wants to exceed everyone. In the other arts, however, it is the artist, the one who is clever and good, who does not try to outdo other artists, but only the ignorant. The musician does not try to exceed other musicians, but only the unmusical; the doctor does not try to exceed other doctors, but only the "nondoctor." (Socrates here seems to be thinking of Thrasymachus' own conception of an artist as one who does not make mistakes. The doctor is the person who makes the right diagnosis and prescribes the right treatment. The musician is the person who plays the right notes.) "In any branch of knowledge or ignorance," Socrates asks, "do you think that a knowledgeable person would intentionally try to outdo other knowledgeable people or say something better or different than they do, rather than doing or saying the very same thing as those like him?" (350a) Thrasymachus responds that "perhaps" this is so. But, Socrates continues, the knowledgeable person, the person who possesses the art, is the one who is clever and good; it is the bad and ignorant person who tries to outdo everyone. It turns out that the just person, who does not try to outdo everyone, is the clever and good person. (He is the one who understands that justice is an art; in the case of the ruler, the ruling art.) The unjust person is bad and ignorant. (He lacks the ruler's art, which he confuses with the wage-earner's art, or the art of self-enrichment.)

Thrasymachus objects to all of this. "I could make a speech about it," he says, "but if I did, I know that you'd accuse me of engaging in oratory" (350d–e). So at this point he "checks out" of the argument. He'll answer so as to please Socrates, rather than state his own view. What Thrasymachus does here is very similar to what Callicles does in the *Gorgias*, and it has the same effect on the elenchus. For the elenchus to work, as I have said previously, the interlocutor must say what he believes. If the interlocutor does not express his own beliefs, he is not really refuted. Thrasymachus plays along, but he is not engaged; "enjoy your banquet of words," he says at one point; "Have no fear, I won't oppose you" (352b). At the conclusion of Socrates' argument he repeats the remark: "let that be your banquet, Socrates, at the feast of Bendis," he says sarcastically (354a). Socrates proceeds with his questions after 350e, but the dialogue has effectively ceased.

Socrates has two more arguments in favor of justice. The first is that even unjust people need justice if they are to pursue their plans. Even a band of thieves needs to cooperate or the thieves will fall out with each other: "injustice ... causes civil war, hatred, and fighting among themselves, while justice brings friendship and a sense of common purpose" (351d). Even within a single individual, injustice causes dissension and discord: "it make him incapable of achieving anything, because he is in a state of civil war and not of one mind ... it makes him his own enemy" (352a). This brief portrait of psychic discord recalls Socrates' point in the *Gorgias* about the parts of the soul, a point that looks forward to *Republic* IV for its full explanation. The final argument that Socrates offers on behalf of justice recalls the earlier argument with Polemarchus. There (335b–e) Socrates had argued that justice was "human virtue" and that it could not be the function of justice to harm another person, which would make that other person worse in human virtue. Here Socrates makes use of the notion of function, *ergon*, which is what each thing can do uniquely or best. Eyes have a function, which is to see; ears have a function, which is to hear; pruning knives have a function, which is to prune vines; and so on. Corresponding to each function there is a virtue. The human soul has a function: "taking care of things, ruling, deliberating and the like" (353d) and, in a more general sense, living. The virtue associated with this function is justice. The person with a just soul will live well and be happy, and the person with an unjust soul will be unhappy.

Critique of Socrates' Arguments

There is widespread dissatisfaction with these arguments. Socrates expresses his dissatisfaction at the end of Book I when he says that it was his fault for shifting from the question, what is justice, to the question whether justice or injustice is more profitable. Glaucon and Adeimantus, Plato's half-brothers, who take over the role of interlocutors at the start of Book II and retain it for the rest of the *Republic*, express dissatisfaction, saying that they want to be truly convinced that "it is better in every way to be just than unjust" (357a), but that Socrates hasn't accomplished this. They demand, and get, not just a new set of arguments, but a new kind of argument from Socrates. There are many points about the individual arguments that could be questioned. In the case of the final argument, Socrates' slide from the claim that the function of the soul is "taking care of things, ruling, deliberating, and the like" to the claim that living is the function of the soul is questionable. We would expect, if taking care of things, ruling and deliberating were the function of the soul, that wisdom, not justice, would be the appropriate virtue. When Socrates says that justice is the virtue of the soul, that raises the question whether wisdom and justice are the same thing, which is the question of the unity of the virtues. The long argument about the virtuous person not wanting to outdo other virtuous persons seems to work at most if we are talking about virtues as ideals or perfections, or in cases such as mathematics where there is only one right answer. One mathematician won't try to outdo another in getting the right answer, though even there one mathematician may attempt to find the answer more quickly or elegantly. Certainly if we are talking about actual musicians, one may well attempt to outdo another in his or her performance of a particular piece; certainly one doctor may well attempt to outdo another in arriving at the correct diagnosis quickly and efficiently. And, we may ask, in what sense does the nonmusical person or the nondoctor attempt to outdo the musician or doctor? The analogy seems to be flawed.

Conclusion

Despite these and other weaknesses in the arguments in *Republic* I,
we learn a good deal about Socrates' views of justice and the ruling
art from them. The chief things we learn are that:

Justice is not a matter of obedience to a few, easily statable rules
("tell the truth; pay your debts").
Justice does not harm others, but rather improves them, specifically makes them more just.
Just rule is an art, which aims at the well-being of the ruled.
The just ruler is like a doctor, a ship's captain, or a shepherd in
this respect.
Justice is a beneficial quality of both the just state and the just
soul.

The comparison between the doctor, ship's captain, and the just
ruler indicates that justice involves expert knowledge. Herein lies
Socrates' critique of Athenian democracy in a nutshell. The Athenians assume that the business of ruling is something in which any
citizen can participate; hence, they elect people to many positions
by lot, and the position of general, which one might think involved
expert knowledge, by popular vote. But the art of ruling is in
Socrates' view a matter of expert knowledge, and only one who has
mastered this art should hold office.

The concept of the knowledgeable ruler, the possessor of the art
of ruling, is of central importance to Socrates' conception of justice.
The ruling art is the art of producing happiness among the ruled;
not the appearance of happiness, in the form of pleasure, but
genuine happiness, of the sort produced by virtue. It is only the
knowledgeable ruler who has the right to rule. Socrates may in fact
find Athenian democracy an acceptable form of government, in the
absence of a knowledgeable ruler, though he would prefer a republic of moral inquiry, in which everyone was aiming at the genuine
good. Still, if a knowledgeable ruler could be found, Socrates would
think it unjust for Athens to refuse to grant such a person political
power. This idea of the knowledgeable ruler is of course developed
in Books II–X of the *Republic*, but the germ of the doctrine of the
philosopher-king is to be found in the ideal of the moral expert in
the elenctic dialogues.

8

From Socrates to Plato

Up to now we have been examining the philosophy of Socrates, as it has been found in the elenctic dialogues of Plato. These dialogues are more commonly referred to as the "Socratic" or "early" dialogues. Interpreters have contrasted the philosophy of these dialogues with the philosophy presented in another group of dialogues, somewhat misleadingly known as the "middle" dialogues. (The designation is misleading because some of the dialogues described as "middle" – the *Cratylus*, *Phaedo*, and *Symposium* – seem to have been written at about the same time as most of the elenctic dialogues. The term "middle" represents, not a temporal distinction, but a doctrinal one.)[1] Interpreters differ on the grounds for distinguishing the two groups of dialogues. Most base the distinction on the ground that, in the "middle" dialogues Plato advances a theory of "separately existing Forms," whereas in the "early" or elenctic dialogues Socrates has "no such theory."[2] It is not uncommon for interpreters who distinguish the elenctic dialogues from the "middle" dialogues on doctrinal grounds to claim that the elenctic dialogues represent the thought of the historical Socrates whereas the "middle" dialogues represent the thought of Plato. This distinction is often accompanied by a theory of Plato's development as a philosophical writer: Plato began his career as a disciple of Socrates, producing or reproducing arguments in defense of Socrates' views; only in midlife did he begin to use the character Socrates he had developed to state his own views.[3] It is sometimes stated that the distinction between the two groups of dialogues is a sharp one, that in them Plato presents "philosophies so different that they could not have been depicted as cohabiting the same brain throughout unless it had been the brain of a schizophrenic."[4] It has been stated that the distinction is sharp in another respect, that it occurs abruptly, at *Meno* 81a, where Socrates introduces the doctrine of recollection.[5]

In this chapter I argue for a different position. The doctrines of the "middle" dialogues do differ, I agree, from the doctrines of the elenctic dialogues, but the differences are not as sharp as some interpreters have claimed, and they are not introduced at the same time. Though there are some genuine contradictions between the doctrines advanced in some elenctic dialogues and the doctrines advanced in some "middle" dialogues, for the most part the doctrines of the "middle" dialogues grow out of the doctrines of the elenctic dialogues. The development from the elenctic to the "middle" dialogues is gradual, and there is quite a lot of continuity between the two groups. Though some of the philosophy of the elenctic dialogues may well originate with the historical Socrates, we cannot say for certain how many of the doctrines of those dialogues belong to Socrates and how many belong to Plato. Socrates does become a spokesman for the philosophy of Plato, but it is not possible to specify a precise point at which that happens.

The *Apology* vs. the *Republic*

We can see the difference on which some interpreters have insisted if we contrast the *Apology* and the *Republic*. In the *Apology* Socrates presents himself as a person with only human wisdom, the awareness of the extent of his own ignorance. He puts forward very few philosophical claims at all. He does describe his elenctic method, and he does urge his fellow Athenians to pursue wisdom, truth, and the best state of their souls rather than wealth, reputation, and honors, but he does not say what wisdom looks like. He does present two accounts of the fate of the soul after death at the end of the dialogue, but he does not choose between them. In most respects, the Socrates of the *Apology* behaves like the barren Socrates of the *Theaetetus*. The Socrates of the *Republic*, in contrast, is fertile. He does not practice the elenchus much, if at all, after Book I. Instead, he puts forward hypotheses in several areas. One of these hypotheses is the theory of separate Forms, including the Form of the good. He distinguishes between knowledge and belief or opinion and connects that distinction with the theory of Forms. He has a theory of the nature of the soul that divides it into three parts:

reason, spirit, and appetite. He presents an argument for the immortality of the soul, or at least its rational part, in Book X. He has a theory of the nature of virtue that connects the virtues with the parts of the soul. He has a political theory that divides the state into three classes, which parallel the three parts of the soul. The ruler in this state is described as a philosopher-king; the philosopher-king knows the Forms, and in particular the Form of the good. None of these theories is to be found in the *Apology*. In the *Republic* Socrates is happy to share these theories with his interlocutors. In the *Apology* he appears to have no such theories to share.

The contrast between the barren Socrates of the *Apology* and the fertile Socrates of the *Republic* is as sharp as anyone could like. The question raised by the comparison between the two dialogues is, how do we get from the barren Socrates of the *Apology* to the fertile Socrates of the *Republic*? The answer lies in the fact that the *Apology* is not a typical elenctic dialogue. Socrates in the elenctic dialogues is not simply the barren practitioner of the elenchus. Consider, for example, the *Euthyphro*, discussed in Chapter 4. The *Euthyphro* is an elenctic dialogue, but it contains a version of the theory of Forms. The Forms of the *Euthyphro* are not the separate Forms of the "middle" dialogues, but they are the ancestors of those Forms. Or consider the *Protagoras*. It is true that the dialogue ends in perplexity, in the manner of a typical elenctic dialogue. (It does seem, however, that the perplexity is easily resolved. As Socrates states at the end of the dialogue, he has been arguing that virtue cannot be taught, but also that it is knowledge. Protagoras has been arguing that virtue can be taught, but he has been denying that it is knowledge. The solution to this problem would seem to be for Socrates to abandon his view that virtue cannot be taught, and for Protagoras to abandon his view that it can. Both would then have consistent positions.) In the body of the dialogue, however, Socrates defends the intellectualist view we discussed in Chapter 5. Or consider the *Gorgias*, discussed in Chapter 6. The *Gorgias* is an elenctic dialogue, without a doubt. Socrates tries his best to refute his interlocutors, who hold views diametrically opposed to his own. He defends the superiority of the just life, a life based on self-control, to the life of unrestrained pursuit of pleasure. He presents a myth of the judgment of souls in the after-life to support his position. He not only states a position, he defends it with fervor. Or consider the *Meno*. The *Meno* starts off like a typical elenctic dialogue, but when Meno questions the very possibility that the elenchus can lead to the truth Socrates presents the doctrine of recollection to show that it can.

The *Meno* also ends not with perplexity, but on a positive note, with the claim that virtue is right opinion. Because the *Gorgias* and *Meno* do not end in perplexity in the manner of the typical elenctic dialogue and because they introduce features, such as the doctrine of recollection and the myth of the after-life that link them with the "middle" dialogues, they are often regarded as "transitional" dialogues. It has been argued that other dialogues also anticipate developments in the "middle" dialogues. Charles Kahn has urged that the dialogues concerned with the definition of ethical terms be regarded as "threshold" dialogues, part of a single literary project, to be read "ingressively," with the culmination of the *Republic* in mind.[6] In several dialogues that are clearly elenctic, then, Socrates introduces constructive philosophical theories. Most of these theories anticipate the theories of the *Republic*. In the remainder of this chapter we shall see how they do so.

Method

Of course, there is one aspect of the elenctic dialogues that distinguishes them from the "middle" dialogues. In the elenctic dialogues Socrates practices the elenchus; in the "middle" dialogues this method changes and gradually disappears. As Robinson writes:

> Three things happen to the elenchus in the middle and later dialogues. First ... it loses its irony. Second, it is incorporated into the larger whole of dialectic, which somewhat changes its character. Though still negative and destructive in essence, it is harnessed to the car of construction. Though still moral in its purpose, the ultimate moral end recedes a great deal, and a large scientific programme occupies the middle view. Third, while often referred to and recommended, it gradually ceases to be actually depicted in the dialogues. Refutations take less of the total space.[7]

It should not come as a surprise that the elenctic dialogues differ from those dialogues that are not elenctic, for the group of elenctic dialogues was distinguished precisely because in this group Socrates practices the elenchus. As I argued in Chapter 2, it is the practice of the elenchus, rather than an early date or some other criterion, that distinguishes those dialogues thought to be "Socratic" from those thought not to be. As Robinson points out, however, the transition from the method of elenchus to other, more constructive methods, in particular the method of hypothesis, is a gradual one. The *Meno* shows us both methods in operation together. There is no reason why Socrates should have abandoned the method of elenchus. We saw that in the late *Sophist* the Eleatic Visitor praises the method as a way of clearing the mind of false beliefs. There is no contradiction between the method of elenchus and the method of hypothesis, though the method of hypothesis is constructive in its aim and the method of elenchus is destructive. The dialogues simply shift their focus from one method to another.

Metaphysics: the Theory of "Separate" Forms

As noted above, the way in which most interpreters distinguish the "middle" dialogues from their predecessors is that the "middle" dialogues contain the theory of "separate" Forms, whereas their predecessors do not. It is sometimes said that the "middle" dialogues are metaphysical whereas the elenctic dialogues are purely ethical. This distinction has its origin in a claim made by Aristotle. Socrates, says Aristotle, sought universal definitions, but he "did not make the universals or the definitions exist apart; his successors, however, gave them separate existence, and this was the kind of thing they called Ideas" (*Metaphysics* M.4, 1078b30–32). It may seem that Aristotle is denying that Socrates had any theory of Forms or Ideas at all. This interpretation runs up against the fact that Socrates in the elenctic dialogues refers to Forms or Ideas on several occasions. As we saw in Chapter 4, one such occasion is *Euthyphro* 5c–d and 6d–e, where Socrates first asks for the Idea of piety, and then reminds Euthyphro that this is what he wants. He uses the term *idea* as a name for what he is seeking in both passages (5d4, 6d11.) If Aristotle is construed as saying that only Plato used the term "Idea" to refer to his Forms, then this passage shows that he is mistaken.

Aristotle might better be read as saying that Socrates had a theory of universals but not a theory of *separate* Forms. Forms are mentioned in several elenctic dialogues. As was stated in Chapter 4, in the *Euthyphro* and *Meno* he describes them as what he is looking for in his search for definitions. In the *Hippias Major* he states that it is by justice that just people are just, and that this justice *is* something, and likewise for wisdom and beauty (287c–d). In the *Protagoras* he asserts that justice and piety are both "things" that exist (330c–d). As was stated earlier, Socrates believes that Forms are universals, characteristics of things, causes, and standards. They are what Socrates is seeking in his definitions; that is, they are essences. One can argue about whether the Socratic references to Forms in the elenctic dialogues constitute a theory.[8] However one decides that question, the references are metaphysical in nature.

Metaphysics: Being and Becoming

The contrast between the elenctic dialogues and the "middle" dialogues is not a contrast between dialogues that have no metaphysics and those that have a metaphysics; it is a contrast concerning the nature of that metaphysics. The Forms of the "middle" dialogues are said to be "separate" from their participants; the Forms of the elenctic dialogues are not. As Plato uses the term "separate" to mark this distinction, he also uses the phrase "itself in itself" to characterize Forms. Plato emphasizes the separate existence of Forms when he introduces the theory at *Phaedo* 100b and *Symposium* 211a and when he opens the theory to criticism at *Parmenides* 130b–c.

What does Plato mean by this claim? The answer to this question does not lie in the theory of Forms itself, so much as in another doctrine that Plato introduces in the "middle" dialogues: the doctrine of two worlds, or of "being and becoming." In *Republic* VII, in Plato's explanation of the allegory of the cave, Plato refers to "the upward journey of the soul to the intelligible realm" (517b). At *Phaedrus* 247c–d he describes a "place beyond heaven," a place "without color and without shape and without solidity," containing "a being that really is what it is, the subject of all true knowledge, visible only to intelligence, the soul's steersman." R. E. Allen summarizes this Platonic concept of separation and of the two worlds that give rise to it as follows:

> The philosophy of the middle dialogues is a nest of coupled contrasts: Being and Becoming, Appearance and Reality, Permanence and Flux, Reason and Sense, Body and Soul, Flesh and the Spirit. Those contrasts are rooted in an ontology of two Worlds, separated by a gulf of deficiency. The World of Knowledge, whose contents are the eternal Forms, stands to the World of Opinion, whose contents are sensible and changing, as the more real stands to the less real, as originals stand to shadows and reflections. The visible world is an image, unknowable in its deficiency, of an intelligible world apprehended by reason alone.[9]

The doctrine of two worlds, of a world of "becoming," composed of phenomena in perpetual flux, and a world of "being," composed of unchanging, eternal Forms, is not present in the elenctic dialogues (though it is hinted at in the doctrine of Recollection in the *Meno*). The Forms of the elenctic dialogues are "in" the objects they characterize. In the dialogues that refer to the early theory of Forms there is one world, not two. The Forms of the elenctic dialogues are properties, characteristics of things; the Forms of the "middle" dialogues are separately existing substances. If there is a "red line" distinguishing Socratic metaphysics from Platonic it is not the existence of Forms, but their separation from the sensible world and the distinction between being and becoming that is responsible for it.

The references in the elenctic dialogues to the Forms occur primarily in the context of definition. Forms are what definition is about. The theory of Forms in the elenctic dialogues is in some sense a logical theory. That does not mean that it is not also a metaphysical one. In the "middle" dialogues its use is wider. In particular, it underwrites Plato's theory of knowledge, as we shall see below. The theory of Forms in the "middle" dialogues is also referred to with a kind of religious devotion that is absent in the elenctic dialogues. Allen makes this point when he says that, in introducing the Form of Beauty in the *Symposium*, "Plato's prose suddenly bursts into dithyrambs, in the manner of a choric ode,"[10] and when he says a few lines later, "this is a metaphysical description which is also a hymn."[11] Allen also states that "Plato's emphasis in the *Symposium* and *Republic* on vision and rebirth has a certain analogy to the ritual of the Eleusinian Mysteries, which celebrated fertility and purification, and culminated in a Beholding, or *Epopteia*, where the sacred objects of the cult were exposed to the wondering eyes of the worshippers suddenly, in a blaze of light, and the worshippers were assured of their kinship to the god and their salvation."[12]

Plato's description of the ascent of the philosopher to the Form of the good in the allegory of the cave in *Republic* VII certainly has this same religious tone. When Vlastos says that Plato's "personal religion centers in communion with divine, but impersonal Forms. It is mystical, realized in contemplation,"[13] he is making the same point. Plato was a philosopher of the rationalist bent, and a sober one at that; but he was capable of flights of religious devotion that are unsurpassed and rarely equaled in philosophy. And the focus of his religious devotion was not the gods of Greek religion, but the Forms, and in particular the Form of the good.

Metaphysics: The Form of the Good

In the elenctic dialogues Socrates on occasion mentions the Form of the good, usually in the company of the Form of the beautiful (*to kalon*). At *Protagoras* 332b he asks whether there is such a thing as beauty, and immediately after that whether there is such a thing as goodness. In the *Gorgias*, at 506d, he speaks of good as "that by which, when it's present in us, we are good." Similarly, at *Hippias Major* 287c he says that it is "by the good [that] all good things are good." This concern with the good continues in the *Cratylus, Phaedo,* and *Symposium*. At *Cratylus* 439c–d Socrates asks Cratylus "are we or aren't we to say that there is a beautiful itself, and a good itself, and the same for each one of the things that are?" At *Phaedo* 65d he asks Simmias whether there is such a thing as the Just itself, and then he repeats the question for "the Beautiful and the Good." At 75d he refers to "the Beautiful itself, The Good itself, the Just, the Pious, and, as I say, ... all those things which we mark with the seal of 'what it is,' both when we are putting questions and answering them." At 100b Socrates states, "I assume the existence of a Beautiful, itself by itself, of a Good and a Great and all the rest." In the *Symposium*, at 206a, Diotima gets Socrates to admit that everyone loves the good and wants it to be their own forever.

There is no doubt that Socrates regards the good, along with the beautiful, as a Form. In the dialogues that grant the Forms separate existence, he assigns the good separate existence, saying that is "itself," "what it is," and "itself by itself." The good, along with the beautiful, is the Form that gives value to the things that participate in it. Only in the *Republic*, however, does Socrates assign a special role to the good in the hierarchy of the Forms. This special role may be hinted at in Book V, at 452e, where he says that "it's foolish to take seriously any standard of what is fine and beautiful other than the good." It is developed, however, in the three analogies of sun, divided line and cave in Books VI and VII. The good is thought to be, not only the cause of the intelligibility of the other Forms, but of their being, and it is said to have a status superior to being. It is the unhypothetical first principle from which all explanation originates.

There is nothing like this account of the good in the elenctic dialogues. Some interpreters have, however, suggested that there is an anticipation of the account of the Form of the good in the *Lysis*. In the *Lysis* Socrates investigates the nature of friendship with two young interlocutors, Lysis and Menexenus. Because of their youth,

Socrates has to play both roles in the elenctic argument: he proposes definitions of friendship, and then criticizes them. Late in the
dialogue, after several failed attempts to explain what a friend is,
Socrates makes use of a complex formula to explain friendship, or
what is beloved. Whoever is a friend is a friend *to* someone, *for the
sake of* something and *on account of* something. For example, a sick
person is a friend to a doctor for the sake of health and on account of
disease. Health, that for the sake of which the sick man befriends the
doctor, is a good thing. Disease, on the other hand, is bad. The sick
man is described as a friend, not just of a doctor, but of medicine,
for the same reason. Medicine, again, is considered good, in that
it produces health. So health is a friend, and disease is an enemy.

We desire health for the sake of some higher good (presumably
happiness). So happiness will be dear to us as well. But can there
be an infinite series of "for the sake of" relationships? Socrates asks,
"don't we have to arrive at some first principle which will no longer
bring us back to another friend, something that goes back to the
first friend, something for the sake of which we say that all the rest
are friends too?" (219c–d) What could this first principle, this "first
friend" (*prōton philon*) or first beloved, be? It is this first principle,
the first friend, Socrates says, that is the real object of our love or
friendship, it is what is "truly a friend" (219d). Aren't all our concerns directed, not at those things which have value as means to the
end, but to the end itself? "The real friend is surely that in which
all these so-called friendships terminate" (220b).

Then comes the question that makes this passage seem relevant
to the Form of the good in the *Republic*. Socrates asks, "But then is
the good a friend?" (220b) We love the good *on account of* the bad,
but not *for the sake of* anything higher. We love the good for its own
sake. It is an intrinsic good. It is the "first friend," the *prōton philon*,
and we love everything else for the sake of it. This passage tells us
something that the *Republic* also tells us, that the good is the ultimate source of value, and it tells us something about the good that
is not explicit in the *Republic*: that the good is the ultimate object of
love. It also argues that there cannot be an infinite regress of objects
of love; there must be something that we love for its own sake. The
metaphysical and epistemological framework that characterizes the
good in the *Republic* is missing, however. The passage does not
assert that the good is of a different order of being from other things,
or that it is the unhypothetical first principle from which all explanation proceeds, or that it is the object of the highest form of inquiry,
dialectic. So this passage in the *Lysis* may be an anticipation of the

Form of the good in the *Republic*, but it does not reveal much about its (admittedly rather mysterious) nature.

Epistemology

The fundamental epistemological distinction on which the elenctic dialogues rely is the distinction between knowledge and ignorance. Knowledge is the cognitive state that Socrates is seeking; ignorance is the state that he professes that he is in. As the elenchus shows, it is also the state that his interlocutors turn out to be in. In the *Gorgias*, however, at 454d, Socrates augments this basic distinction with another, that between knowledge and conviction. Knowledge is infallible. Conviction, on the other hand, is fallible; it can be true or false. In the *Meno*, at 97b, Socrates distinguishes between knowledge and true or right belief. That knowledge and true belief are different is one of the few things that Socrates says he would claim to know. In the *Meno*, right opinion is convertible into knowledge: "true opinions, as long as they remain, are a fine thing and all they do is good, but they are not willing to remain long, and they escape from a man's mind, so that they are not worth much until one ties them down by (giving) an account of the reason why" (97e–98a). One may have knowledge and opinion concerning the same objects. To use an example from the *Meno*, one person may know the road to Larissa while another may have only right opinion about it.

The *Meno* introduces the doctrine of recollection, according to which everyone has true beliefs latent in one's soul, beliefs that can be converted into knowledge by questioning. Many interpreters think of this doctrine as Platonic, rather than Socratic, and the *Meno* as the dialogue in which the transition from Socrates to Plato begins to take place. In the *Phaedo*, at 72e, Socrates links the doctrine of recollection with the theory of separate Forms, which as we have seen is a doctrine that many interpreters see as the distinctive characteristic of Plato's "middle" dialogues. This is one reason why the *Meno* is often described as a "transitional" dialogue. The doctrine of recollection is referred to in the *Phaedrus* as well, at 249c.

In the *Apology* Socrates stated that he possessed only human wisdom, which consisted in awareness of the fact that he was ignorant of the first principles of ethics. He held that only the god is wise, and he may have thought that the gap between divine wisdom and human ignorance was unbridgeable. The doctrine of recollection offered an account of how that gap might be bridged. It described the soul as a traveler between two worlds, the world we experience with our senses and the world we experience after death. In the *Phaedo* those two worlds are identified as the world of phenomena and the world of Forms. In the "middle" dialogues there are actually two accounts of how this gap might be bridged. The second account is ascent. In the *Symposium*, from to 210a to 212b Diotima describes a ladder of ascent in which the lover rises in stages from the love of a single beautiful body to an experience of the Form of beauty itself. In *Republic* VII, 514a–517c, Socrates describes an ascent from a cave, representing the sensible world, to the world outside the cave, representing the intelligible world, wherein the ultimate object of cognition is the good, represented by the sun. Plato never explains how these two accounts, recollection and ascent, are to be reconciled with each other.

The elenctic dialogues, therefore, distinguish three, or possibly four, cognitive states. At one extreme there is ignorance; at the other there is knowledge, and intermediate between them is opinion, one species of which is true opinion. The "middle" dialogues, and in particular the *Republic*, develop these distinctions and add to their number, in light of the ontology of two worlds, the world of phenomena and the world of the Forms. In *Republic* V Socrates distinguishes between philosophers and "lovers of sights and sounds" (476b). The lovers of sights and sounds love all sorts of beautiful sounds, colors, and shapes, but they are unable "to see and embrace the nature of the beautiful itself" (ibid.). The beautiful itself is a unity, "and the same account is true of the just and the unjust, the good and the bad, and all the forms. Each of them is itself one, but because they manifest themselves everywhere in association with actions, bodies and one another, each of them appears to be many" (476a). Those who believe in beautiful things, but not in the beautiful itself, are living in a dream: they mistake the likeness of a thing for the thing itself. The person who can see both the beautiful and the things that participate in it is, by contrast, awake. This person has knowledge; the lover of sights and sounds has only opinion. Knowledge has for its object reality, in this case the beautiful itself. The opposite of knowledge is ignorance, which has the opposite of reality, not-being, as its object. In between these two opposite states is opinion, which has as its object something intermediate between reality and complete unreality. Knowledge is of what is real, and is infallible. Opinion is of this intermediate something, and is fallible.

What is this intermediate something? It is the sensible participant in the intelligible Form. Here we see the same distinctions as were made in the elenctic dialogues at work: knowledge, ignorance, and, intermediate between them, belief or opinion.

What Socrates tells us in this passage is that, because opinion is fallible, it cannot have the same object as knowledge, which is infallible. Knowledge is of intelligible Forms; opinion is of sensible particulars and their qualities. Let me give an example. I have a favorite symphony: Shostakovich's Fifth. I have a favorite recording of this symphony: the 1959 Bernstein recording, with the fourth movement taken at a breakneck pace. When I listen to this recording, or in fact to any performance of the Shostakovich Fifth, I would say that I can hear beauty. But it is beauty embodied in a particular work. What can I say to someone who does not hear what I hear? Suppose this person has a different conception of beauty than I do. Suppose he or she does not appreciate classical music, or Shostakovich. How could I prove to such a person that this work is a manifestation of pure beauty? I might want to argue with this person, but in the end I must admit that I am only defending my opinion about the work. Socrates imagines someone with genuine expertise, someone who knows what beauty is apart from its participants. Such a person would have knowledge, not opinion. Such a person would say that if one is trying to define beauty by means of an example, whether it be Shostakovich's Fifth Symphony or the Parthenon or something else, one is making a mistake, the same kind of mistake that Euthyphro, Laches, and Meno make when they first attempt to define a term.

The distinction between knowledge and opinion is in fact rooted in that Socratic criticism of definitions of the sort that Euthyphro and others make. Euthyphro, Laches, and Meno begin their attempts at definition with an example. The example may not be a particular thing; it may be a universal, but one that is too narrow to capture the complete nature of the term. Euthyphro is of the *opinion* that prosecuting his father on a charge of murder is pious and just, but because he does not know the definition of piety he cannot know that for a fact. So the distinction drawn by Socrates in *Republic* V between knowledge and opinion has its origin in the elenctic dialogues. And yet … Socrates does not explicitly say that Euthyphro has only opinion. The contrast he draws here and in most of the elenctic dialogues is between knowledge and ignorance. That is the distinction he draws in the *Apology* when he limits knowledge of the nature of virtue to the gods. In the

Protagoras he virtually equates ignorance with false belief. It is in the *Gorgias* and *Meno* that he introduces the concept of an intermediate state between knowledge and ignorance. Socrates in the *Republic* does something different with the knowledge/belief distinction than he does in the elenctic dialogues. For Socrates in *Republic* V, one cannot have knowledge and opinion about the same objects. Knowledge is reserved for the Forms; opinion is reserved for their sensible participants.

In the divided line (VI, 509d–511e), the second of three analogies Socrates uses to explain the nature of the good, he distinguishes four cognitive states. The lowest state, imagination, is concerned with images of objects, "first, shadows, then reflections in water ... and everything of that sort" (509e–510a). The second level, belief, is concerned with "the originals of these images, namely, the animals around us, all the plants, and the whole class of manufactured things" (510a). The third level, the first part of the intelligible world, uses objects in the sensible world as images of the Forms. Geometers, says Socrates in a passage that evokes the examination of the slave in the *Meno*, "make their claims for the sake of the square itself and the diagonal itself, not the diagonal they draw" (510d). They use hypotheses to explain things (think here of the definitions, axioms and postulates of Euclidean geometry), but they leave the hypotheses unexplained. Socrates calls this stage "thought." The highest stage, understanding, dispenses with visual images altogether and ascends from hypotheses to "the unhypothetical first principle of everything," the good (511b). The method the soul uses is dialectic, which, he explains later in Book VII, enables the philosopher to give an account of the nature of the good that can withstand all criticism (534b–d).

Plato does not in general make use of all of these cognitive divisions: usually he focuses on the basic distinctions between knowledge, belief, and ignorance. Knowledge is cognition of Forms, and ultimately of the Form of the good; belief is cognition of phenomena, the sensible images of the Forms; and ignorance is false belief. These distinctions, as noted above, can all be found in the elenctic dialogues. What is new in the "middle" dialogues is the correlation of the cognitive states with the two-worlds ontology of separate Forms. Plato makes his epistemology congruent with his ontology. I suspect that he developed his ontology of separate Forms first, and then adapted the epistemology of the elenctic dialogues to fit it; but conceivably it might have been the other way around.

Psychology

"Psychology" literally means "account" (*logos*) of the "soul" (*psychē*). For Socrates, this account had two aspects: the immortality of the soul and the structure of the soul. The first aspect bears primarily on Plato's metaphysics and epistemology; the second aspect bears primarily on his moral theory (though it has an impact on his metaphysics and epistemology as well). Let us consider the question of immortality first. It is sometimes said that Socrates had little interest in this question.[14] That is not so. Perhaps the earliest mention of the question of immortality is found in Plato's *Apology*. At the end of the *Apology* Socrates offers two alternative accounts of the fate of the soul after death. On one alternative, the soul enters a state of perpetual unconsciousness. This state is described as akin to a long, sound sleep, but it is also described as extinction. On the other alternative, the soul is transferred to another location, which resembles the after-life as described by Homer in *Odyssey* 11, with one important difference. Socrates' inhabitants of the underworld retain their rational faculties. Socrates can converse with them, which he describes as "extraordinary happiness" (41c). The first possibility, that of everlasting loss of consciousness, is dropped in the *Crito*. There Socrates mentions a dream he has had in which "a beautiful and comely woman dressed in white" comes to him and, quoting Homer, says, "may you arrive at fertile Phthia on the third day" (44a–b) which he takes to be a reference to his death and transfer to the underworld. At the end of the dialogue the laws refer to "our brothers, the laws of the underworld" (54c), who, it is said, "will not receive you [Socrates] kindly" when he arrives there if he violates his social contract with the laws of Athens. At the end of the *Gorgias*, as noted in Chapter 6, Socrates describes in a myth the judgment of souls after death in the underworld. This myth connects the *Gorgias* with the *Apology*, which also refers to a judgment of souls, and even names several of the same judges (Minos, Rhadamanthus, and Aeacus). Similar references to post-mortem judgment occur in the myths at the end of the *Phaedo* (107e) and *Republic* (X, 615a–616b).

Neither the *Apology* nor the *Gorgias* refers to reincarnation, though both refer to immortality. When reincarnation is introduced, in the *Meno*, it is not in the form of a myth, but the context is definitely religious in nature: it is attributed to certain "priests and priestesses" and to "the divine among our poets" (81a–b). When recollection is mentioned in the *Phaedo* it is as part of a rational argument for the immortality of the soul, not as part of a myth. In the *Phaedrus* it is introduced as part of a myth that explains the cognition of general terms: "a human being must understand speech in terms of general forms, proceeding to bring many perceptions together into a reasoned unity. That process is the recollection of the things our soul saw when it was traveling with god, when it disregarded the things we now call real and lifted up its head to what is truly real instead" (249b–c). According to the scheme described in the *Phaedrus*, knowledge is concerned with Forms. According to the doctrine of recollection, we do not experience Forms directly when we are incarnate; we must recollect a previous experience. This requires that the soul exist before it is incarnated. Socrates connects this requirement with other arguments for the immortality of the soul to produce a cycle of reincarnation. Once the doctrine of the immortality of the soul is introduced in the *Apology* and *Crito* it recurs in the *Gorgias, Meno, Phaedo, Republic, Phaedrus, Timaeus*, and *Laws*. Likewise, once the doctrine of reincarnation is introduced it becomes a regular feature of Plato's thought. Reincarnation might be considered a Platonic doctrine, but the immortality of the soul is a doctrine that links the elenctic and later dialogues. Socrates introduces new proofs for the immortality of the soul in the *Republic* (X, 608d–611b) and *Phaedrus* (245c–e), and he develops a theory of the complexity of the soul in the *Republic*, but the doctrine of immortality is a recurring feature of Plato's work from the early dialogues to the latest.

Let us consider next the structure of the soul. In the elenctic dialogues, as we have previously seen, there is a hint at the complexity of the soul in the *Gorgias*, at 493a–b, where Socrates introduces the idea that the soul has parts, specifically reason and appetite, and that it is the task of reason to exercise control over the appetites, a view that gets developed in *Republic* IV, 435d–441c. For the most part, however, Socrates in the elenctic dialogues treats the soul as if it were a single, simple entity, consisting solely of the faculty of reason. He may allow in the *Protagoras* that there are irrational forces – pleasure and pain, love, anger and fear – that conflict with reason (352b–c), but it may be that he regards this as the mistaken view of the many. Socrates does not *assert* that the soul is simple in the elenctic dialogues, or that it is equivalent to reason, but he does treat it in that way. Once the soul is divided into parts, however, that changes. He must consider whether the entire soul is immortal or just the rational part. Plato may not have reached a settled opinion on this matter until the late *Timaeus*, if then. (*Timaeus* 69c–72d talks about a mortal part of the soul. 90a–d suggests that the rational part of the soul is, or can be, immortal; but the passage is not altogether clear.)

Moral Theory

It has been argued[15] that Socratic intellectualism, discussed in Chapter 5, is in conflict with the moral psychology of *Republic* IV. According to intellectualism, all of the virtues are actually knowledge or wisdom; according to *Republic* IV wisdom is distinct from the other virtues. According to intellectualism, all desire is for the good; according to *Republic* IV there are irrational desires. This seems to be correct. Socrates does defend intellectualism in the dialogues we discussed in Chapter 5 and he does appear to reject it in Republic IV. This is a genuine conflict, an incompatibility. Plato did retain the Socratic claim that no one does wrong willingly even in his late work (see in particular *Laws* V, 731c and IX, 860d), but in the *Republic* he accepts the existence of irrational desires. If intellectualism were the only moral theory contained in the elenctic dialogues, the contrast between Socratic ethics and Platonic ethics would be clear. It is not, however, the only moral theory present in the elenctic dialogues.

In the *Crito*, as we discussed in Chapter 6, Socrates presents the analogy between physical and psychological health, and argues that the good life, which is the just life, is the life of psychological health. In the *Gorgias* he develops and defends these claims against the objections and the alternative views of his interlocutors. In the *Gorgias* psychological health is defined as proper order in the soul. As we have seen, this notion of order requires the concept of parts of the soul, which is hinted at in the *Gorgias*, at 493a–b. In the *Gorgias* only two parts of the soul are distinguished, reason and appetite; in *Republic* IV Socrates adds spirit. The *Gorgias* emphasizes the importance of self-control, rational control over the appetites, as the central virtue. In *Republic* IV the virtue responsible for self-control is justice, which is the proper order among the parts of the soul. The difference between these two claims is slight, since justice and self-control or temperance are very closely related to each other in the *Republic*. Justice is proper order of the parts of the state and soul; temperance is harmony between the parts. If the theory of intellectualism contrasts sharply with the theory of *Republic* IV, the theory of happiness as psychic order in the *Gorgias* leads directly to it. The seeds of the *Republic* theory of the virtuous life are present in the elenctic dialogues.

Political Theory

In Chapter 7 we discussed two aspects of Socratic political theory. The first aspect was Socrates' desire to create a republic of moral inquiry. Socrates wanted the Athenians to stop pursuing wealth, reputation, and honors and to start pursuing wisdom, truth, and the best state of their souls. The way to pursue these goals was through elenctic argument: as Socrates says at *Apology* 38a, the greatest good for a human being is "to discuss virtue every day … for the unexamined life is not worth living." Socrates exemplified the life he thought all Athenians should lead by examining others; as he stated at *Gorgias* 521d, he thought he was the only Athenian of his day who practiced the true art of politics. Socrates was aware that the Athenian people were unlikely to abandon their current pursuits and convert to a life of philosophy, but he thought of that as an ideal. The second aspect of Socratic political theory was his search for a moral expert. Socrates believed that what qualified someone to rule was not citizenship, wealth, or heredity but knowledge. He searched for someone who had knowledge of the first principles of ethics. He believed that, if such a person could be found, that person ought to be the ruler in the city. If a knowledgeable person or persons could be discovered, any government other than rule by that person would be undesirable, perhaps illegitimate.

In the *Republic* Plato reconceives Socrates' idea of a republic of moral inquiry, but he does not modify his view that the moral expert should rule. He apparently realized that a state in which everyone was engaged in the search for virtue would be impractical. Someone, in fact most people in the city, would need to grow the food for the city, house its inhabitants, clothe them, and provide shoes for them. Because he accepted a principle that labor should be carried out by specialists who did only one job, this required farmers, carpenters, tailors, and shoemakers. Eventually other specialists were added to the workforce, including a military class, from which a class of rulers was drawn. Plato envisioned a class society. Each class practiced the virtues of justice and temperance, but the military class was distinguished for its courage and the ruling class for its wisdom. It was to the ruling class that the task of investigating the nature of virtue fell. Though Plato modified the conception of a republic of moral inquiry, he retained the Socratic idea that it was knowledge that qualified a ruler to rule. The rulers of Plato's state were characterized not by their active pursuit of virtue, but by their actual possession of knowledge of virtue and the good. They were to be the moral experts for which Socrates searched, but never claimed that he had found. The philosopher rulers of the *Republic* were the descendants of the moral experts Socrates sought in all of the elenctic dialogues. The Socratic search for moral wisdom culminated in the philosopher-king. To become a philosopher-king one would have to take a rigorous ten year sequence of courses in mathematics, followed by five years of dialectic, and no one would qualify as philosopher-king until he or she could offer a definition of the good that could withstand all possible criticism, so the likelihood of a philosopher-king just "popping up" would seem to be extremely small. On the other hand, Plato's Academy, with its emphasis on mathematical learning, may have been, at least in aspiration, a training-ground for potential philosopher-kings. The political ideal of the *Republic* was a republic of virtue in the sense that every member of the society possessed at least some virtue and contributed to the proper functioning of the state and to the well-being of the whole, but it would be a republic of moral inquiry only in the sense that the philosopher-kings in training would actively seek knowledge of virtue and the good, not in the Socratic sense that every member of society actively sought moral wisdom. It was based on the Socratic idea that the wise should rule, but not on the Socratic idea that everyone in the state might, theoretically, become wise.

Conclusion

I have been describing in this chapter the transformation of the character Socrates in the elenctic dialogues into the Platonic Socrates of the "middle" dialogues, primarily the *Republic*. I am confident that by the time Plato wrote the *Republic*, with its tripartite soul, complex theory of virtue, sharp distinction between knowledge and opinion, theory of separate Forms, concept of the good and account of the philosopher-king, this transformation of the character Socrates into a spokesman for Plato had been completed. I am also confident that the Socrates of the *Republic* is far removed from the barren Socrates represented in the elenctic dialogues and in particular in the *Apology*. As I said at the outset of this chapter, however, Socrates, as he is characterized in the elenctic dialogues, is not simply barren. He is also fertile, with answers to the questions he raises for others. The roots of the theory of separate Forms, the signature doctrine of the Platonic Socrates, are to be found in the search for definitions of ethical terms in the elenctic dialogues. The key distinction between the Socratic and the Platonic theory of Forms lies in the concept of separation, which is introduced in the *Cratylus*, *Phaedo*, and *Symposium* and remains thereafter a key concept of Platonism. The Form of the good is to be found in the elenctic dialogues, and the good as the object of love is discussed in the *Lysis*. The *Meno* distinguishes between knowledge and right opinion, anticipating the *Republic's* fourfold classification of cognitive states. There are places in the elenctic dialogues, such as the *Protagoras*, where Socrates presents a theory of virtue, intellectualism, that differs from the theory presented in the *Republic*. In other elenctic dialogues, however, Socrates presents views that anticipate the *Republic*. The account of the happy life as the life of the wise person, whose soul is healthy and just, can be found in the *Crito* and *Gorgias*. The ideal of the philosopher-king is in essence the Socratic ideal of the moral expert. The ideal of the person who possesses the "royal art," the political art that makes people happy, is found in the *Euthydemus*.

The ideas that distinguish the "middle" dialogues from the elenctic dialogues are not introduced all at once. The transformation of Socrates the barren inquirer into Socrates the confident theoretician is a gradual one, which has several landmarks. Throughout this transformation, however, there is a guiding principle that shapes the discussion: the ideal of a quest for wisdom, truth, and the best possible state of one's soul, to which Socrates exhorts the Athenians in the *Apology*. Throughout the elenctic dialogues Socrates carries on a search for wisdom, which he says is the only life worth living for people. I believe that this ideal of a philosophical life, a life of inquiry into wisdom, is something that Plato inherited from the historical Socrates. I also believe he inherited from the historical Socrates his elenctic method, however much he may have developed it and used it for his own purposes. How much more he may have inherited from Socrates is something that, as I said at the outset of this book, it is impossible to determine. It is possible that several of the theories introduced in the elenctic dialogues originate with Socrates; it is possible that all of them originate with Plato. It is possible that the gradual introduction into the elenctic dialogues of doctrines that foreshadow the doctrines of the *Republic* was part of a literary project that Plato conceived at the beginning of his career. It is also possible that Plato developed his various doctrines over a period of time. It is possible that he was influenced in this development by his encounter with Pythagorean philosophy on his first voyage to Sicily in 387. Where the truth lies in this controversy cannot be known.

It is possible that Plato began his career as a disciple of Socrates, and that he developed his own distinctive doctrines over time. I think it is clear, however, that the development of those doctrines began in the elenctic dialogues. If we think of Socrates not as the historical figure behind the dialogues but as the character in the elenctic dialogues, then Platonic doctrine, such as is found in the "middle" dialogues originates with Socrates in the elenctic dialogues. Charles Kahn has written that "the dialogues are all Platonic."[16] They are also, however, Socratic. They represent the thought of a character through which Plato presents his philosophical reflections to the world. The Socrates of the elenctic dialogues is not the Socrates of the *Republic*, though he is moving in the direction of that Socrates. The philosophy of Socrates, the character in the elenctic dialogues, is worthy of study, not simply as the anticipation of the philosophy of Plato, but for its own sake. Emerson said that "Socrates and Plato are the double star which the most powerful instruments will not entirely separate."[17] This is true; however, there is enough separation to create room for the philosophical study of the Socrates of the elenctic dialogues.

9

Socrates' Legacy

Throughout this book we have focused on Socrates as portrayed by one of his associates, Plato. In this chapter we shall look at Socrates as he has been portrayed by other authors throughout the centuries. Socrates has been seen by later writers in four basic ways: as a virtuous man, an exemplar of the philosophical life; as an ignorant inquirer (the barren Socrates); as an exemplar of wisdom (the fertile Socrates); and as a martyr. There are two periods in particular in the history of the West in which the philosophy of Socrates has been intensively studied: antiquity and the nineteenth century. Philosophy in antiquity was understood not only as an academic study but as a way of life, and the life of Socrates was seen by many philosophers as paradigmatic of that life. With the advent of Christianity the focus shifted somewhat to Socrates as a virtuous man and martyr. The cultural debate about Socrates in the Christian era was concerned with him not only as an individual but as a representative of ancient Greek philosophy and culture in general. The question raised in antiquity and debated into the modern age concerned the relation between classical culture and Christianity. In the nineteenth century Socrates became a crucial figure in philosophy in his own right once again, though the connection with Christianity was not lost. One focus of the portrayal of Socrates in the twentieth century has been his relationship to Athenian democracy.

This survey is highly selective; it does not attempt to tell the story of the cultural influence of Socrates in literature and the arts. This chapter will also not include the scholarly study of Socrates. Especially since the nineteenth century Socrates has been the subject of intense scrutiny by classical scholars. One project of these scholars has been the attempt to recover the historical Socrates from the testimony of his associates and later interpreters, to solve what is usually referred to as the "Socratic problem." As I noted above, in Chapter 2, I do not believe this problem has a solution. This scholarly debate was not in general the primary concern of the philosophers I write about in this chapter, though some of the more recent philosophers do discuss it. The scholarly study of Socrates, and in particular the various attempts to solve the Socratic problem, from Friedrich Schleiermacher to Gregory Vlastos, is worth a volume in its own right.

Beginning with Plato, each of the authors I shall discuss used Socrates for his own purposes. Because Socrates left no written legacy, he could be molded to fit the concerns of other philosophers. This is not to say that if Socrates had left a written legacy, all controversy over the interpretation of his philosophy would have ceased. That is simply not the way things are in philosophy. Still, the fact that Socrates did not leave a written record of his philosophical teachings has made it easier for subsequent writers to use Socrates in service of their own philosophies.

Xenophon's Socrates

Before turning to the reception of Socrates in later Greek and Roman philosophy it is necessary to discuss Xenophon's portrait of Socrates. As was mentioned in Chapter 2, Xenophon wrote four works featuring Socrates: an *Apology* and *Symposium*, thought to be indebted to Platonic models, the *Oeconomicus*, a treatise on estate management, and the *Memorabilia*, his major Socratic work.[1] Xenophon may have written these works in part to correct the portrait of Socrates offered by Plato. Plato's Socrates, as we have seen, was the practitioner of the elenchus, who refuted his interlocutors and left them in a state of perplexity. Xenophon's Socrates practices the elenchus also, but only as the first stage of the educational process. When a person has become a Socratic associate, Xenophon's Socrates replaces the elenchus with more constructive educational methods. These are not devoid of philosophical interest; in *Memorabilia* IV.vi Xenophon's Socrates offers definitions of several of the terms Plato's Socrates had sought to define without success in his elenctic dialogues. Xenophon's Socrates is interested, not in refutation, but in producing young men who are *kalos kagathos*, admirable and good.

There is a story in Diogenes Laertius (2.48) of Socrates accosting Xenophon in the streets of Athens and asking him if he knows where a number of different foods can be found. Finally, Socrates asks Xenophon if he knows where young men become admirable and good, and when Xenophon replies that he does not, Socrates says, "follow me and learn." Xenophon's Socrates uses irony considerably less frequently than does Plato's.[2] He is also unaware of the Platonic Socrates' profession of ignorance. Xenophon's Socrates admits to being an expert in the education of youth, a subject he has devoted his life to (Xenophon, *Apology* 20–21). What Xenophon's Socrates and Plato's have in common is their depiction of Socrates as a man who excelled all others in virtue, who led an exemplary life.

The Reception of Socrates in the Ancient World

Socrates acquired a preeminent status in antiquity, due in large part to the depiction of him in the works of Plato and Xenophon. This is not to say that there was no criticism of Socrates. Criticism began, of course, with the first portrait of Socrates in history: Aristophanes' *Clouds*. Plato's *Apology* was written in part to counteract Aristophanes' depiction of Socrates. Sometime after 390 a certain Polycrates wrote a pamphlet purporting to contain Anytus' prosecution speech at Socrates' trial. The pamphlet is now lost, but it is thought that the opening chapters of Book I of Xenophon's *Memorabilia* respond to the charges of Polycrates. This pamphlet may have been the origin of the political interpretation of the trial, for Polycrates accused Socrates of having educated Alcibiades and Critias (Xenophon, *Memorabilia* I.ɪɪ.12).

It became fashionable in the years following the rise of various ancient schools of philosophy for doxographers, writers who recorded the opinions of various philosophers, to trace the lineage of these schools back to Socrates. Two schools resisted this genealogy. The Pyrrhonian skeptics saw Pyrrho (c. 365–c. 275) as the originator of their philosophy. The Epicureans saw Epicurus (341–270) in the same way. The Epicureans had little good to say about any rival philosophers; they wanted all the credit for any philosophical truth to go to their master. They thought it necessary not only to build him up, but to run down all of his rivals, including Socrates. "The Epicureans displayed a hostility to Socrates that is virulent even by the extreme standards of ancient polemic."[3]

Aristotle himself was not critical of Socrates, but his followers "were either silent about Socrates, ... or determinedly malevolent. Aristoxenus, according to Porphyry, is said to have written a life of Socrates that was more vicious than the accusations of Meletus and Anytus."[4] The reasons for the hostility of the Aristotelians are something of a mystery.

More common than such criticism is the high status of Socrates among his associates and in other, later schools of philosophy. During Socrates' lifetime a number of philosophers became his associates. These have become known as "the Socratic circle." Some of these associates wrote dialogues in which Socrates is the leading character. Apart from the works of Plato and Xenophon, these dialogues are now lost, except for a few fragments.[5] Plato was not the inventor of the Socratic dialogue, though his dialogues became the best-known and most read examples of that genre. (The preservation of Plato's dialogues may be due to their literary and philosophical quality, but it no doubt helped that Plato founded a school, the Academy, in which those dialogues were not only studied but preserved for posterity.) In the first generation following the death of Socrates the leading figure among these associates was Antisthenes (c. 445–c. 365). Antisthenes saw Socrates as an example of moral strength, a quality that was preeminent for Xenophon as well. There seems to have been a debate within the Socratic circle concerning the human good, with Antisthenes championing moral strength and self-sufficiency and Aristippus (c. 435–c. 356) defending pleasure. Antisthenes was quoted as saying, "I would rather go mad than enjoy pleasure."[6] Doxographers traced the Cynic school back to Socrates by way of Antisthenes; Plato is alleged to have referred to the Cynic Diogenes of Sinope as "Socrates gone mad" (Diogenes Laertius 6.54). Aristippus was thought to be the founder of the Cyrenaic school of philosophy, which held that the immediate experience of pleasure was the good. It may seem surprising that two philosophers with such different, mutually opposed views of the good should have been Socrates' associates, but it should not be. We can see some evidence for each view in the discussion of hedonism in Plato's *Protagoras* and the arguments against hedonism in the *Gorgias*. It is likely that Socrates encouraged debate among his associates. It is possible that, as the portrait of Socrates as barren suggests, he refrained from stating his own view. We do not know the extent to which these two philosophers attributed their views to Socrates, but part of the reason that Socrates played such a powerful role in ancient and modern philosophy is that he is not identified with either of these philosophical doctrines.

For the Stoics, Socrates' exemplary life stemmed from his philosophical principles. The Stoic Socrates was an intellectualist. He held that virtue was knowledge and that virtue was sufficient for a good life. The Stoics took seriously the Socratic argument in the *Euthydemus* and *Meno* that there is no good except virtue, the nature of which is wisdom.[7] They constructed a picture of the person who lived such a life, who infallibly made the correct moral choices: they referred to this person as "the sage." The sage, thought the Stoics, was the only sane person in a world of madness. Who could live up to this impossibly high standard? The Stoics, modestly, did not put forward Zeno of Citium (c. 334–c. 262), the founder of their school, or Chrysippus of Soli (c. 279–c. 206), its greatest early proponent, as candidates for the sage. If anyone qualified, they thought, it was Socrates. The doxographic tradition derived Stoicism from Socrates by way of the Cynic philosophers, but a more direct route seems possible. It seems that Zeno began his career as a philosopher by reading Xenophon's *Memorabilia*, which led him to study in the Academy. The Stoics were so favorably disposed toward Socrates that it is said that they were willing to be called "Socratics."[8] Epictetus (c. 55–135 CE) shows the influence of Socrates most clearly. As Long writes, "no other philosopher is named nearly as often … it is Socrates who primarily authorizes everything Epictetus is trying to give his students in terms of philosophical methodology, self-examination, and a life model for them to imitate."[9] As Epictetus himself writes, "Socrates became fully perfect … by not paying attention to anything but his reason in everything that he met with. You, even if you are not yet Socrates, ought to live as someone wanting to be Socrates" (*Handbook*, 51).[10]

The Socrates that the Stoics appropriated was the intellectualist Socrates, a version of the fertile Socrates. The Academic skeptics appropriated the barren Socrates, and used him to combat the dogmatism of the Stoics.[11] The Stoics held that some perceptions, which they called "gripping presentations," were certain, infallible. The Academic skeptics held that, on the contrary, nothing was infallible: there was no such thing as a gripping presentation. It was always possible to be mistaken. The academic skeptics went further than anything the Platonic Socrates says by advocating a suspension of judgment, *epochē*, as a result of the uncertainty of matters. This battle over the question of the certainty of our judgments was a major focus of Hellenistic and Roman philosophy.

Academic skepticism owes its origin to Arcesilaus, who was the head of Plato's Academy from c. 273 to c. 242. Arcesilaus derived his skeptical philosophy from a reading of Plato's Socratic dialogues, and he seems to have been the first philosopher to emphasize the skeptical side of Socrates' thought.[12] Arcesilaus modeled his own life on the life of Plato's Socrates, but he went further than Socrates: whereas Socrates confined his skepticism to ethics, Arcesilaus read Socrates as saying that he had knowledge of just one thing, namely that he knew nothing; and Arcesilaus denied that he, Arcesilaus, knew even that. This understanding of Socratic skepticism became commonplace in later centuries. Arcesilaus wrote nothing; we know about his views because of their description in several sources, most prominently in works of the Roman philosophical writer, Cicero (106–43), himself a proponent of Academic skepticism.

The Christian Reception of Socrates

With the advent of Christianity the conversation about Socrates changes. The strands previously found remain the same: on the one hand, there is a strand that is hostile to Socrates, while on the other there is a strand that is favorable. The nature of the judgments made concerning Socrates change, however: now Socrates is judged, not as a philosopher in the context of ancient philosophy in general, but in relation to Christian thought and morality. One strand of Christian thinking is hostile to Greek philosophy in general: the Christian writer Tertullian (160–230 CE) saw Greek philosophy as the source of false beliefs. "What has Athens to do with Jerusalem?" he asked, famously; "what concord is there between the Academy and the Church? ... Away with all attempts to produce a mottled Christianity of Stoic, Platonic and dialectic composition ... With our faith, we desire no further belief" (*Prescription against Heretics*, 7). Tertullian traced his attempt to banish Greek philosophy from Christian belief to a remark of the apostle Paul in Colossians 2.8, "see that no one beguile you through philosophy and vain deceit, after the tradition of men."

Tertullian was reacting against a Christian tradition of seeing in Greek philosophy a precursor of Christian faith. For numerous early Christian writers, including Justin Martyr, Clement of Alexandria, and Origen, Greek philosophy was something that could be used to make Christianity seem credible to a Greek audience. Plato was an especially attractive source: his doctrine of the immortality of the soul helped to explain the Christian promise of eternal life, and his account of the creation of the world by a wise and benevolent craftsman deity seemed to resemble the account of creation in Genesis. Then there was the example of Socrates, tried and convicted of impiety and put to death in a way that resembled, in some respects, the trial and death of Jesus. This was a comparison that was to be made over and over again, down through the centuries, and not only by Christian writers. It was common among Christian interpreters to see Socrates as a monotheist, an opponent of pagan religion. Was Socrates to be embraced as a human counterpart of Jesus, a victim of injustice and evidence of the human tendency to reject the truth? Or was Socrates to be seen as a representation of all that was wrong with pagan thought? How did Socrates, the philosophical world's model of a sage, compare to Christian models? Two problems stood out for Christians in the life of Socrates: his homoerotic tendencies and his *daimonion*, his "divine sign." Though Plato attempts to make it clear in the *Symposium* that Socrates' interest in youths was chaste (Alcibiades' failed seduction attempt testifies to this, and his remark at 216d that "it couldn't matter less to him whether a boy is beautiful"), still Socrates' response to Charmides at *Charmides* 155d attested to his erotic interest in young males, and his pursuit of Alcibiades was well known. Christians disapproved of pederasty. Was Socrates a pederast? And what was to be made of his *daimonion*, the voice that Socrates confessed came to him on occasion and forbade him from doing certain things, some of minor importance but others of major, such as entering Athenian political life? Was Socrates possessed by a demon? Demons were universally regarded as agents of evil in Christian scripture. Or was his *daimonion* something more akin to a guardian angel, indicating that Socrates was blessed by God? These issues dominated the Christian discussion of Socrates not just in the ancient world, but in subsequent eras as well.

The Christian concern with the trial, conviction, and execution of Socrates brought about a shift of focus in the way he was treated. Down to this point the focus of the study of Socrates had been on Socrates' methods and teachings. Was he a dogmatic philosopher or an ignorant inquirer? Was he fertile or barren? This is not to say that the questions surrounding the trial, conviction and execution had been neglected; numerous *Apologies* of Socrates were composed during this period. In the Christian era, however, it was no longer necessary to look to Socrates, or any other philosopher for that matter, for the content of morality. Christians relied on the teachings of Jesus for that. Instead of dialectic, in the form of the elenchus, Christians relied on the interpretation of Jesus' words. Reasoned discourse concerning interpretation was not out of place, but it was no longer necessary to argue dialectically in order to reach the fundamental truths of ethics themselves. Those had been declared in the Sermon on the Mount and in other canonical texts. Instead of focusing on the methods and teachings of Socrates, those Christian thinkers who referred to him could focus on his trial, conviction, and execution. Socrates seemed to be a model of unjust punishment, and Christian apologists could use him as a parallel both to the trial and death of Jesus and to the persecution of his Christian followers. Socrates the philosopher declined in importance; Socrates the martyr increased.

Socrates from the Middle Ages to the Enlightenment

In the period following the collapse of the Roman Empire in the West in the fifth century interest in Socrates declined. The revival of philosophy in the twelfth century was spurred by the renewed appropriation of Aristotle's works; though Plato's *Crito* and *Phaedo* were available in Latin translation, Socrates was not a focus of philosophical discussion.[13] Socrates was understood primarily as he was depicted in Aristotle's works. That is how he is referred to in St. Thomas Aquinas. During the Renaissance there was a great increase in interest in Socrates, first with renewed interest in Cicero's philosophical works and subsequently with the recovery in the West of Plato's works. Plato emerged as a rival to Aristotle as the leading philosopher of antiquity, and his more literary approach to philosophy won the enthusiastic support of humanist interpreters critical of the methods of medieval Scholastic philosophy. Marsilio Ficino (1433–1499), translator of the *Symposium* and founder of the Florentine Academy, named after Plato's Academy, saw Socrates as a model of virtue to rival Christian models. The humanist thinkers of the Renaissance did not quarrel openly with Christianity, but they did tend to see classical culture, and Socrates as its exemplar, as worthy of serious consideration in its own right.

This appreciation of classical culture and Socrates continued to concern writers in the Reformation. One thinker of the Reformation era who tried to integrate Socrates and Christianity was Erasmus (1466–1536). Erasmus wrote several works in which Socrates was discussed. There is a charming colloquy, "The Godly Feast," in which one of the characters utters a line that has been much quoted: "I can hardly refrain from saying, 'Saint Socrates, pray for us.'"[14] Martin Luther, although he makes some grudging remarks in favor of Socrates in various places in his writings, wholeheartedly rejected this attempt by Erasmus to integrate classical culture and Christianity, saying, "even if Cicero or Socrates had sweated blood, that would not make it pleasing to God."[15] Thus he reiterated the claim originally made by Tertullian that only the Christian faith was relevant to the question of salvation.

In the period from the Reformation to the Enlightenment writers, including philosophical writers, continually refer to Socrates in terms that reflect but do not advance much the preceding discussion. As with earlier thinkers, these writers adapt the figure of Socrates to the ideals that they themselves favor. For Montaigne (1533–1592), Socrates is a model of natural virtue. For the freethinker Anthony Collins (1676–1729) he is a model of freethinking. For Benjamin Franklin he was an example for emulation. For Voltaire he was a rationalist opponent of superstition and political oppression. As the demand for freedom from the *ancien regime* and the dogmatism of the church grew in intensity, Socrates became more and more associated with these popular causes: he remained a saint, as he had been for Erasmus, but a secular one. There is criticism of Socrates in this period too, but by and large the philosophers of this period who are studied today – Hobbes, Descartes, Spinoza, Locke, Berkeley, Leibniz, Hume, and Kant – do not pay a great deal of attention to him. He is referred to occasionally, but he is not the central figure he was for the ancients. Modern philosophy, with its emphasis on epistemology, does not draw its inspiration from the example or the teaching of Socrates.

The Nineteenth Century

In the nineteenth century philosophical interest in Socrates underwent a remarkable revival. Three major philosophers, Hegel, Kierkegaard, and Nietzsche offered portraits of Socrates that stood in dialectical relation to each other. Each defined Socrates in relation to his own philosophy, as other philosophers have done. Because each had different, often opposed, highly original philosophies, they produced rival appreciations of Socrates. Nietzsche did not know Kierkegaard's work, which was not translated from Danish until the twentieth century, but both Kierkegaard and Nietzsche knew, and in different ways responded to, the interpretation of Hegel. Socrates is *important* for each of these thinkers; both Hegel and Nietzsche treat Socrates as introducing a new era in philosophy. For Kierkegaard in particular, Socrates is essential to his own response to modernity and to Christianity. If the ancient world produced a "golden age" in the interpretation of Socrates, with rival schools battling for his legacy and offering different interpretations of his thought and influence, then the nineteenth century might be said to be a second golden age in Socrates interpretation.

Hegel

G. W. F. Hegel believed in progress. He thought that the history of the world was a history of ascent from a primitive beginning to the culmination of the present day. He did not think of this progress in materialistic terms, for instance from the discovery of fire to electricity to nuclear power, but in conceptual terms. It is debated whether he saw this progress as the working of a single intelligence, a ruling intellect in control of all of history, which might be called God or Reason, but he thought that history could be described as a series of successive ages, defined by different conceptions of reality. He saw these ages as introduced by revolutionary individuals, whom he described as "world-historical" in their significance. He applied this view of progress to ethics and political philosophy as well as to history, and in his *Lectures on the History of Philosophy* he applied it to the history of philosophy. These lectures were edited and published after Hegel's death, based on notes he left from his professorship at the University of Berlin.

In Hegel's lectures we hear a voice which is familiar to us today: the voice of the professor. In this case, the professor is a man with a system, which he used to interpret the history of philosophy. Hegel's account of Socrates is one that a modern student of Socrates would find familiar. He deals with many of the points that a modern professor would deal with in discussing Socrates. He does not agree with modern scholarship in every detail, and his discussion throughout is shaped by his big idea, the idea of progress, but one can see in his presentation of Socrates an ancestor of views that can be found today. Hegel and modern students of Socrates are part of a single conversation. Hegel's discussion of Socrates is lengthy and detailed, 65 pages in the translation of E. S. Haldane. Hegel actually apologizes for the length of his treatment at the end of the section.[16]

Hegel begins his discussion of Socrates by calling him "not only a most important figure in the history of Philosophy – perhaps the most interesting in the philosophy of antiquity, but ... also a world-famed personage. For a mental turning-point exhibited itself in him in the form of philosophic thought" (384).[17] As opposed to his philosophical predecessors, who, Hegel thinks, thought but did not focus on the nature of thought, Socrates turned his attention inward, to the "I" that thinks. He sees this "I" as the source of morality, which he distinguishes from the customary, traditional ethics of the Greeks, which he calls "Sittlichkeit." Hegel thought that Socrates' fellow Athenians drew their sense of moral obligation from their culture, unreflectively; Socrates drew his sense from within himself: not himself as an individual, but himself as a representative of universal thought. "In him we see pre-eminently the inwardness of consciousness that in an anthropological way existed in the first instance in him, and became later on a usual thing" (391).

Socrates explores the nature of morality by means of dialectic, which he says "has two prominent aspects, the one the development of the universal from the concrete case" (think for example of Euthyphro's initial attempt to define piety in terms of prosecuting wrongdoers such as his father), "and the exhibition of the notion which implicitly exists in every consciousness" (think in this case of the doctrine of recollection), and "the causing of confusion between" the universal and the concrete (think of the perplexity produced in so many of the elenctic dialogues) (398). Socrates represented himself as ignorant, which Hegel refers to as "the celebrated Socratic irony" (ibid.). He "taught those with whom he associated to know that they knew nothing; indeed, what is more, he himself said that he knew nothing" (399). In other words, he behaved like the barren Socrates. But he also elicited from his interlocutors "the thought which is already contained in the consciousness of the individual" (402); that is, he acted as a midwife. This process is individual in that it involves individual interlocutors, but it is also universal, which can be seen when, under Socrates' guidance, the interlocutor learns how to separate the universal concept from the concrete example in which it is embedded: "the child, the uncultured man, lives in concrete individual ideas, but to the man who grows and educates himself, because he thereby goes back into himself as thinking, reflection becomes reflection on the universal and the permanent establishment of the same" (403). The main tendency of the Socratic dialogues was negative: "to show the bewilderment and confusion which exist in knowledge" (404–5). "Philosophy must," Hegel says in a famous assertion, "begin with a puzzle in order to bring about reflection; everything must be doubted, all presuppositions given up, to reach the truth" (406). The other side of Socrates' method, "the affirmative, ... is nothing but the good in as far as it is brought forth from consciousness through knowledge ... His knowledge for the first time reached this abstraction" (ibid.). With this discovery, which Hegel interprets as the beginning of reflective morality, "the spirit of the world ... begins to change" (407).

This discovery of the conceptual, reflective nature of morality, something that is now generally accepted, was perceived as a threat to traditional morality. For the Athenians, tradition and culture, expressed ultimately in the laws of the state, were absolute. Socrates' response to this was to question the absoluteness of the law. "Consciousness, in the perception of its independence, no longer immediately acknowledges what is put before it, but requires that this should first justify itself to it" (409). As a result, "the State has lost its power ... Morals have become shaken, because we have the idea present that man creates his maxims for himself" (ibid.). This rise of reflective morality produces a crisis, which leads to Socrates' trial. Socrates undermines the validity of the law; he pokes holes in traditional morality by counter-examples that show that the laws of custom are not universal (think here of Socrates showing Cephalus in *Republic* I that telling the truth and paying one's debts are not always just). Unfortunately, Socrates cannot flesh out his abstract conception of the good; though he rocks the foundations of traditional morality, he cannot point to a morality of consciousness that will replace it.

"The contemporaries of Socrates, who came forward as his accusers before the Athenian people, laid hold on him as the man who made known that what was held as absolute was not absolute ... Because Socrates makes the truth rest on the judgment of inward consciousness, he enters upon a struggle with the Athenian people as to what is right and true" (426). Who was right in this struggle? One might expect Hegel to say that Socrates was right, because he had discovered the higher source of morality. What Hegel says, however, is that both sides in the dispute were correct. Aristophanes was justified in portraying Socrates in the *Clouds* as an enemy of the state; the Athenian people were right to object to his "daemon" as an inward principle of judgment. Socrates threatened the foundation of the state, its religion: "it would undoubtedly in the first place mean the subversion of the Athenian State, if this public religion on which everything was built and without which the State could not subsist, went to pieces" (439); but that is just what Socrates threatened, by placing the individual conscience above the law. Socrates was a threat to the law of the state and its religion. "Is it then to be wondered at that Socrates was found guilty?" (440).

Not only was Socrates guilty, but he had to be put to death. By refusing to propose an alternative punishment (and here, as elsewhere in discussing the trial, Hegel relies on Xenophon's version more than Plato's) he refused to submit to the authority of the state: "Socrates disclaims the submission to, and humiliation before the power of the people" (442). The Athenian law, however, does not permit this, nor can any state: "the first principle of a State is that there is no reason or conscience or righteousness or anything else, higher than what the State recognizes as such" (443). In spite of this, however, "Socrates was still the hero who possessed for himself the absolute right of the mind, certain of itself and of the inwardly deciding consciousness, and thus expressed the higher principle of mind with consciousness" (444). In general heroes "appear to be violently destroying the laws. Hence individually they are vanquished, but it is only the individual, and not the principle, which is negated in punishment ... His own world could not comprehend Socrates, but posterity can" (ibid.).

Socrates' fate was thus tragic: "in what is truly tragic there must be valid powers on both the sides which come into collision; this was so with Socrates" (446). The tragedy was not just his, however, but Athens': "two opposed rights come into collision, and the one destroys the other. Thus both suffer loss and yet both are mutually justified ... The one power is the divine right, the natural morality ... The other principle, on the contrary, is the right, as really divine, of consciousness or of subjective freedom" (446–7). But the subjective freedom of Socrates was actually vindicated: "for the world-spirit had raised itself into a higher consciousness" (447).

Hegel's account of the trial can certainly be criticized, and on his own principles at that. If the Athenian law cannot recognize the power of individual consciousness, and if in fact individual consciousness is a higher basis of morality than the tradition on which the law is based, then it would seem that both sides do not equally have right on their side. Socrates is, as Hegel states, the hero of the conflict, for his principle ultimately emerges victorious. The old way is submerged in a new version of the law, one that recognizes the individual consciousness. There are many other criticisms of detail that one might wish to make in Hegel's account, but Most's comment, that "Hegel's interpretation of the figure of Socrates is perhaps the only one that can be compared with Plato's, for depth of philosophical penetration and for richness of historical imagination,"[18] is worth serious consideration. Most is surely correct when he states that "it is with Hegel, as much as with Socrates himself, that such nineteenth century philosophers as Kierkegaard and Nietzsche are in dialogue when they write about the Greek philosopher."[19]

Kierkegaard: Socrates as an Individual

Socrates is a hero for Søren Kierkegaard (1813–1855). He refers to him as "the simple wise man ... of all men the greatest ... intellectual hero and martyr."[20] "O noble, simple sage of antiquity," he continues, "the only human being that I acknowledge with admiration as a thinker ... How I have longed ... for one short hour of conversation with you!"[21] Kierkegaard saw his own task in Socratic terms. In one of his final writings, in 1855, he writes, "my only analogy is Socrates. My task is a Socratic task – to revise the conception of what it means to be a Christian."[22] Kierkegaard's task, as he saw it, was to awaken in the complacent minds of his fellow citizens in Copenhagen the awareness of the fact that they were not, as they thought, Christians, as Socrates' task was to awaken in the complacent minds of his fellow Athenians the awareness of the fact that they were ignorant of the truths of ethics.

Kierkegaard began his career under the influence of Hegel, an influence he later repudiated.[23] His first published work was his master's thesis, *On the Concept of Irony, with Special Reference to Socrates.*[24] In his thesis Kierkegaard saw Socrates as an ironist: "what made up the substance of his existence was irony."[25] As Hegel had thought, Socrates rejected the traditional morality of his fellow citizens, but he had no positive moral teaching of his own with which to replace it. His stance was that of "infinite absolute negativity," Hegel's definition of irony.[26] Even in his master's thesis, however, one can discern Kierkegaard moving past the Hegelian conception of Socrates as the inventor of a new stage in the history of ethics. Socrates, thinks Kierkegaard at this stage of his life, had no positive teaching at all: "He is like a hyphen in world history ... he, in a certain sense, is in world history and then again *is not* ... he is the nothing with which the start had to be made."[27] This is not a rejection of Socrates on Kierkegaard's part: "Socrates is not mini-mized by my interpretation but rather becomes a hero ... The old Greek civilization had outlived itself, a new principle was about to enter ... The new principle has to fight for its life, world history needs a new obstetrician. Socrates fills this position."[28]

Kierkegaard soon heightened his critique of Hegel. Kierkegaard objected to Hegel's view of Socrates as a world-historical person, whose life was to be understood in terms of its contribution to the unfolding of the system. Socrates, for Kierkegaard, was an indi-vidual. He did not fit into a grand scheme that depicted the growth in human society of reason or freedom. Socrates, the individual, was in fact for Kierkegaard a counter-example to Hegel's systematic understanding. Kierkegaard opposed Hegel's presentation of Chris-tianity as a stage, albeit the highest stage, in the unfolding of the system. Christianity was not an objective truth, to be expressed in systematic terms. Christianity was a subjective truth, "an objective uncertainty held fast in an appropriation-process of the most pas-sionate inwardness."[29] This inward appropriation-process is faith. With respect to the question of the immortality of the soul: "Socrates ... puts the question objectively in a problematic manner: *if* there is an immortality ... On this 'if' he risks his entire life ... The bit of uncertainty that Socrates had helped him because he himself con-tributed the passion of the infinite ... It is possible that there was more truth in the Socratic ignorance as it was in him, than in the entire objective truth of the System."[30] (A few pages later he makes the same claim about Socrates' faith in God.) Socrates' God was not the God of Christianity, who became a human being in time and suffered death on the cross, a God who is the "ultimate paradox," but he is still a God requiring faith.

In *The Sickness unto Death* (1848) Kierkegaard revises the estima-tion of him in *The Concept of Irony* as an ironist pure and simple:

> Socrates was certainly an ethical teacher (the Classical age claims him absolutely as the discoverer of ethics); he was the first one, as he is and remains the first in his class; ... But on the other hand ... Socrates is not an essentially religious ethicist, still less a dogmatic one ... Socrates ... never really gets to the determinant we know as sin ... What determinant is it then that Socrates lacks in determining what sin is? It is will, defiant will. The Greek intellectualism was too happy, too naïve, too aesthetic, too ironical, too witty ... too sinful to be able to get it into its head that a person knowingly could fail to do the good, or knowingly, with knowledge of what was right, do what was wrong.[31]

Kierkegaard sees Socrates' intellectualism, with its rejection of the idea of sin, as a defect in relation to Christianity. Yet Socrates retained his status for Kierkegaard as the model individual thinker: "I for my part tranquilly adhere to Socrates. It is true, he was not a Christian; that I know, and yet I am thoroughly convinced that he has become one … I can very well call Socrates my teacher."[32]

Nietzsche

Nietzsche's attitude toward Socrates is often said to be ambivalent.[33] In an oft-quoted passage, he remarks, "Socrates … stands so close to me that I am practically always waging a battle with him."[34] Nietzsche discusses Socrates in the first work he published, *The Birth of Tragedy* (1872), and one of the latest, *Twilight of the Idols* (1888). His estimation of Socrates' influence does not change much, if at all, but in the earlier work it is presented in a less polemical tone than in the later. For Nietzsche the acme of Greek culture is the tragic drama of Aeschylus and Sophocles. He describes tragedy as the product of two forces, which he calls the Apollonian and Dionysian. He describes the Dionysian force as akin to intoxication. In *Twilight of the Idols* he associates it with the reproductive force and the pain of childbirth, which is represented as holy ("What I Owe to the Ancients," sec. 4[35]), and in general with "the eternal joy of becoming, beyond all terror and pity" in the face of pain and sorrow (sec. 5). According to Nietzsche, tragedy was destroyed by the playwright usually considered the third of the three great Athenian tragedians: Euripides, with the assistance of Socrates. Socrates elevated knowledge, the product of reason, above the Dionysian force of instinct as a guide to life. Nietzsche, by training a classical scholar, describes Socrates in terms directly recalling Plato's *Apology*:

> It was Socrates who expressed most clearly this radically new prestige of knowledge and conscious intelligence when he claimed to be the only one who acknowledged to himself that he knew nothing. He roamed all over Athens, visiting the most distinguished statesmen, orators, poets and artists, and found everywhere merely the presumption of knowledge. He was amazed to discover that all these celebrities lacked true and certain knowledge of their callings and pursued those callings by sheer instinct. The expression "sheer instinct" seems to focus perfectly the Socratic attitude. From this point of view Socrates was forced to condemn both the prevailing art and the prevailing ethics. Wherever his penetrating gaze fell he saw

nothing but a lack of understanding, fictions rampant, and so was led to deduce a state of affairs wholly discreditable and perverse. (*The Birth of Tragedy*,[36] sec. 13)

It would be hard to imagine a better summary of the barren Socrates.

But Nietzsche's Socrates was not simply barren. Nietzsche summarizes "the Socratic maxims: 'Virtue is knowledge; all sins arise from ignorance; only the virtuous are happy,'" which he calls "three basic formulations of optimism" and which he says "spell the death of tragedy" (sec. 14). Socrates does not simply bring an end to tragedy: "we are certainly not entitled to see in Socrates merely an agent of disintegration" (ibid.) Though Nietzsche refers to Socrates as a "despotic logician" (ibid.), he also describes him as "the prototype of an entirely new mode of existence," the theoretical man. "His mission is to make existence appear intelligible and thereby justified" (sec. 15). "We cannot help viewing Socrates as the vortex and turning point of Western civilization," he states; "Socrates represents the archetype of the theoretical optimist, who, strong in the belief that nature can be fathomed, considers knowledge to be the true panacea and error to be radical evil. To Socratic man the one noble and truly human occupation was that of laying bare the workings of nature, of separating true knowledge from illusion and error" (ibid.). In other words, Socrates was the prototypical scientist, "the mystagogue of science" (ibid.).

Late in his life, in *The Twilight of the Idols*, Nietzsche discusses "The Problem of Socrates." He begins with a famous reflection on Socrates' final words, as recounted in Plato's *Phaedo*: "Crito, we owe a cock to Asclepius; make this offering to him and do not forget" (118a). Asclepius was the god of healing, and Nietzsche took the remark, the significance of which has been much debated, to be a Socratic comment on the nature of human life, namely that it was a sickness from which death was the release. Socrates, Nietzsche says, "*wanted* to die: not Athens, but he himself chose the hemlock; he forced Athens to sentence him" (sec. 12). Socrates, says Nietzsche, was a symbol of decline, of decadence. He launches an attack on Socrates, beginning in section 3 with his personal appearance. Behind this attack, however, is an aim which goes beyond the surface: "I seek to comprehend what idiosyncrasy begot that Socratic equation of reason, virtue and happiness: that most bizarre of all equations, which moreover is opposed to all the instincts of the earlier Greeks" (sec. 4). Socrates was, according to Nietzsche, a member of the lowest class; his use of dialectic, he suggests, was a

kind of class warfare against the noble classes. "one chooses dialectic only when one has no other means" (sec. 6). For Nietzsche,
Socrates' use of dialectic was an act of violence: "does he," Nietzsche
asks, "enjoy his own ferocity in the knife-thrusts of his syllogisms?"
(sec. 7) For Nietzsche, Socrates' method was an act of revenge
against the powerful in his society. (Think here of the Socratic critique of Callicles in the *Gorgias*.)

But this critique is only one side of Nietzsche's interpretation of
Socrates. "It is ... all the more necessary," he says, "to explain his
fascination. That he discovered a new kind of *agon* [contest], that he
became its first fencing master for the noble circles of Athens, is one
point. He fascinated by appealing to the agonistic impulse of the
Greeks – he introduced a variation into the wrestling match between
young men and youths" (sec. 8). But Socrates did not merely invent
a new form of blood sport: "Socrates understood that all the world
needed him ... everywhere the instincts were in anarchy ... 'The
impulses want to play the tyrant; one must invent a *counter-tyrant*
who is stronger'" (sec. 9). The counter-tyrant, of course, was reason:
"rationality was then hit upon as the savior; neither Socrates nor
his 'patients' had any choice about being rational ... there was
danger, there was but one choice: either to perish or – to be *absurdly
rational*" (sec. 10). Nietzsche thought this use of reason as a cure to
the anarchy of the appetites was a form of self-deception. When he
wrote *Twilight of the Idols* Nietzsche was fully on the side of instinct
in opposition to reason as the key to a happy life. Socrates was not
the cure to a disease, but another sign of decadence: "Socrates was
a misunderstanding: *the whole improvement-morality, including the
Christian, was a misunderstanding.* The most blinding daylight;
rationality at any price, life, bright, cold, cautious, without instinct,
in opposition to the instincts – all this too was a mere disease,
another disease, and by no means a return to 'virtue,' to 'health,' to
happiness. To *have* to fight the instincts – that is the formula of
decadence: as long as life is *ascending*, happiness equals instinct"
(sec 11).

The Twentieth Century

Karl Popper's Socrates

One of the persistent features of appreciations of Socrates in the
twentieth century is the view of him as a defender of democracy.

We can see this view in Karl Popper's *The Open Society and its Enemies*, first published in 1945. The date of publication perhaps gives a key to the book's polemical tone. It was composed during the Second World War, when the institution of democracy was literally under attack by totalitarian forces. The "open society" of the title was the society of liberal democracy, represented by Pericles' "funeral oration": a society based on the free exchange of ideas and rational criticism. (Criticism was the essential feature of Popper's own philosophy of science: science advances by rational criticism of bold hypotheses.) The enemy of the open society was, of course, the closed society, which Popper interpreted as the result of a desire to return to an imagined past, a tribal society governed by a strict understanding of shared traditions. Popper saw Plato, Hegel, and Marx as the chief philosophical proponents of the closed society.

Popper saw Plato as the ancient world's great enemy of Pericles' open society and the *Republic* and *Laws* as his expressions of that enmity. Socrates, of course, was the spokesman for Plato's antidote to the open society in the *Republic*; it might seem that he would be characterized in the same way as Plato, as a proto-totalitarian. Yet Popper exempts Socrates from this charge. Socrates was the greatest contributor to the "faith of the open society, the faith in man, in equalitarian justice, and in human reason."[37] True, Socrates was a critic of Athenian democracy, but "Socrates' criticism was a democratic one, and indeed of the kind that is the very life of democracy."[38] True, Socrates was tried because of his association with people like Critias, oligarchic opponents of Athenian democracy (Popper accepts the "political" interpretation of the trial of Socrates). Yet this did not show that he shared their anti-democratic sentiments; rather, as a teacher, he hoped to convert and reform them.[39] Socrates had no sympathy with the practices of the Thirty, and he tried to show this at his trial. He proved his loyalty to Athens by remaining in prison: "his fearlessness, his simplicity, his modesty, his sense of proportion, his humor never deserted him."[40] How did Plato turn such a defender of ideal democratic values into a spokesman for totalitarianism? He betrayed him, just as Critias and Charmides had done. He may have done so out of a sincere desire to improve the lot of the Athenian democrats, but he betrayed him nonetheless.

The portrayal of Socrates as a supporter of democracy was especially prevalent in the United States. This was true of popular as well as scholarly appreciations. Socrates was seen not just as a democrat but as a liberal one: as Melissa Lane writes, "Socrates was virtually always invoked on a single side. Thus, he was cast as a resister of McCarthyism; an advocate of black civil rights; and a protestor against the Vietnam war – in the last two cases also as a civil disobedient when necessary to defend higher constitutional or moral values."[41] Socrates was a hero of free speech; free speech was a feature of democracy, the open society; therefore Socrates must have been a proponent of democracy. Socrates did not think that virtue could be restricted to a certain gender or class; therefore he must have thought virtue was, at least in theory, available to everyone. This was also seen as a democratic belief.

I. F. Stone's Socrates

One interpreter who does not buy the interpretation of Socrates as a friend of democracy is the investigative reporter I. F. Stone. In the preface to his book, *The Trial of Socrates*, Stone describes how, forced into retirement by health issues, he set out to write a history of freedom of thought and speech. This pursuit led him to classical Greece and the trial of Socrates. The study reawakened a youthful interest in philosophy and the classics. Dissatisfied with studying the sources in translation, he taught himself Greek. His problem was that the trial of Socrates seemed to him to have been an egregious affront to freedom of thought and speech. "It horrified me as a civil libertarian ... It was a black mark for Athens and the freedom it symbolized ... I could not defend the verdict when I started and I cannot defend it now ... But I wanted ... to give the Athenian side of the story, to mitigate the city's crime and thereby remove some of the stigma the trial left on democracy and on Athens."[42]

Stone reaches a conclusion about Socrates that is opposed to that of Popper and many of Socrates' defenders in the twentieth century. Stone's Socrates is no defender of democracy, but an extreme elitist, a monarchist in fact, an admirer of the Homeric king Agamemnon. Socrates had no faith in the wisdom of common people, the foundation of democracy. Stone does not accept the key point in Socrates' critique of democracy, the claim that it puts unqualified people in charge of the government, because he does not accept the premise of Socrates' argument, which is that qualification for office is a matter of expert knowledge, demonstrated by the ability to define the key terms of political rule, such as justice. Stone holds that the inability to define these terms is no sign of lack of virtue: didn't Socrates himself demonstrate his courage on the battlefield, though he never proved able to define the term? Stone dismisses the Socratic search for definitions as "a wild goose chase."[43]

Stone rejects the view, which Socrates states in Plato's *Apology*, that he was tried because he was suspected of being an atheist who practiced natural philosophy, an idea that goes back to Aristophanes. "It was the political, not the philosophical or theological, views of Socrates which finally got him into trouble."[44] Socrates was tried because the democracy had been overthrown twice, in 411 and 404, and had faced a third threat in 401. Socrates had not taken the democratic side in these revolts; he had "remained in the city" on each occasion and associated with tyrants such as Critias and Charmides. Stone accepts Xenophon's account of his motives for behaving haughtily before the jury, antagonizing them rather than trying to win their favor: that he had decided, in effect, to commit "suicide by trial" rather than face the vicissitudes of old age. He might have won acquittal by appeal to the Athenian love of free speech, by turning the tables on the prosecutors and making the trial about Athens and not himself. "When Athens prosecuted Socrates, it was untrue to itself."[45] The charges against him were vague; he was not accused for any acts, but for his beliefs. "I do not believe in your so-called freedom of speech," Stone says Socrates might have said to the jurors, "but you do ... I do not believe in democracy. But you do."[46] By convicting and executing him for speaking freely, Socrates might have argued, the Athenians were behaving like the tyrants they hated. Freedom of speech was a basic principle of Athenian democracy: the Athenians had not one but four words for it. Socrates could not appeal to free speech because neither he nor Plato believed in it; but had he done so he might have been acquitted.

The value of Stone's work lies in part on his providing "a fresh pair of eyes" on the problem of Socrates. Stone looks at the same sources that classical scholars examine, but he reaches radically different conclusions about them. The reason is that he approaches the study of these sources from the perspective of an investigative journalist and partisan of democracy, eager to find the "true story" of the trial, convinced that Plato did not tell it. He looks at Socrates' trial from the perspective of a twentieth-century liberal, someone we might refer to today as a democratic socialist, but he also tries to tell the story of the trial from the perspective of the democratic jurors of the fourth century. The value of this fresh perspective on texts that are so familiar to scholars that they may have come to take them for granted should not be underrated. The story Stone tells is not new, but it was new to him, and one can find his sense of discovery on almost every page. The book was generally harshly reviewed by scholars,[47] and with good reason. But beyond the errors in judgment pointed out by his critics, there lies the fact that this ardent democrat, late in life, was motivated to reopen the "Socrates case" and bring his journalistic skills to bear on it. The fact that Stone pursued this quest is testament to the enduring power to awake in thoughtful people an interest in a trial that took place 2400 years ago, of a man who was as controversial in his own times as he remains in ours. As Tony Long has said, "what matters most about Socrates is the fact that we never tire of him or stop wanting to talk to him and get mad with him."[48] This was true of Alcibiades in Plato's *Symposium* and it remains true today.

Notes

Preface

1 Malcolm Schofield, "Socrates on Trial in the USA," in T. P. Wiseman, ed., *Classics in Progress: Essays on Ancient Greece and Rome* (Oxford and New York: Oxford University Press, 2002), 282.

1 Socrates' Times and Trial

1 Unless otherwise indicated, all dates in this book are BCE.
2 I use the term "associate" to refer to all of those people who spent time with Socrates. This includes students, friends, and fellow philosophers.
3 All references to Plato's dialogues are to a standard pagination, called "Stephanus pagination," after a Renaissance edition of Plato's works. All translations of Plato are from J. M. Cooper, ed., *Plato: Compete Works* (Indianapolis and Cambridge: Hackett Publishing, Inc., 1997).
4 The Greek word *nomizōn* can also mean "honoring" or "recognizing."
5 The Greek phrase here translated "gentleman" is *kalos kagathos*. This is a standard description of an excellent life. The word *kalos* is difficult to translate. It may mean, in some contexts, "beautiful" in an aesthetic sense. Some translators use "fine" to capture the range it covers. In the phrase *kalos kagathos*, however, it has a distinctly moral tone, which I translate "admirable." A life that is *kalos* is one that is beautiful, fine, in being legitimately worthy of admiration.
6 For a discussion of the rival interpretations of the trial, see Mark Ralkowski, "The Politics of Impiety: Why was Socrates Prosecuted by the Athenian Democracy?" in John Bussanich and Nicholas D. Smith, eds. *The Bloomsbury Companion to Socrates* (London and New York: Bloomsbury Academic, 2013), 301–327 and 371–378.
7 Myles Burnyeat, "The Impiety of Socrates," *Ancient Philosophy* 17 (1997), 4.
8 Again, the Greek phrase is *kalos kagathos*.

2 Socratic Method

1 The best evidence we have for the dating of Plato's works comes from studies of Plato's style, begun in the late nineteenth century and continuing to the present. These studies tend to agree on a classification of Plato's works as early, middle, and late. There are controversies, based not on style but on the content of the dialogues, about the placement of some of the works within or between the three groups.
2 Richard Robinson, *Plato's Earlier Dialectic*, 2nd edn. (Oxford: Clarendon Press, 1953), 7. The account of the elenchus in this chapter generally follows Robinson's account. See also Hugh H. Benson, *Socratic Wisdom: The Model of Knowledge in Plato's Early Dialogues* (New York and Oxford: Oxford University Press, 2000), Part 1 (17–95).
3 Robinson, *Plato's Earlier Dialectic*, 10–15.
4 Ibid., 7.
5 F. M. Cornford, *Plato's Theory of Knowledge* (London: Routledge & Kegan Paul, Ltd, 1935), 2.
6 R. E. Allen, "Plato's Earlier Theory of Forms," in Vlastos, ed. *The Philosophy of Socrates* (Garden City, New York: Anchor Books, Doubleday & Company, 1971), 334.

3 Knowledge and Ignorance

1 Robinson, *Plato's Earlier Dialectic*, 51: "the impression vaguely given by the early dialogues as a whole is that Socrates thinks that there is no truth whatever about X that can be known before we know what X is."
2 David Sedley, *The Midwife of Platonism* (Oxford: Clarendon Press, 2004), 1.
3 Myles Burnyeat, "Socratic Midwifery, Platonic Inspiration," originally in the *Bulletin of the Institute of Classical Studies* 24 (1977), 7–16; Reprinted in Benson, ed. *Essays on the Philosophy of Socrates* (New York and Oxford: Oxford University Press, 1992), 57. Though Burnyeat argues that the midwife analogy of Socrates is a Platonic invention, he admits that in the *Theaetetus* "a fresh start [is] prepared by the return to the style and method of the early dialogues," and "Socrates himself, instead of being a mouthpiece for Platonic views, is restored to something like his original role as the man who knows nothing on his own account but has a mission to help others by his questioning. All this can be understood as a move 'back to Socrates' for the purpose of a dialogue which is critical in intent and deliberately restrained in its positive commitments" (58).
4 There is a debate among interpreters as to whether "irony" is the correct term for the behavior Thrasymachus attributes to Socrates. Without going into the debate, I accept the conclusion that it is. The point, however, whether we call it irony or not, is that Socrates is concealing opinions that he denies that he has.

4 Piety

1 See e.g. Peter T. Geach, "Plato's *Euthyphro*: An Analysis and Commentary," *The Monist* 50 (1966), 369–382. Geach refers to the priority of definition principle as the "Socratic fallacy" (371).

2 Mark McPherran, "Piety, Justice and the Unity of Virtue," *Journal of the History of Philosophy* 38 (2000), 301, n. 9.

3 Alexander Nehamas, *The Art of Living: Socratic Reflections from Plato to Foucault* (Berkeley, Los Angeles and London: University of California Press, 1998), 37.

4 Franco Trivigno, "The Moral and Literary Character of Hippias in Plato's *Hippias Major*," *Oxford Studies in Ancient Philosophy* 50 (2016), esp. 32–40. Trivigno applies the *eirōn/alazōn* distinction primarily to Hippias and Ion. I extend it to Euthyphro and, in fact, to all of Socrates' interlocutors who claim to have expert knowledge.

5 R. E. Allen, *Plato's 'Euthyphro' and the Earlier Theory of Forms* (London: Routledge & Kegan Paul Ltd., 1970), 20–23.

6 On this point, and on the general account of Forms in the *Euthyphro*, see my "Socrates Metaphysician," in *Oxford Studies in Ancient Philosophy* 27 (2004), 1–14, and "Socratic Metaphysics," in Bussanich and Smith, eds. *The Bloomsbury Companion*, 68–93 and 337–338.

7 "Reverence" is a rather free translation of *gera*, which literally means, "gifts of honor."

8 For a discussion of this point, see Thomas C. Brickhouse and Nicholas D. Smith, *Plato's Socrates* (New York and Oxford: Oxford University Press, 1994), 26.

5 Virtue

1 Alcibiades describes Socrates' profession of a poor memory as a joke at 336d.

2 On this point see Terry Penner, "The Historical Socrates and Plato's Early Dialogues: Some Philosophical Questions," in Annas and Rowe, eds. *New Perspectives on Plato, Ancient and Modern* (Washington, D.C.: Center for Hellenic Studies. Distributed by Harvard University Press, 2002), 196.

3 The argument that Socrates puts forward is similar to one in the *Euthydemus* (278e–282a).

4 Terence Irwin, *Plato's Ethics* (New York and Oxford: Oxford University Press, 1995) 56, refers to them as "assets." The Stoics referred to them as "preferred indifferents."

5 Irwin, *Plato's Ethics*, 57, distinguishes between a moderate and an extreme version of this argument. I think the moderate version is correct; he thinks Socrates is committed to the extreme version. I think the issue turns on the question whether the notion of "good" changes in the course of the

argument. Wealth is a good in the sense of something that, rightly used, can be beneficial for its possessor. Wisdom is good in the sense that it is infallibly beneficial; it cannot, unlike wealth, be misused. If "good" means "infallibly beneficial," then wisdom is the only good. If "good" means "something that, rightly used, can be beneficial," then wealth is a good. I suggest that the sense of "good" changes from the beginning of the argument to the end.

6 Happiness

1 It is a strange comment by someone who listens to what he regards as his divine voice. The apparent conflict between these two aspects of Socrates: his rationalist approach to philosophy and his reliance on his sign, has been the target of much critical discussion. For an example see the essays in Smith and Woodruff, eds. *Reason and Religion in Socratic Philosophy* (Oxford and New York: Oxford University Press, 2000).
2 Gregory Vlastos calls this Socrates' rejection of the *lex talionis*, the principle of "an eye for an eye," and he regards it as one of the most significant features of his ethical theory. See his *Socrates: Ironist and Moral Philosopher* (Cambridge: Cambridge University Press, 1991), 179–199. Specifically, however, it is not a rejection of reciprocity or retribution (though Socrates does reject the retributory theory of punishment) but the rejection of returning a wrong for a wrong. Two wrongs, Socrates holds, don't make a right.
3 For instance see Benson, *Socratic Wisdom*, 82.
4 In *Plato at the Googleplex: Why Philosophy won't go Away* (New York: Pantheon, 2014), 9, 126, Rebecca Goldstein attributes to the Athenian people an "Ethos of the Extraordinary," a belief that "the unexceptional life is not worth living." This belief that it is the exceptional life that matters, which she traces back to Achilles in the *Iliad*, links the Socratic and the Calliclean conception of morality. It is interesting to note that Socrates was the mentor of Alcibiades, Goldstein's favorite example of the ethos of the extraordinary, and perhaps the best example from Athenian history of a man answering to Callicles' description of the superior man.
5 Plato made the first of three voyages to Sicily in about 387. It is thought that he was influenced by Pythagorean philosophers he met in Italy on this voyage, and that this influence shows up in the myths of the *Gorgias* and the doctrine of recollection in the *Meno*. If that is so, it would date these two dialogues to after 387, perhaps around the time Plato founded the Academy.
6 As Goldstein notes, "There is an entire moral theory contained in this passage" (392).
7 "Socratic Ethics and Moral Psychology," in Fine, ed. *The Oxford Handbook to Plato* (New York and Oxford: Oxford University Press, 2008), 162.

Other scholars who see an inconsistency between the moral psychology of the *Protagoras* and that of the *Gorgias* include Terence Irwin, *Plato's Ethics* (New York and Oxford: Oxford University Press, 1995), 111–116, and John Cooper, "Socrates and Plato in Plato's *Gorgias*," in Cooper, *Reason and Emotion* (Princeton: Princeton University Press, 1999), esp. 51–75. Cooper attributes the change in moral psychology in the latter part of the *Gorgias* to Callicles and not Socrates. That is a view I do not accept.

7 The State

1 On this controversy see the discussion of the views of Karl Popper and I. F. Stone in Chapter 9.
2 For instance, Verity Harte, "Conflicting Values in Plato's *Crito*," *Archiv für Geschichte der Philosophie* 81 (1999), 117–147, and Roslyn Weiss, *Socrates Dissatisfied: An Analysis of Plato's* Crito (Oxford and New York: Oxford University Press, 1998).
3 This is the third condition that Socrates has placed on a life's being worth living in the *Crito*. Earlier (at 47e) he has stated that life is not worth living if one's body is corrupted, and (at 47e–48a) that life is not worth living if the part of us that is concerned with just actions is corrupted. Here he adds that, even if one's body and soul are not corrupted, one's life will not be worth living if one lives in a badly governed state.
4 As Brickhouse and Smith have pointed out in *Socrates on Trial* (Princeton: Princeton University Press), 137–153, and *Plato's Socrates*, 141–155), the jury may not suggest a penalty other than the one proposed by the prosecution or an alternative proposed by Socrates. I do not think that this fact prevents Socrates from speculating what he might do if, contrary to fact, the jury suggested that he be banned from continuing to philosophize. In any case Socrates himself would be free to propose that he be ordered to cease philosophizing. The passage in the *Apology* may be taken to indicate the reason why he would never make such a proposal.
5 Thus Popper and Vlastos; see Chapter 9, "The Reception of Socrates in the Ancient World."
6 This is the view of Richard Kraut, in *Socrates and the State* (Princeton: Princeton University Press, 1984), 7–9, 208, 226–228, 232, 237, 243–244, 268, 307.
7 For more on the Socratic circle see Chapter 9.
8 On this question see, for instance, Vlastos, *Socrates*, 248–251.
9 This appears to be another case of the priority of definition principle in action.
10 The wage-earner's art seems to be an exception to the Socratic principle that no art benefits the artist.

8 From Socrates to Plato

1 The story of the creation of three groups of dialogues based on stylistic distinctions and the modification of those groups by doctrinal considerations is told by Charles Kahn, in "On Platonic Chronology," in Annas and Rowe, *New Perspectives on Plato, Modern and Ancient* (Washington, D.C.: Center for Hellenic Studies, 2002), 93–97. In this chapter I put "middle" in scare quotes to indicate that I am talking about those dialogues that are considered to be "middle" based on doctrinal, not stylistic considerations.

2 Vlastos, *Socrates*, 47–48.

3 I criticize this view, which I refer to as the "biographical hypothesis," in "Why did Plato Write Socratic Dialogues?" in McPherran, ed. *Wisdom, Ignorance and Virtue: New Essays in Socratic Studies* (Edmonton: Academic Printing & Publishing, 1997), especially 111–114.

4 Vlastos, *Socrates*, 46.

5 W. K. C. Guthrie, trans., *Plato:* Protagoras *and* Meno (London: Penguin Books, Ltd., 1956), 24–25.

6 Kahn, *Plato and the Socratic Dialogue* (Cambridge: Cambridge University Press, 1996), 59–65.

7 Robinson, *Plato's Earlier Dialectic*, 19.

8 I have argued that it does: see my "Socrates Metaphysician" and "Socratic Metaphysics."

9 Allen "Plato's Earlier Theory of Forms," 332–333.

10 Allen, *Plato's 'Euthyphro' and the Earlier Theory of Forms*, 151.

11 Ibid., 152.

12 Ibid., 152–153.

13 Vlastos, *Socrates*, 49.

14 Thus Penner: "On the question of the immortality of the soul, there is little interest in the Socratic dialogues." "Socrates and the Early Dialogues," 125.

15 By Penner "Socrates and the Early Dialogues" and "The Historical Socrates."

16 "Did Plato Write Socratic Dialogues?" originally in *Classical Quarterly* 31 1981), 305–320; reprinted in Benson, ed. *Essays on the Philosophy of Socrates* (New York and Oxford: Oxford University Press, 1992), 47.

17 "Plato; or, the Philosopher," in *The Complete Works*, Vol. IV: Representative Men: Seven Lectures, number 2 (1904), quoted in Bartleby. com/90/0402, an electronic source.

9 Socrates' Legacy

1 On Xenophon's debts to Plato see Kahn, *Plato and the Socratic Dialogue*, 393–401.

2 Gregory Vlastos once dismissed Xenophon's portrait of Socrates with these words: "Xenophon's is a Socrates without irony and without paradox. Take these away from Plato's Socrates, and there is nothing left." "Introduction: The Paradox of Socrates," in Vlastos, ed. *The Philosophy of Socrates* (Garden City, NY: Doubleday and Company, 1971), 1. The characterization is apt, but overstated; the dismissal is not justified, as was shown by Donald Morrison, in "On Professor Vlastos' Xenophon," *Ancient Philosophy* 7 (1987), 9–22.

3 A. A. Long, "Socrates in Later Greek Philosophy," in Morrison, ed. *The Cambridge Companion to Socrates* (Cambridge: Cambridge University Press, 2011), 369.

4 Ibid., 368.

5 The story of the associates of Socrates and the dialogues they wrote is told by Kahn, *Plato and the Socratic Dialogue*, 1–35.

6 Ibid., 7.

7 See the discussion of the *Meno* argument in Chapter 5, "The Hypothesis that Virtue is Knowledge." There was a debate among the Stoics as to whether "goods" other than virtue had any form of positive value at all; see Long, "Socrates in Hellenistic Philosophy," *Classical Quarterly* 38 (1988), 164–169, and Long, "Socrates in Later Greek Philosophy," 364.

8 Long, "Socrates in Later Greek Philosophy," 370.

9 Long, *Epictetus: A Stoic and Socratic Guide to Life* (Oxford: Clarendon Press, 2002), 67.

10 As translated by Nicholas P. White (Indianapolis: Hackett Publishing, Inc., 1983).

11 As is often noted, the Academics did not refer to themselves as skeptics, as the Pyrrhonians did.

12 According to Long, "Socrates in Hellenistic Philosophy," 157–158.

13 James Hankins, "Socrates in the Italian Renaissance," in Trapp, ed. *Socrates from Antiquity to the Enlightenment* (Aldershot, Hampshire and Burlington, VT: Ashgate Publishing Company, 2007), 179.

14 As quoted in Spiegelberg, *The Socratic Enigma* (Indianapolis: The Bobbs-Merrill Company, Inc., 1964), 62.

15 Ibid., 65.

16 As Glenn Most notes: "Socrates in Hegel," in Trapp, ed. *Socrates in the Nineteenth and Twentieth Centuries* (Aldershot, Hampshire and Burlington, VT: Ashgate Publishing Ltd., 2007), 5.

17 Quotations of Hegel are from the *Lectures on the History of Philosophy*, Vol. 1. E. S. Haldane, trans. (Lincoln and London: University of Nebraska Press, 1995).

18 Most, "Socrates in Hegel," 2.

19 Ibid., 3.

20 *Christian Discourses and Journals*, No. 1079 (1850), as quoted in Spiegelberg, *The Socratic Enigma*, 304.

21 Ibid., 305.

22 Ibid.

23 He later remarked that when he wrote his master's thesis he was a "Hegelian fool." George Pattison, "A Simple Wise Man of Ancient Times: Kierkegaard on Socrates," in Trapp, ed. *Socrates in the Nineteenth and Twentieth Centuries*, 20.

24 Quotations are taken from Spiegelberg, *The Socratic Enigma*.

25 *On the Concept of Irony*, as quoted in Spiegelberg, *The Socratic Enigma*, 291.

26 Pattison, "A Simple Wise Man of Ancient Times," 21.

27 *On the Concept of Irony*, as quoted in Spiegelberg, *The Socratic Enigma*, 292.

28 Ibid, 293.

29 Søren Kierkegaard, *Concluding Unscientific Postscript*, David Swenson and Walter Lowrie, trans. (Princeton: Princeton University Press, 1941), 182.

30 Ibid., 180–181.

31 "The Socratic Definition of Sin," *The Sickness unto Death*, Walter Lowrie, trans. (Princeton: Princeton University Press, 1954), 219–221.

32 *The Point of View* (1848–1849), in Spiegelberg, *The Socratic Enigma*, 303.

33 C. C. W. Taylor, *Socrates: A Very Short Introduction* (Oxford and New York: Oxford University Press, 1998), 97.

34 James I. Porter, "Nietzsche and 'The Problem of Socrates,'" in Ahbel-Rappe and Kamtekar, eds. *A Companion to Socrates* (Malden, MA: Blackwell Publishing Ltd., 2009), 406, quoting "a note jotted down in 1875." See also C. C. W. Taylor, *Socrates*, 97.

35 *The Twilight of the Idols*, in Kaufmann, ed., *The Portable Nietzsche* (New York: Viking Press, 1954).

36 *The Birth of Tragedy and the Genealogy of Morals*, Francis Golffing, trans. (Garden City, New York: Doubleday & Company, Inc., 1956).

37 *The Open Society and its Enemies, Volume I: The Spell of Plato* (London: Routledge & Kegan Paul Ltd., 4th edn. 1962), 189.

38 Ibid.

39 Ibid., 191.

40 Ibid., 194.

41 "'Gadfly in God's Own Country': Socrates in Twentieth-Century America," in Trapp, ed. *Socrates in the Nineteenth and Twentieth Centuries*, 207. For two scholarly treatments of Socrates which disagree on whether Socrates was democratic or oligarchic in his sympathies, see Gregory Vlastos, "The Historical Socrates and Athenian Democracy," *Political Theory* 11 (1983), 495–516, and E. M. Wood and N. Wood, "Socrates and Democracy: A Reply to Gregory Vlastos," *Political Theory* 14 (1986), 55–86. For Vlastos, Socrates is democratic, or at least "demophilic" in his political philosophy; for the Woods, he is oligarchic.

42 I. F. Stone, *The Trial of Socrates* (Boston and Toronto: Little, Brown and Company, 1988), xi.

43 Ibid., ch. 6.
44 Ibid., 138–139.
45 Ibid., 197.
46 Ibid., 212.
47 For a (mostly) positive appreciation of the book, see Myles F. Burnyeat, "Cracking the Socrates Case," *New York Review of Books*, March 31, 1988, 12–18.
48 Long, "Socrates in Later Greek Philosophy," 378.

Bibliography

Ancient Sources

Aristophanes. *Clouds*. Peter Meineck, trans. Indianapolis and Cambridge: Hackett Publishing, Inc. 2000.

Aristotle. *Complete Works*. Jonathan Barnes, ed. 2 vols. Princeton: Princeton University Press. 1984.

Cicero. *Tusculan Disputations*.

Diogenes Laertius. *Lives of the Eminent Philosophers*.

Plato. *Complete Works*. J. M. Cooper, ed. Indianapolis and Cambridge: Hackett Publishing, Inc. 1997.

Thucydides. *History of the Peloponnesian War*. *The Landmark Thucydides*. Robert Strassler, ed. New York, London, Toronto, Sydney: Free Press. 1996.

Xenophon. *Memorabilia, Oeconomicus, Symposium, Apology*. E. C. Marchant and O. J. Todd, trans. Cambridge: Harvard University Press. 1923.

Modern Sources

Ahbel-Rappe, Sara and Kamtekar, Rachana, eds. *A Companion to Socrates*. Malden, MA: Blackwell Publishing Ltd. 2009.

Allen, R. E. "Plato's Earlier Theory of Forms," in Vlastos, ed. *The Philosophy of Socrates*, 319–34.

_____. *Plato's 'Euthyphro' and the Earlier Theory of Forms*. London: Routledge & Kegan Paul Ltd. 1970.

Annas, Julia and Rowe, Christopher, eds. *New Perspectives on Plato, Modern and Ancient*. Washington, D.C.: Center for Hellenic Studies. Distributed by Harvard University Press. 2002.

Benson, Hugh H. *Socratic Wisdom: The Model of Knowledge in Plato's Early Dialogues*. New York and Oxford: Oxford University Press. 2000.

_____. ed. *Essays on the Philosophy of Socrates*. New York and Oxford: Oxford University Press. 1992.

Brickhouse, Thomas C. and Smith, Nicholas D. *Socrates on Trial*. Princeton: Princeton University Press. 1989.

_____. *Plato's Socrates*. New York and Oxford: Oxford University Press. 1994.

Burnyeat, Myles. "The Impiety of Socrates." *Ancient Philosophy* 17 (1997), 1–12.

_____. "Socratic Midwifery, Platonic Inspiration," originally in the *Bulletin of the Institute of Classical Studies* 24 (1977), 7–16. Reprinted in Benson, ed. *Essays on the Philosophy of Socrates*, 53–65.

Bussanich, John and Smith, Nicholas D., eds. *The Bloomsbury Companion to Socrates*. London and New York: Bloomsbury Academic. 2013.

Cooper, John. "Socrates and Plato in Plato's *Gorgias*," in *Reason and Emotion*. Princeton: Princeton University Press. 1999, 29–75.

Cornford, F. M. *Plato's Theory of Knowledge*. London: Routledge & Kegan Paul, Ltd. 1935.

Devereux, Daniel. "Socratic Ethics and Moral Psychology," in Fine, ed. *The Oxford Handbook to Plato*), 139–164.

Emerson, Ralph Waldo. "Plato; or, the Philosopher," in *The Complete Works*, Vol. IV: Representative Men: Seven Lectures, no. 2 (1904), quoted in Bartleby.com/90/0402, an electronic source.

Fine, Gail, ed. *The Oxford Handbook to Plato*. New York and Oxford: Oxford University Press. 2008.

Geach, Peter T. "Plato's *Euthyphro*: An Analysis and Commentary." *The Monist* 50 (1966), 369–82.

Goldstein, Rebecca. *Plato at the Googleplex: Why Philosophy won't go Away*. New York: Pantheon. 2014.

Guthrie, W. K. C., trans. *Plato: Protagoras and Meno*. London: Penguin Books, Ltd. 1956.

Hankins, James. "Socrates in the Italian Renaissance," in Trapp, ed. *Socrates from Antiquity to the Enlightenment*.

Harte, Verity. "Conflicting Values in Plato's *Crito*," *Archiv für Geschichte der Philosophie* 81 (1999), 117–147.

Hegel, G. W. F. *Lectures on the History of Philosophy, Vol. 1*. E. S. Haldane, trans. Lincoln and London: University of Nebraska Press. 1995.

Irwin, Terence. *Plato's Ethics*. New York and Oxford: Oxford University Press. 1995.

Kahn, Charles. "Did Plato Write Socratic Dialogues?" originally in *Classical Quarterly* 31 1981), 305–320; reprinted in Benson, ed. *Essays on the Philosophy of Socrates*, 35–52.

_____. *Plato and the Socratic Dialogue*. Cambridge: Cambridge University Press. 1996.

_____."On Platonic Chronology," in Annas and Rowe, eds. *New Perspectives on Plato*, 93–127.

Kaufmann, Walter, ed. *The Portable Nietzsche*. New York: Viking Press. 1954.

Kierkegaard, Søren. *Concluding Unscientific Postscript*. David Swenson and Walter Lowrie, trans. Princeton: Princeton University Press. 1941.

_____. *The Sickness unto Death*. Walter Lowrie, trans. Princeton: Princeton University Press. 1954.

Kraut, Richard. *Socrates and the State*. Princeton: Princeton University Press. 1984.

_____, ed. *The Cambridge Companion to Plato*. Cambridge: Cambridge University Press. 1992.

Lane, Melissa. "'Gadfly in God's Own Country': Socrates in Twentieth-Century America," in Trapp, ed. *Socrates in the Nineteenth and Twentieth Centuries*, 205–226.

Long, A. A. "Socrates in Hellenistic Philosophy." *Classical Quarterly* 38 (1988), 150–171.

_____. *Epictetus: A Stoic and Socratic Guide to Life*. Oxford: Clarendon Press. 2002.

_____. "Socrates in Later Greek Philosophy," in Morrison, ed. *The Cambridge Companion to Socrates*.

McPherran, Mark. "Piety, Justice and the Unity of Virtue." *Journal of the History of Philosophy* 38 (2000), 299–328.

_____, ed. *Wisdom, Ignorance and Virtue: New Essays in Socratic Studies*. Edmonton: Academic Printing & Publishing, 1997. Also *Apeiron* 30.

Morrison, Donald. "On Professor Vlastos' Xenophon." *Ancient Philosophy* 7 (1987), 9–22.

_____. ed. *The Cambridge Companion to Socrates*. Cambridge: Cambridge University Press. 2011.

Most, Glenn. "Socrates in Hegel," in Trapp, ed. *Socrates in the Nineteenth and Twentieth Centuries*, 1–17.

Nehamas, Alexander. *The Art of Living: Socratic Reflections from Plato to Foucault*. Berkeley, Los Angeles and London: University of California Press. 1998.

Nietzsche, Friedrich. *The Birth of Tragedy and the Genealogy of Morals*, Francis Golffing, trans. Garden City, New York: Doubleday & Company, Inc. 1956.

_____. *Twilight of the Idols*, in Kaufmann, ed., *The Portable Nietzsche*, 463–563.

Pattison, George. "A Simple Wise Man of Ancient Times: Kierkegaard on Socrates," in Trapp, ed. *Socrates in the Nineteenth and Twentieth Centuries*, 19–35.

Penner, Terry. "Socrates and the Early Dialogues," in Kraut, ed. *The Cambridge Companion to Plato*, 121–169.

_____. "The Historical Socrates and Plato's Early Dialogues: Some Philosophical Questions," in Annas and Rowe, eds. *New Perspectives on Plato*, 189–212.

Popper, Karl. *The Open Society and its Enemies, Volume 1: The Spell of Plato.* 4th edn. London: Routledge & Kegan Paul Ltd. 1962.

Porter, James. "Nietzsche and 'The Problem of Socrates,'" in Ahbel-Rappe and Kamtekar, eds. *Companion*, 406–425.

Prior, William J. "Why did Plato Write Socratic Dialogues?" in McPherran, ed. *Wisdom, Ignorance and Virtue*, 109–123.

_____. "Socrates Metaphysician." *Oxford Studies in Ancient Philosophy* 27 (2004), 1–14.

_____. "Socratic Metaphysics," in Bussanich and Smith, eds. *The Bloomsbury Companion*, 68–93 and 337–338.

Ralkowski, Mark. "The Politics of Impiety: Why was Socrates Prosecuted by the Athenian Democracy?" in Bussanich and Smith, eds. *The Bloomsbury Companion*, 301–327 and 371–378.

Robinson, Richard. *Plato's Earlier Dialectic.* 2nd edn. Oxford: Clarendon Press. 1953.

Schofield, Malcolm. "Socrates on Trial in the USA," in Wiseman, ed. *Classics in Progress*, 263–283.

Sedley, David. *The Midwife of Platonism.* Oxford: Clarendon Press. 2004.

Smith, Nicholas D. and Woodruff, Paul B., eds. *Reason and Religion in Socratic Philosophy.* Oxford and New York: Oxford University Press. 2000.

Spiegelberg, Herbert. *The Socratic Enigma.* Indianapolis: The Bobbs-Merrill Company, Inc. 1964.

Stone, I. F. *The Trial of Socrates.* Boston and Toronto: Little, Brown and Company. 1988.

Trapp, Michael ed. *Socrates from Antiquity to the Enlightenment.* Aldershot, Hampshire and Burlington, VT: Ashgate Publishing Company. 2007a.

_____, ed. *Socrates in the Nineteenth and Twentieth Centuries.* Aldershot, Hampshire and Burlington, VT: Ashgate Publishing Ltd. 2007b.

Trivigno, Franco. "The Moral and Literary Character of Hippias in Plato's *Hippias Major.*" *Oxford Studies in Ancient Philosophy* 50 (2016), 31–65.

Vlastos, Gregory. "Introduction: the Paradox of Socrates," in Vlastos, ed. *The Philosophy of Socrates*, 1–21.

_____. "The Historical Socrates and Athenian Democracy." *Political Theory* 11 (1983), 495–516.

_____. *Socrates: Ironist and Moral Philosopher.* Cambridge: Cambridge University Press. 1991.

_____. ed. *The Philosophy of Socrates.* Garden City, New York: Anchor Books, Doubleday & Company. 1971.

Wiseman, T. P., ed. *Classics in Progress: Essays on Ancient Greece and Rome.* Oxford and New York: Oxford University Press. 2002.

Wood E. M., and Wood, N. "Socrates and Democracy: A Reply to Gregory Vlastos," *Political Theory* 14 (1986), 55–86.

Recommended Reading

The literature on Socrates is enormous. The Bibliography is limited to works actually cited in the text. Rather than attempting to provide a complete listing of relevant works, which would take many pages and which might well prove impossible, I want to mention a few books that the reader might wish to look at in taking the next step beyond this volume. I do not list below books or articles that are already mentioned in the Bibliography.

General historical background

John Boardman, Jasper Griffin, and Oswyn Murray, eds. *The Oxford History of the Classical World* (Oxford and New York: Oxford University Press, 1986)

On Socrates' Athens

Bettany Hughes, *The Hemlock Cup: Socrates, Athens and the Search for the Good Life* (London: Random House, 2010)

On Athenian law

Douglas M. MacDowell, *The Law in Classical Athens* (Cornell: Cornell University Press, 1978)

On Socratic piety

Mark McPherran, *The Religion of Socrates* (University Park, PA: The Pennsylvania State University Press, 1996)

On definition and Forms

R. M. Dancy, *Plato's Introduction of Forms* (Cambridge: Cambridge University Press, 2004)

On reverence

Paul Woodruff, *Reverence: Renewing a Forgotten Virtue*, 2nd edn. (New York and Oxford: Oxford University Press, 2014)

On the *Gorgias*

E. R. Dodds, *Plato: Gorgias* (Oxford: Clarendon Press, 1959). Introduction and Appendix

On Socratic perplexity

Gareth B. Matthews, *Socratic Perplexity* (Oxford and New York: Oxford University Press, 1999)

On ancient philosophy as a way of life

Pierre Hadot, *Philosophy as a Way of Life* (Oxford and Cambridge, MA, 1995)

On Socratic moral psychology

Thomas C. Brickhouse and Nicholas D. Smith, *Socratic Moral Psychology* (Cambridge: Cambridge University Press, 2010)

On the *Republic*

Julia Annas, *An Introduction to Plato's* Republic (Oxford: Clarendon Press, 1981)

On the death of Socrates, with special emphasis on its treatment through history

Emily Wilson, *The Death of Socrates* (Cambridge: Harvard University Press, 2007)

Index